Frederick Douglass 1818-1895

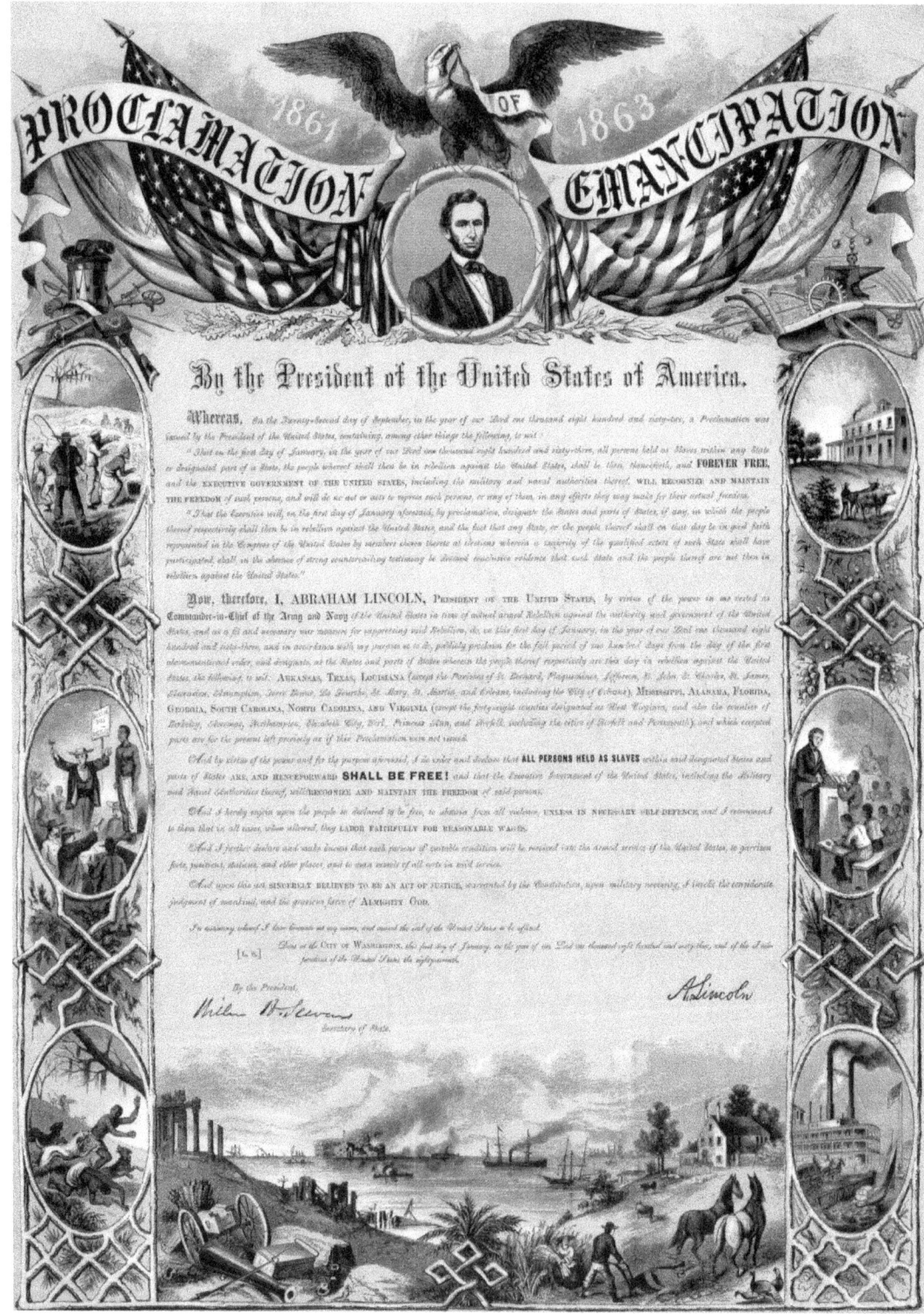

Uncle Tom's Companions

Or, Facts Stranger Than Fiction.
A Supplement to Uncle Tom's Cabin:
Being Startling Incidents in the Lives of Celebrated Fugitive Slaves:

CONTENTS

PREFACE……………………………...…………..…7

FREDERICK DOUGLASS……………………….……12

CHAPTER I. THE MASTER AND HIS SLAVES…………………………………………..…….49

CHAPTER II LIFE STAKED FOR LIBERTY……………………………………………....54

CHAPTER III. HOPE SUPPORTS, AND FREEDOM AWAITS HIM…………………………………………..…....59

CHAPTER IV. WILLIAM WELLS BROWN…….80

CHAPTER V. HENRY BIBB……...………………108

CHAPTER VI. PETER'S LOT GROWS HARDER THAN BEFORE……………………………………………..150

CHAPTER VII. THE MASTER PUNISHED, AND THE SLAVE SET FREE…………………..…..303

CONCLUDING OBSERVATIONS. ……………158

APPENDIX……………………………………..161

PREPARED FOR PUBLICATION
By
HISTORIC PUBLISHING

All materials found within this title have been proofed and prepared for publication by Historic Publishing. No part of this publication may be reproduced, distributed, or transmitted in any form or by any means, including: photocopying, recording, or by any other electronic or mechanical methods without the express written consent of Historic Publishing.

©2017 (Edited Materials) All Rights Reserved

UNCLE TOM'S COMPANIONS
OR,
FACTS STRANGER THAN FICTION.
A SUPPLEMENT
TO
Uncle Tom's Cabin:
BEING STARTLING INCIDENTS IN THE LIVES OF
CELEBRATED FUGITIVE SLAVES.

BY
J. PASSMORE EDWARDS,
[1823-1911]
Editor of "The Biographical Magazine.
&
FREDERICK DOUGLASS

LONDON:
EDWARDS AND CO., 2, HORSESHOE COURT
LUDGATE-HILL.
MDCCCLII.
T. C. JOHNS, PRINTER,
Wine Office Court, Fleet Street.
1852

PREFACE.

IF ever a nation were taken by storm by a book, England has recently been stormed by "Uncle Tom's Cabin." It is scarcely three months since this book was first introduced to the British Reader, and it is certain that at least 1,000,000 copies of it have been printed and sold. The unexampled success of "Uncle Tom's Cabin" will ever be recorded as an extraordinary literary phenomena. Nothing of the kind, or anything approaching to it, was ever before witnessed in any age or in any country. A new fact has been contributed to the history of literature--such a fact, never before equaled, may never be surpassed. The pre-eminent success of the work in America, before it was reprinted in this country, was truly astonishing. All at once, as if by magic, everybody was either reading, or waiting to read, "the story of the age," and "a hundred thousand families were every day either moved to laughter, or bathed in tears," by its perusal.

This book is not more remarkable for its poetry and its pathos, its artistic delineation of character and development of plot, than for its highly instructive power. A great moral idea runs beautifully through the whole story. One of the greatest evils of the world--slavery--is stripped of its disguises, and presented in all its naked and revolting hideousness to the reading world. And that Christianity, which consists not in professions and appearances, but in vital and vitalizing action, is exhibited in all-subduing beauty and tenderness in every page of the work. If ever a book had a mission, that book is "Uncle Tom's Cabin." Its mission is to attract all readers to it by virtue of its many charms, and after attracting them, warm them with an enthusiasm, and fill them with a love of Humanity--and unmistakably and admirably has this mission so far been fulfilled. And it will continue to be fulfilled as the years pass away, and the empire of Injustice gradually crumbles before the advancing tide of a Christianized Civilization. "Uncle Tom's Cabin" will not only be read by Englishmen, and those who talk the English language, all the world over, but it will be translated into all the principal languages of Europe, and become a household book for ages.

This book, as it is now well known, depicts with graphic force Negro life in the United States. That it does this with as much truth as vigor, will be seen by a perusal of "Uncle Tom's Cabin." But as the truthfulness of the delineations of Mrs. Stowe's book has been called into question, and the inferences drawn therefrom disputed by the Times newspaper, and other authorities, such a book as "UNCLE TOM'S COMPANIONS" was demanded. It has been said that "Uncle Tom's Cabin" is an exaggeration, that it misrepresents Slavery and Slaveholders, and that its influence must be prejudicial in riveting more closely the chains of the poor slave, and protracting the hour of his emancipation.

The Times, in speaking of Mrs. Stowe and her book, says--"That she will convince the world of the purity of her own motives, and of the hatefulness of the sin she denounces is equally clear; but that she will help in the slightest degree towards the removal of the gigantic evil that afflicts her soul, is a point upon which we may express the greatest doubt; nay, is a matter upon which, unfortunately, we have very little doubt at all, inasmuch as we are certain that the very readiest way to rivet the fetters of slavery in these critical times, is to direct against all slaveholders in America, the opprobrium and indignation which such works as 'Uncle Tom's Cabin' are sure to excite. . . . . The gravest fault of the book has, however, to be mentioned. Its object is to abolish slavery. Its effect will be to render slavery more difficult than ever of abolishment. Its very popularity constitutes its greatest difficulty. It will keep ill-blood at boiling point, and irritate instead of pacifying those whose proceedings Mrs. Stowe is anxious to influence on behalf of humanity." The long and elaborate review concludes with the following words--"Liberia, and similar spots on the earth's surface, proffer aid to the South, which cannot be rejected with safety. That the aid may be accepted with alacrity and good heart, let us have no more 'Uncle Tom's Cabins' engendering ill-will, keeping up bad blood, and rendering well-disposed, humane, but critically placed men their own enemies and the stumbling-blocks to civilization, and to the spread of glad tidings from Heaven."

Mrs. Stowe has either told the truth or she has not. If she has told the truth, it was right and proper that she should tell it, whether slaveholders were offended or pleased. The Times admits that slavery is an evil. If so, let the evil be exposed, whoever may be displeased. But if, on the other hand, Mrs. Stowe has not described truly, if her pictures be false, and her reflections erroneous, then will her book in the long run be considered of little value, and be soon consigned to the oblivion it merits. But Mrs. Stowe has not overdrawn the picture, she has only painted slave life as it is, and because she has spoken truly, the influence of her book "will be vast and immeasurable."

The object I have in writing "Uncle Tom's Companions," is to vindicate "Uncle Tom's Cabin," and to refute the unjust criticisms of the Times, and all who think with that paper. I have done this by simply narrating passages in the lives of fugitive slaves--of men who have passed through the fiery furnace of slavery, and escaped, though not unhurt, to the land of freedom--of men, some of whom are now in England, and who cannot return to their native country on account of the Fugitive Slave Law. I have drawn no imaginary picture, I have summoned no ideal characters on the scene, and thrown around them the hues of my own fancy; but I have called as my witnesses men, living men--men who have walked, or who are now walking, the streets of London, but who a few years ago, suffered all the horrors which slavery inevitably inflicts. And they are not witnesses whose names are unknown. No, but those of Frederick Douglass, Dr. Pennington, the Rev. Mr. Garnett, William

Wells Brown, and others, with whose views, or whose writings, a large proportion of the English public are familiarized: These men have been, and are "Uncle Tom's Companions." They were his companions in slavery and in suffering, and it is right that their story should be told, and their testimony recorded, so that the general character of "Uncle Tom's Cabin" may be vindicated, for the sake of truth and humanity.

That "Uncle Tom's Cabin" should be so eagerly sought after and read, both in America and England, and produce the profound sensation it has, is the greatest compliment the age could pay to itself. All have contributed to give the book an enthusiastic reception; cheap editions and dear editions have followed each other with unexampled rapidity amongst us. Publishers of classical literature and publishers of trashy periodicals have sent forth editions of the book. Half-a-guinea editions and sixpenny editions have met with a rapid sale. And the most cheering fact of all is, that low publishers, who have hitherto only sent forth desolating streams of reading to the poorest classes of the community, have recently vied with each other in sending forth cheap editions of this wondrous work, and thereby showing that there was higher power of appreciation in the nation's heart than they were aware of, and that a poisoned cheap literature has only flourished in the absence of something sweeter and purer. Mrs. Stowe's work has not only sent vibrations along the chords of England's universal heart, but it has already familiarized large portions of our population with a story tender in pathos, pure in sentiment, and elevating in aim. Whatever may be the evils which fester in the midst of our dirty alleys and neglected homes, it is encouraging and full of hope to know that there is a heart ready to beat in unison with the good and the pure, among the lowest and most neglected of our population. Well may the benevolent and the philanthropic be grateful to Mrs. Stowe for what she has already done in England! She has touched the hidden cells of feeling of many a degraded outcast, and awoke in him that latent and moral life which exists, and which is inextinguishable in every heart, however degraded. Though England is renowned for its churches and its Bibles, it is well known that untold numbers of its population know nothing of Christianity and its power to save. And for years past praise-worthy exertions have been made by the Established Church, and other Christian communities, to diffuse the blessings of the Gospel among the most ignorant and wretched; but unfortunately but little practical good has hitherto resulted therefrom. Perhaps the means which have been used were and are unequal to the task to be performed. But "Uncle Tom's Cabin" will do, to a great extent, what sermons and tracts could not accomplish. It will be read or listened to by the lowest; and will, by virtue of its peculiar excellence, soften, and subdue, and purify. And many will see the workings and development of vital Christianity, as exhibited in the character of Uncle Tom, and the incarnate purity of the beautiful Eva, who would have no conception of such things by exhortations and tracts. Consequently, whether "Uncle Tom's Cabin" does its work in America or not, it is already doing a work here which no agency before accomplished.

As for "Uncle Tom's Cabin" being read by almost everybody everywhere, and not to a greater or less extent answer its purpose, is unreasonable and absurd. It is as well to say, that the flowery breath of spring awakens no cheerfulness, or the voluptuous swell of music yields no pleasure. The Pure and the Beautiful must, by virtue of their intrinsic excellence, influence for good all who are brought within their charmed circle.

There is something in the instantaneous effect produced by "Uncle Tom's Cabin" approaching the sublime. A gentle woman moves her pen, and stirs races. She speaks, and millions are charmed by her melodious accents. Clay, the modern disciple of Compromise, has frequently lashed audiences into a storm by his eloquence; and Webster, who was heaven-born, but slavery-corrupted, has frequently spoken ponderous words to a listening Senate; but their voices awoke no echoes in the universal heart--sent no electric currents through the great arteries of public opinion like "Uncle Tom's Cabin." It will be seen, by-and-bye, that this gentle woman will do more to uproot slavery, than conventions and associations, and premature legislative action. She will do so by creating around Slavery an atmosphere of sentiment too pure for so vile a thing to live in. Has she not already upheaved a tide of feeling in her own country? And has not her book carried with it in this country, publishers, readers, newspapers, lecturers, theatres, and public opinion. And back a wave of that public opinion, charged with mingled sympathy and indignation, has gone to America, to add to the volume, of influence directed against slavery there.

The unbounded success of "Uncle Tom's Cabin," intimates the growth of an important element of moral power in those modern days. It shows what woman can do, and indicates what she is destined to do for the elevation of the race. It has been said and sung, "that they who rock the cradle rule the world"--meaning thereby that woman wields an immense power in forming the minds and training the characters of the world's most illustrious sons. And it is so, and ever has been. The sages and heroes of the earth, have in their proudest moments of triumph and glory, principally attributed their success to the moral influence of their mothers. This must have been so, by the relationship necessarily existing between mother and child. But during the last few years, woman has been exerting another influence on the world. This she has been doing through the medium of that mightiest of all agencies--Literature. The age of Books and Newspapers has yet to come. Literature, though now mightier than the Pulpit and the Platform, and much mightier than both combined, grows in importance and power daily, and will continue to grow as the volume of years increase. And it is through this Literature that woman is destined to exert her potent strength in moulding the character and directing the destinies of man. To do this, it is not necessary that she should pour out high-sounding periods, but paint life as she sees and feels it; to speak, it may be, in monosyllables--but in syllables pregnant and vitalized with the essence of her soul, and then she will see, and the world will acknowledge her transcendent ability. The most powerful things are the most simple and silent. How silent is sunlight--and yet how powerful. Equally silent and equally powerful, in the moral world, is the sunlight of woman's life and genius, when directed through the atmosphere of literature. A notable instance is this "Uncle Tom's Cabin." It is a simple story about simple people. There is no king, or noble lord, or pompous baronet, figuring in its pages. Its heroes and heroines are not taken from courtly circles. The pride and pomp of fashionable life, and the gorgeous display of fashionable aristocratic circles, and all the other gilded machinery, which are the staple materials of ordinary novels, are scarcely alluded to in Mrs. Stowe's work. No: the title of her book is "Uncle Tom's Cabin; or, Life among the Lowly,"-- a title evidently too plebeian for British publishers, as we have not seen it adopted by any of them. Instead of parading before us the externally great, and the accidentally aristocratic, she induces us to walk with her in the midst of the most degraded of the human race--of men and women kept in servile bondage and shameful ignorance. She talks to us of their sorrows and sufferings, of their vices and virtues, of their wrongs and rights; and she talks in so simple a strain, that she enlists our most powerful sympathies in their behalf. She does it in a way that none but a woman could do. Mary Howitt, Mrs. S. C. Hall, George Sand, Mrs. Child, Eliza Cook, the author of "Jane Eyre," and other living female writers, have given the world beautiful and captivating books--books distinguished as much for mental ability, as the moral purpose which pervades them. But that cluster of geniuses must now acknowledge another, and a greater star than any amongst their number. No one more triumphantly vindicates the significance of literature than Mrs. Stowe, as no one before has so effectively used it.

J. P. E.

FREDERICK DOUGLASS.

The most remarkable fugitive slave, and one of the most remarkable men in America, is Frederick Douglass. He possesses powers of mind and oratorical ability which would render him popular anywhere. He is one of the most eloquent speakers living, and he can wield his pen with as much effect as he can his tongue. His intense energy of character and moral bravery are acknowledged by all. His integrity and dignity of life and actions have long stamped him as one of the most extraordinary citizens of the United States. "If there is a man on earth," says Dr. Campbell "he is a man." To give our readers an idea of what this man was a little after he escaped from slavery, and to sharpen their curiosity to know what they can of his previous perilous and romantic life, we cannot do better than give a few passages from an address, delivered by W. Lloyd Garrison, in Boston, in 1845. "In the month of August, 1841," says he, "I attended an anti-slavery convention in Nantucket, at which it was my happiness to become acquainted with Frederick Douglass. He was a stranger to nearly every member of this body, but having recently made his escape from the southern house of bondage, and feeling his curiosity excited to ascertain the principles and measures of the abolitionists--of whom he had heard a somewhat vague description while he was a slave--he was induced to give his attendance on the occasion alluded to, though at that time a resident in New Bedford.

"Fortunate, most fortunate occurrence! fortunate for the millions of his manacled brethren yet panting for deliverance from their awful thralldom! fortunate for the cause of negro emancipation and of universal liberty! fortunate for the land of his birth, which he has done much to save and bless! fortunate for the large circle of friends and acquaintances whose sympathy and affection he has strongly secured by the many sufferings he has endured; by his virtuous traits of character, by his ever abiding remembrances of those who are in bonds, as being bound with him! fortunate for the multitudes in various parts of our republic whose minds he has enlightened on the subject of negro slavery, and who have been melted to tears by his pathos, or roused to virtuous indignation by his stirring eloquence against the enslavers of men! fortunate for himself, as it at once brought him into the field of public usefulness, 'gave the assurance of a MAN,' quickened the slumbering energies of his soul and consecrated him to the great work of breaking the rod of the oppressor and letting the oppressed go free.

"I shall never forget his first speech at the convention; the extraordinary emotion it excited in my own mind, the powerful impression it created upon a crowded auditory, completely taken by surprise; the applause which followed from the beginning to the end of his felicitous remarks. I think I never hated slavery so intensely as at that moment; certainly my perception of the enormous outrage which is inflicted by it on the godlike nature of its victims, was rendered far more clear than ever. There stood one, in physical proportion and stature commanding and erect, in natural eloquence a prodigy, in soul manifestly 'created but a little lower than the angles,' yet a slave, aye, a fugitive slave, trembling for his safety, hardly daring to believe that on the American soil, a single white person could be found who would befriend him at all hazards, for the love of God and humanity. Capable of high attainments as an intellectual and moral being, needing nothing but a comparatively small amount of cultivation to make him an ornament to society and a blessing to his race--by the law of the land, by the voice of the people, by the terms of the slave code, he was only a piece of property, a beast of burden, a chattel personal, nevertheless!

"A beloved friend from New Bedford prevailed on Mr. Douglass to address the convention. He came forward to the platform with a hesitancy and embarrassment, necessarily the attendants of a sensitive mind in such a novel position. After apologizing for his ignorance, and reminding the audience that slavery was a poor school for the human intellect and heart, he proceeded to narrate some of the facts in his own history as a slave, and in the course of his speech gave utterance to many noble and thrilling reflections. As soon as he had taken, his seat, filled with hope and admiration, I rose, and declared that Patrick Henry, of revolutionary fame, never made a speech more eloquent in the cause of liberty, than the one we had just listened to from the lips of that hunted fugitive. So I believed at that time--such is my belief how: I reminded the audience of the peril which surrounded this self-emancipated young man at the North, even in Massachusetts, on the soil of the Pilgrim Fathers, among the descendants of revolutionary sires; and I appealed to them, whether they would ever allow him to be carried back into slavery, law or no law, constitution or no constitution. Their response was unanimous, and in thunder-tones, 'No!' 'Will you succor and protect him as a brother-man--a resident of the old Bay State?' 'YES!' shouted the whole mass, with an energy so startling, that the ruthless tyrants south of Mason and Dixon's line, might almost have heard the mighty burst of feeling, and recognized it as the pledge of an invincible determination on the part of those who gave it, never to betray him that wanders, but to hide the outcast, and firmly to abide the consequences."

Frederick Douglass was born in Tuckahoe, near Hillsborough, and about twelve miles from Easton, in the county of Talbot, Maryland. But when he was born no one knows. Slaves never know when they were born, and are as ignorant of such times as horses. Frederick Douglass says he never met with a slave who knew how old he was, or could tell his birthday. When one jockey asks another, in this country, how old may be the horse which is about to be sold, the answer is, "three or four years last fall." It is precisely in this way that the ages of slaves are estimated in America. And this one fact speaks volumes of the real state and degradation of the slave there.

Frederick Douglass says, that a want of information concerning his own age when he was a boy, was a source of great unhappiness to him. White boys could tell their ages, and be felt uneasy and degraded that he could not. The nearest guess which he is now enabled to give of his ago is, that he supposes he was born sometime during the year 1828.

His father was a white man, and rumor went so far as to say that his father was his master. This is not at all unlikely, as it frequently happens, in the slave-holding states, that the father and the master are one. Frederick was separated from his mother while he was an infant. It was a custom in that part of Maryland to part mothers from their children at a very early age. This no doubt, is done to hinder the development of the child's affection towards the mother, and to blunt and destroy the natural affection of the mother for the child. He never saw his mother more than a few times in his life. What need is there for any imagination to invent ideal disadvantages of slavery, when this one fact is acknowledged? The most tender and the strongest feeling in the human heart is that of a mother's love for her offspring. It is a feeling as strong, yea, even stronger than life itself--a feeling from which the mother derives unutterable joy, and the child immeasurable advantage. But this of all other feelings is trodden under foot and spurned at in America. But poor slave as Douglass mother was, the infamous exactions imposed upon her, did not crush every spark of maternal love in her breast. He says he never remembers seeing his mother by daylight. When she saw him it was at night time. But she died when he was seven years of age; but as he never enjoyed much of her soothing presence he did not probably feel the loss very poignantly.

Instead of being a privilege to have one's master for a father, it is a great disadvantage to the poor slave. This arises from the jealousy which the young mulatto excites in the breast of the master's wife. Douglass says, "the master is frequently compelled to sell this class of his slaves, out of deference to the feelings of his white wife. And cruel as the deed may appear, for a man to sell his own children to human flesh mongers, it is often the dictate of humanity for him to do so; for unless he does this, he must not only whip them himself, but must stand by and see one white son tie up his brother, of but a few shades darker complexion than himself, and ply the gory lash to his naked back."

One of Douglass masters was called Anthony, and though a cruel man himself, he had an overseer more cruel still. The overseer's name was Plummer, who was a miserable drunkard, a profane swearer, and a savage monster. This man was hardened by a long life of slave-holding. He even took pleasure in whipping a slave. Douglas says, "I have often been awakened at dawn of day by the most heart-rending shrieks of an aunt of mine, whom he used to tie up to a joist, and whip upon her naked back till she was literally covered with blood. No words, no tears, from his gory victim, seemed to move his iron heart from its bloody purpose. The louder she screamed, the harder he whipped; and where the blood ran fastest, there he whipped; and where the blood ran fastest, there he whipped longest." Here is a statement recorded by an eye-witness, which no doubt, if related by Mrs. Stowe in her "Uncle Tom's Cabin," would have excited the indignation of the "Times," for its "stimulating" character. The same authority may doubt it now. But why doubt it? Does not familiarity breed contempt? Can we expect grapes from thorns and figs from thistles? Is not the slaveholder himself demoralized by the inhuman system he sustains? And if so, is it unreasonable to suppose that overseers should be inhuman? And if inhuman, is it net unreasonable to suppose that such statements as the above are exaggerations? In fact, such things cannot easily be exaggerated; and well might Douglass say, "It was a most terrible spectacle. I wish I could commit to paper the feelings with which I beheld it."

Douglass soon got under the tender mercies of another overseer, whose name was Severe, who was rightly named and, who soon died. He was followed by another whose name was Hopkins, who remained but a short time, because he was not sufficiently severe. Mr. Hopkins was succeeded by Mr. Austin Gore, "a man possessing in an eminent degree all those traits of character indispensable to what is called a first-rate overseer." This Mr. Gore was a grave man, and though a young man, he indulged in no jokes, said no funny words, seldom smiled. His acts were in perfect keeping with his words. Overseers will sometimes indulge in a witty word, even with the slaves; not so with this Mr. Gore. He was "dressed in a little brief authority," and must have made "e'en angels weep," and poor slaves at the same time. "He spoke but to command, and commanded but to be obeyed; he dealt sparingly with his words, and bountifully with his whip; never using the former, while the latter would answer as well. When he whipped, he did so from a sense of duty, and feared no consequences. He did nothing reluctantly, no matter how disagreeable; always at his post, never inconsistent. He never promised but to fulfill. He was a man of the most inflexible firmness and stone-like coolness. He was of all overseers most dreaded by the slaves. His presence was painful; his eye flashed confusion, and seldom was his sharp shrill voice heard without producing horror and trembling in their hearts."

Such is a passing sketch of a consistent man, whose barbarity was only equaled by the consummate coolness with which he committed the grossest and most savage deeds. He once undertook to whip a slave of the name of Demby. He had given Demby but a few stripes, when, to get rid of the scourging, he ran and plunged into a creek, and stood there at the depth of his shoulders, refusing to come out. "Gore told him that he would give him three calls, and that if he did not come out at the third call, he would shoot him. The first call was given. Demby made no response, but stood his ground. The second and third calls were made with the same result. Mr. Gore then, without consultation or deliberation by any one, not even giving poor Demby an additional call, raised his musket to his shoulder, taking deadly aim at his standing victim, and in an instant poor Demby was no more, his mangled body sank out of sight, and blood and brains marked the water where he had stood.

"A thrill of horror flashed through every soul upon the plantation, excepting that of Mr. Gore. He was asked by Colonel Lloyd, why he resorted to this extraordinary expedient? His reply was (as well as I remember) that Demby had become unmanageable--that he was setting a bad example to the other slaves--one which, if suffered to pass without some such demonstration on his part, would finally lead to the total subversion of all rule and order upon the plantation. He argued, that if one slave refused to be corrected, and escaped with his life, the other slaves would soon copy the example; the results of which would be the freedom of the blacks, and the enslavement of the whites. Mr. Gore's defense was satisfactory. He was continued in his station as overseer upon the same plantation. His fame as an overseer went abroad. His horrid crime was not even submitted to judicial investigation. It was committed in the presence of slaves, and they of course could neither institute a suit, nor testify against him; and thus the guilty perpetrator of one of the bloodiest and most foul murders goes unvisited by justice, and uncensored by the community in which he lives." In order to substantiate the fact, and to leave no doubt on the reader's mind, Mr. Douglass gives all its particulars. He says, "Mr. Gore lived in St. Michael's, Talbot county, Maryland, when I left there; and if he is still alive, he very probably lives there now; and if so, he is now, as he was then, as highly esteemed and as much respected as though his guilty soul had not been stained with his brother's blood.

"I speak advisedly when I say that killing a slave, or any colored person, in Talbot county, Maryland, is not accounted as a crime, either by the courts or the community. Mr. Thomas Lanman, of St. Michael's, killed two slaves, one of them he killed with a hatchet, by knocking his brains out. He used to boast of the commission of the awful deed. I have heard him do so, laughingly, saying, among other things, that he was the only benefactor of the country in the company, and that when others had done as much as he had done, we should be relieved of the d----d niggers."

Mr. Douglass goes on to say "the wife of Mr. Giles Hicks, living but a short distance from where I used to live, murdered my wife's cousin, a young girl between fifteen and sixteen years of age, mangling her person in the most horrible manner, breaking her nose and breastbone with a stick, so that the poor girl expired in a few hours afterwards. She was immediately buried, but had only been in her untimely grave a few hours, before she was taken up and examined by the coroner, who decided that she had come to her death by beating. The offence for which this girl was thus murdered was this--She had been set that night to mind Mrs. Hicks' baby, and during the night she fell asleep, and the baby cried. The girl having lost her rest for several nights previous, did not hear the crying. They were both in the room with Mrs. Hicks. Mrs. Hicks finding the girl slow to move, jumped from her bed, seized an oak stick from the fire-place, and with it broke the girl's nose and breastbone, and thus ended her life. I will not say that this most horrid murder produced no sensation in the community. It did produce a sensation, but not enough to bring the murderess to punishment. There was a warrant issued for her arrest, but it was not served. Thus she escaped not only punishment, but even the pain of being arraigned before a court for her horrid crime.

"Whilst I am detailing bloody deeds which took place during my stay on Colonel Lloyd's plantation, I will briefly narrate another, which occurred about the same time as the murder of Demby by Mr. Gore.

"Colonel Lloyd's slaves were in the habit of spending a part of their nights and Sundays in fishing for oysters, and in this way made up the deficiency of their scanty allowance. An old man, belonging to Colonel Lloyd, while thus engaged, happened to get beyond the limits of his master's plantation, and on the premises of Beal Bondly. At this trespass Mr. Bondly took offence, and, with his musket, came down to the shore, and blew its deadly contents into the poor old man.

"Mr. Bondly came over to see Colonel Lloyd the next day, whether to pay him for his property, or to justify himself in what he had done, I know not; at any rate, this whole fiendish transaction was soon hushed up. There was little said about it, and nothing done. It was a common saying, even among little white boys, that it was worth a half cent to kill a nigger, and a half cent to bury one."

Had Mrs. Stowe detailed such circumstances as these, it would have been said that her "pictures were too stimulating," and her "delineations too highly colored and exaggerated," and that, consequently, she would defeat her purposes, and that the slave's fetters would be fastened still closer on her account. But we have here detailed facts not fictions; and these facts are given by an eye-witness, whose statements can be relied on, as much as those of any pro-slavery man in America.

Mr. Horace Greeley, a man of great mental endowments, and high moral respectability, said, in the "New York Tribune," (a paper which circulates more copies daily than the "Times") a little after Frederick Douglass' life was published, "We highly prize all evidence of this kind, and it is becoming more abundant. Douglass seems very just and temperate. We feel that his view, even of those who have injured him most, may be relied on. He knows how 'to allow for motives and influences.' " Such is the endorsement of Mr. Horace Greeley's opinion of the truths contained in Frederick Douglass' narrative. Another authority, as high as that of Mr. Greeley's--Mr. Wendell Phillips, says, in a letter to Douglass, "In reading your life, no one can say that you have unfairly picked out some rare specimens of cruelty. We know that the bitter drops, which even you have drained from the cup, are no incidental aggravations, no individual ills, but such as much mingle always and necessarily in the lot of every slave. They are the essential ingredients, not the occasional results of the system." Mr. Lloyd Garrison, another man who is as much celebrated for his virtuous character, as for his intense hatred of the "peculiar institution," which it is the peculiar glory of America to possess, says, in the preface to Douglass' life, that every word it contains may be relied on for its truthfulness. The men whose names I have here mentioned are as respectable as any of the writers in the "Times" newspaper. That paper has impugned the character of Mrs. Stowe's book, because it is exaggerated, and yet that book does not contain instances more diabolical than those related by Douglass. The most barbarous incident detailed in "Uncle Tom's Cabin" is the death of Uncle Tom himself, and the means used to bring it about. He was flogged to death and his murderer was not arraigned before a court of justice. If he had been, there was no evidence to prove the fact, as the evidence of a slave is no evidence in the Southern States. This is quite consistent. Take away from a man over himself, ignore his individuality and humanity, and then take his evidence on oath before a court of justice, would be folly. It would be admitting him a man in the one instance and not in the other.

It so happens that where barbarous transactions take place, very frequently there is no white man near, and certainly no friendly white man. And it is quite evident, and quite reasonable to believe, that where one murder gets circulated, ten or more are heard nothing of; and it is not for a moment unreasonable to suppose, that in those great cotton plantations of the South, where the slave is held in such low estimation as a man, and where cruel hard-hearted overseers are permitted to have uncontrolled sway over him, that he should frequently fall a victim to the passion or caprice of those above him. We have just recorded five instances which occurred within a brief period, in a comparatively small portion of the slave-holding states. And as Mr. Douglass has given the names of the places, and the parties, without meeting with any authentic contradiction, we are bound to believe what he says, and in believing it, express our deepest detestation of slavery, and condemnation of slave-holders. As a confirmation of Mr. Douglass' evidence, we will give an extract from a Baltimore paper. The "Baltimore American," of March 17, 1845, contains the following--

"SHOOTING A SLAVE.--We learn upon the authority of a letter from Charles county, Maryland, received by a gentleman of this city, that a young man, named Matthews, a nephew of General Matthews, and whose father, it is believed, holds an office at Washington, killed one of his slaves upon his father's farm, by shooting him. The letter states that young Matthews had been in charge of the farm; that he gave an order to the servant, which was disobeyed, when he proceeded to the house, obtained a gun, and, returning, shot the servant. He immediately," the letter continues, "fled to his father's residence, where he still continues unmolested." We give this extract as it is taken from a paper printed near where Douglass formerly lived.

After the above, we think, pardonable digression, we return to the early career of Douglass. He did not remain long on Colonel Lloyd's plantation, and while there, was not, on the whole, treated harshly. He was sufficiently fortunate to become a bit of a favorite of Colonel Lloyd's son Daniel, and was employed in going with him on shooting excursions, and finding the birds after they were shot, or in running errands for Daniel's sisters. His young master would not allow older boys to impose on his "little nigger," and would even go so far as to divide his cakes with him. Douglass says, "I was seldom whipped by my old master, and suffered little from anything else than hunger and cold. I suffered much from hunger, but much more from cold. The hottest summer, and coldest winter, I was kept almost naked--no shoes, no stockings, no jacket, no trousers, nothing but a coarse torn linen shirt, reaching only to my knees. I had no bed. I must have perished with cold, but that during the coldest nights, I used to steal a bag which was used for carrying corn to the mill. I would crawl into this bag, and then sleep on the cold, damp clay floor, with my head in, and feet out. My feet have been so cracked with the frost, that the pen with which I am writing, might be laid in the gashes. We were not regularly allowanced. Our food was coarse corn-meal, boiled, called mush. It was put into a large wooden tray or trough, and set down upon the ground. The children were then called like so many pigs, and like so many pigs they would come and devour the mush,--some with oyster-shells, others with pieces of shingle, some with naked hands, and none with spoons. He that ate fastest got most; he that was strongest secured the best place, and few left the trough satisfied."

Douglass was about eight years old when he left Colonel Lloyd's plantation to go to Baltimore, to live with Mr. Hugh Auld. When the information reached him that he was to go, he danced for joy; and why should he not? He had no home. His mother was dead, and there was nothing particular in Colonel Lloyd's plantation to attract him. He had three days to prepare previous to leaving for Baltimore; and these three days were spent in "washing off the plantation scurf, not so much because he wished to wash, but because Mrs. Lucretia had told him that he must get all the dead skin off his feet and knees before he could go to Baltimore, for the people there were very cleanly." Besides, she was going to give him a pair of trousers. The thought of owning a pair of trousers was great indeed. He says, "It was almost a sufficient motive not only to make me take off what would be called by pig-drovers the mange, but the skin itself. I went at it in good earnest, working for the first time with the hope of reward."

When he got to Baltimore, he found that he had to take care of the little son of Mr. Auld. Here he saw what he had never seen before--a white face beaming upon him with the most kindly emotions--the face of his mistress, Mrs. Sophia Auld. It was a strange sight to him, brightening up his pathway with the light of happiness. He ever afterwards attributed his removal from Colonel Lloyd's plantation as a manifestation of Providence, as it "opened the gateway to all his subsequent prosperity."

His new mistress proved all she appeared, or at least for some time. "Her face was made of heavenly smiles, and her voice of tranquil music." She taught Douglass the A. B. C., and to read words of three or four letters. But just at this part of his progress, her husband found out what was going on, and at once forbade Mrs. Auld to instruct him any further telling her that it was not only unlawful, but unsafe, to teach a slave to read. He said, if you give a nigger an inch, he will take an ell. A nigger should know nothing, but obey his master. Learning would spoil the best nigger in the world, and he was right. For the very small amount of instruction the boy had received from his mistress awoke in him an unquenchable desire to know more. The words of his master sank deep into his heart, and stirred emotions which before slumbered. They were to him a new and special revelation, explaining dark and mysterious things, with which his youthful understanding had struggled. He long entertained doubts about the relative positions of the white man and the black man, and could not imagine why the one should continue the slave of the other. But when he heard that learning would spoil the best nigger in existence, he saw in what consisted the controlling power of the white man over the slave. From that moment, he saw the pathway from slavery to freedom. Though conscious of the difficulty of learning without a teacher, he set out with a high hope and a fixed purpose to learn to read at whatever cost of labor. "All the heaven of great desire" was lit within him. And now began his "pursuit of knowledge under difficulties."

The plan which he adopted, and the one by which he was most successful, was that of making friends of all the little white boys he met in the streets. As many of those as he could he converted into teachers, and used all kinds of maneuvers to entice them to teach him. When he was sent on errands he carried his little book with him, and by going one part of the way quickly, he found time to get a lesson before he returned. He used to carry crusts of bread with him, with which he would tempt the little hungry urchins to assist him to get the more valuable bread of knowledge, for which he was still more hungry. His master and mistress were now suspicious that he was learning to read, and watched him secretly, and threw every possible impediment in his way. But it was now too late. The first step was taken, and his mistress, in teaching him the alphabet, had given him the inch, by which he would take the ell. Little did she know what she was doing at the time. She was sending the first stray beam of sunlight into a soul that had wrapped up within it mighty powers. She was warning into real intellectual life an intellectual giant--a giant who would, in a very few years vindicate his equality with the greatest man in America. She was unknowingly instructing a boy who would soon, as a man, send his fame over the world--who would speak potent words and perform great deeds for humanity--a man who, had he a lighter-colored skin, would, perhaps, soon have filled the President's chair itself. It is not even unlikely now that Frederick Douglass, though a colored man, will, one day, be the President of the United States. For slavery cannot remain much longer in that country. In spite of all that Webster and all the compromise men have done, this question of questions must get uppermost, whether the integrity of the Union be threatened thereby or not. If slavery be abolished during Frederick Douglass' lifetime, then will he stand a good chance of being elected President. I remember hearing him when he came to this country some time since. He spoke at a large London meeting, and I never heard eloquence so-electrical before. I never saw an English audience so excited as it was under his magic words. He would, at one moment, lash the audience into a storm, and in another moment make it as tranquil as a lake without a ripple. When he sat down. Dr. Campbell, the Editor of the "British Banner," got up and said, "That if he were a few years younger, he would have gone around the world to listen to that speech, rather than not have heard it." And there was not a young man in that vast assembly who would not have followed the doctor; This extraordinary speech will form an Appendix to this volume. We give it verbatim, for two reasons, namely, to show what a poor fugitive slave could do in the greatest city of the world a few years after his self-emancipation, and secondly, to familiarize the British reader with the horrors of the slave system in America. Whoever reads this speech will say, that if it does not equal the finest efforts of Burke, whom the boy Douglass so much admired, that the man Douglass, with English cultivation and advantages, would successfully rival the great English orator. Such was the influence of Douglass' thrilling eloquence. And this man, a few years before, was a slave--a poor slave, in a country which boasts of its independence, its liberty, and its greatness! Well might Dr. Channing say "We are keeping in bondage one of the finest races living." O, America, so sure as a God liveth, the day of retribution must come! So vast a crime cannot be perpetrated without punishment.

Frederick Douglass had not long continued reading before he saw and felt his degradation. Just about this time, and he was only about twelve years of age, he got hold of a book entitle "The Columbian Orator," Among other stirring things in this book he with one of Sheridan's mighty speeches on behalf of Catholic Emancipation. This gave tongue to interesting thoughts of his own soul, which had flashed through it, and died away for want of utterance. As he read and contemplated, that very discontent which was alluded to by his master, came "to torment and sting his soul with unutterable anguish." He began to feel that reading was a curse rather than a blessing to him. It opened his eyes to the horrible pit in which he was plunged. He preferred the condition of the meanest reptile to his own. He says, "anything, no matter what, to get rid of thinking. It was everlasting thinking of my condition that tormented me. There was no getting rid of it; it was pressed upon me by every object within sight or hearing; animate or inanimate. The silver trump of freedom had roused my soul to eternal wakefulness. Freedom now appeared, to disappear no more forever. It was heard in every sound, and seen in everything. It was ever present to torment me with the sense of my wretched condition. I saw nothing without seeing it; I heard nothing without hearing it; and felt nothing without feeling it. It looked from every star, it smiled-in every calm, breathed in every wind, and moved in every storm."

The manner in which the future reformer and orator learnt to write is worth recording. The idea of how he might do so was suggested in a ship-yard. Here he frequently saw the ship-carpenters, after hewing and getting a piece of timber ready for use, write on it the name of that part of the ship for which it was intended. When a piece of timber was intended for the larboard side, it would be marked "L;" when a piece was for the starboard side, it would be marked "S," and so on. In this way he learnt to write these and other letters, and immediately, in his way, commenced copying them. After that, when he met with any boy whom he knew could write, he would tell him he could write as well as him. He would be answered with "I don't believe you; let me see you try it." He would then make the letters which he had been so fortunate as to learn, and ask the boy to beat that. In this way he got a great many writing lessons, which it would be impossible for him to get in any other way. During this time his copy book was the board-fence, the brick wall and pavement, and his pen and ink a lump of chalk. He says: "By this time my little master Thomas had gone to school, and learned how to write, and had written over a number of copy-books. These had been brought home, and shown to some of our near neighbors and then thrown aside. My mistress used to go to class-meeting every Monday afternoon, and leave me to take care of the house. When left thus I used to spend the time in writing on the spaces left in Master Thomas's copy-book, crossing what he had written. I continued to do-this until I could write a hand very similar to that of Master Thomas. Thus, after a long tedious effort, I finally succeeded in learning to write."

Soon after this Douglass master died, and he, the slave, was valued with the other property. The stock on the estate was all valued together, men and women, old and young, married and single horses, sheep, and swine. Horses and men, cattle and women, pigs and children, were all held in the same rank in the scale of being by the valuer, and were all subjected to the same narrow examination. Silvery-headed age and sprightly youth, maids and matrons, underwent the same indelicate examination. Poignantly must the young slave have felt the degradation of his situation, when he saw himself held in the same estimation as the brutes. But such is slavery.

It fell to the lot of Douglass to be apportioned to Mrs. Lucretia, a daughter of his late master. In this he was fortunate, as he might have fallen to the portion of Master Andrew, who was a most cruel monster. "A man who," says Douglass, "but a few days before, to give me a sample of his bloody disposition, took my little brother by the throat, threw him on the ground, and with the heel of his boot stamped upon his head, till the blood gushed from his nose and ears." Very soon after this division of property, Mrs. Lucretia died; and a short time after her death, Master Andrew died. Now all the property of his late master fell into the hands of strangers. Not a slave was left free, not even Douglass' old grandmother, who had been a source of wealth to his late master. "If any one thing," says Douglass, "in my experience, more than another, served to deepen my conviction of the infernal character of slavery, and to fill me with unutterable loathing of slaveholders, it was their base ingratitude to my poor old grandmother. She had served my old master faithfully from youth to old age. She had been the source of all his wealth; she had peopled his plantation with slaves; she had become a great-grandmother in his service. She had rocked him in infancy, attended him in childhood, served him through life, and at his death wiped from his icy brow the cold death-sweat, and closed his eyes forever. She was nevertheless left a slave--a slave for life--a slave in the hands of strangers; and in their hands she saw her children, her grandchildren, and her great-grandchildren divided, like so many sheep, without being gratified with the small privilege of a single word as to their or her own destiny. And to cap the climax of their base ingratitude and fiendish barbarity, my grandmother, who was now very old, having outlived my old master and all his children, having seen the beginning and end of all of them, and her present owners finding she was of but little value, her frame already racked with the pains of old age, and complete helplessness fast stealing over her once active limbs, they took her to the woods, built her a little hut, put up a little mud chimney, and then made her welcome to the privilege of supporting herself there in perfect loneliness; thus virtually turning her out to die! If my poor old grandmother now lives, she lives to suffer in utter loneliness; she lives to remember and mourn over the loss of her children, the loss of grandchildren, and the loss of great-grandchildren. The hearth is desolate. The children, the unconscious children, who once sang and danced in her presence, are gone. She gropes her way, in the darkness of age, for a drink of water. Instead of the voices of her children, she hears by day the moans of the dove, and by night the screams of the hideous owl. The grave is at the door. And now, when weighed down by the pains and aches of old age, when the head inclines to the feet, when the beginning and ending of human existence meet, and helpless infancy and painful old age combine together--at this time, this most needful time, the time for the exercise of that tenderness and affection which children only can exercise towards a declining parent--my poor old grandmother, the devoted mother of twelve children, is left all alone, in yonder little hut, before a few dim embers. She stands--she sits--she staggers--she falls--she groans--she dies--and there are none of her children or grandchildren present, to wipe from her wrinkled brow the cold sweat of death, or to place beneath the sod her fallen remains. Will not a righteous God visit for these things?"

Douglass had to change masters several times. In 1832, he left Baltimore, and went and lived with Mr. Thomas Auld, at St. Michael's. This Mr. Auld was a mean man. He kept his slaves without sufficient food. And not to give a slave enough to eat is regarded as the most aggravated development of meanness, even among slaveholders. One of the most extraordinary moral phenomenon among slaveholders is, that those who profess to be religious are frequently the most cruel and mean. In August, 1832, this Mr. Auld attended a Methodist camp meeting, "and there experienced religion." It was thought he would now alter for the better. But if he altered at all, he altered for the worse. For, prior to his conversion, he relied upon his own depravity to shield and sustain him in his barbarity; but after his conversion he found religious sanction and support for his slaveholding cruelty. He made the greatest pretension to piety. He prayed morning, noon and night. His activity at revivals was very great, and he proved himself an instrument in the hands of the church in converting many souls. His house was the preachers' home. But while he stuffed the preachers, he starved his slaves. Such is one of the anomalies of human conduct, and it can only be explained on the principle that "familiarity breeds contempt."

Slaveholders, by treating men as brutes, soon get to think men brutes; and then continue to treat them as brutes, as a matter of course. And so deeply rooted do prejudices get in their nature, that even the softening, sanctifying influences of Christianity make little or no impression on them. How indescribably low must these men be who put on the cloak of Christianity while engaged in a system so "steeped in iniquity,"--a system which has been called by a distinguished critic "the sum of human villainies," "I am filled with unutterable loathing," says Douglass, "When I contemplate the religious pomp and show, together with the horrible inconsistencies which co-exist in the slave states. They have men stealers for ministers, women-whippers for missionaries, and cradle-plunderers for church members. The man who wields the blood-clotted cow skin during the week fills the pulpit on Sunday, and claims to be a minister of the meek and lowly Jesus. The man who robs me of my earning at the end of each week, meets me as a class leader on Sunday morning, to show me the way of life and the path of salvation. he who sells my sister, for purposes of prostitution, stands forth as the pious advocate of purity. He who proclaims it a religious duty to read the Bible, denies me the right of learning to read the name of the God who made me. He who is the religious advocate of marriage, robs whole millions of its sacred influence, and leaves them to the ravages of wholesale pollution. The warm defender of the sacredness of the family relation is the same that scathes whole families--sundering husbands and wives, parents and children, sisters and brothers--leaving the hut vacant, and the hearth desolate. We see the thief preaching against theft, and the adulterer against adultery. We have men sold to build churches, women sold to support the Gospel, and babes sold to purchase Bibles for the poor heathen? All for the glory of God, and the good of souls!

"The slave auctioneer's bell and the church-going bell chime in with each other, and the bitter cries of the heart-broken slave are drowned in the religious shouts of his pious master. Revivals in religion and revivals in the slave-trade, go hand in hand together. The slave prison and the church stand near each other. The clanking of fetters and the rattling of chains in the prison, and the pious psalm and the solemn prayer in the church may be heard at the same time. The dealers in the bodies and souls of men erect their stand in the presence of the pulpit, and they mutually help each other. The dealer gives his blood-stained gold to support the pulpit, and the pulpit, in return, covers his infernal business with the garb of Christianity. There we behold religion and robbery the allies of each other; slavery and piety linked and interlinked; preachers of the Gospel united with slaveholders. A horrible sight, to see devils dressed in angels' robes, and hell, presenting the semblance of paradise!"

Another evidence of the falseness and hypocrisy of this man, who professed to be a follower of Him who was so meek and lowly, so pure and disinterested, may be ascertained from his treatment of a lone young woman. When quite a child she fell into the fire, and burned herself horribly. Her hands got so burnt that she never again had the use of them. She could do very little to gain her own livelihood, and consequently was considered a burden on the estate. She was once given away to Auld's sister; but being a poor gift was quickly returned. And this man--this religious man--would tie up this lame young woman, and whip her with a cow skin on her naked shoulders, causing the warm red blood to drop, and in justification of the bloody deed, he would quote the following passage of Scripture--"He that knoweth his master's will and doeth it not, shall be beaten with many stripes." And he would keep this lacerated young woman tied up in this horrid situation, four or five hours at a time. He was known to tie her up early in the morning and whip before breakfast; leave her, go to his store, return to dinner, and whip her again, cutting her in the places already made raw, with his cruel lash. Another secret of this man's cruelty toward the poor woman was found in the fact of her being almost helpless."

It is not at all likely that a man who would treat a female slave so harshly, would show more mercy to the males. And poor Douglass, like the rest, had much to put up with. One of his greatest faults was letting his master's horse run away, and go down to his father-in-law's farm, which was about four miles from St. Michael's. And Douglass had to go and fetch it and his reason for this kind of carelessness, or carefulness, was that he always managed to get enough to eat when there. No doubt such a desideratum was an inducement for Douglass to let the horse run away and follow him pretty frequently. At last Mr. Auld got so tired with his slave, who always got hungry, if he had not enough to eat, that he determined on letting him out to a "nigger broker" for twelve months. He was accordingly let to a Mr. Covey for one year. This Mr. Covey, who performed such a noble mission in the world, as that of "breaking in" obstreperous niggers, was not, as it might reasonably be expected, distinguished for his humanity. He had acquired a very high reputation for training young slaves--for making them methodical, steady-going workers. When Douglass heard that he was about to be removed to be improved, he was not disheartened, as he knew, from what he had heard, though he should have to work hard under the strictest and severest discipline, that he should have enough to eat, which is not the smallest consideration to a hungry man. During all this time he felt the degradation of his position. He yearned for freedom, and frequently revolved in his mind the best mode of making his escape. Every bit of information that he could get, that would in any way enable him to see how he might get to the land of freedom, was most cordially welcomed.

He left Mr. Auld's house, and went to live with Covey, "the nigger broker," on the 1st of January, 1833. Being accustomed to a city life, and unaccustomed to field employment, he found himself more awkward than a country boy in a large city. He had been in his new home no more than one week, before Mr. Covey gave him a severe whipping, cutting his back, and causing the blood to run, and raising ridges there as large as his finger. Such treatment was not at all likely to reconcile him to the life of a slave, and especially as he had been so impertinent as to wish himself a free man. During the first six months he remained with Mr. Covey, a week did not escape without his being lashed. He was hardly ever free from a sore back. Think of this ye who know what it is to breath the air and enjoy the sunlight of freedom! Think of this young man, possessing sensitive feelings, who was keenly alive to the degradation of his lot, from whose deep heart would frequently bubble up hopes for liberty, who possessed a mind, even then, more capacious and enlightened than his master's--always carrying with him a sore back--a back made sore by frequent whippings. And this while he was worked fully up to the point of endurance. He says, "long before day we were up, our horses fed, and by the first approach of day all were off to the field, both with our hoes and ploughing teams. Mr. Covey gave us enough to eat, but scarce time to eat it. We were often less than five minutes taking our meals, we were often in the fields from the first approach of day till its last lingering ray had left us, and saving fodder time, midnight often caught us in the field binding blades."

"If at any one time of my life more than another," says he, "I was made to drink the bitterest dregs of slavery, that time was during the first six months of my stay with Mr. Covey. We were worked in all weathers. It was never too hot or too cold; it could never rain, blow, or snow too hard for us to work in the field. Work, work,

work was scarcely more the order of the day than the night. The longest days were too short for him. I was somewhat unmanageable when I first went there, but a few months of this discipline soon tamed me. I was broken in body, soul, and spirit; my natural elasticity was crushed; my intellect languished; the disposition to read departed, the cheerful spark that lingered about my eye died; the dark night of slavery closed in upon me."

But he was not altogether crushed. The Godlike in his nature was not altogether effaced. There were still some lingering hopes of freedom, some embers still smoldering's in the depths of his heart, which even, the brutal discipline of Mr. Covey could not quench. Had he been but a little weaker minded man,--did not nature ended him with the elements of that intellectual and moral life, which were inextinguishable,--then would he have remained in slavery, and the world would have lost a great man.

Sunday was his only leisure time, which be spent in a beast-like stupor, between sleep and wakefulness, under some large tree. At times, he would rise up, a flash of freedom would dart through his soul, accompanied with a faint gleam of hope, that flickered for a moment and then vanished. Years afterwards, he said "My sufferings in this plantation seem now more like a dream than a reality."

It seemed at the time that fate delighted to tantalize him. He possessed a nature capable of enjoying freedom, but was not permitted to realize it; and his master's house stood within a few rods of the Chesapeake Bay, whose broad bosom was ever white with sails from all quarters of the globe. These vessels, robed in white canvas, so beautiful to the eye of the painter, were to him so many shrouded ghosts, to terrify and torment him with thoughts of his own wretched condition. He frequently, in the deep stillness of a summer's Sabbath, stood alone upon the lofty banks of that noble bay, and traced with saddened and tearful eye, the countless number of sail moving off to the great ocean. Such a sight powerfully affected him. It would stir the very depths or his soul: at one moment he would wish himself a brute, and at another he would give utterance to his most cherished aspirations; and there, with no audience but the Almighty One, he would pour out his soul's complaint in fervent apostrophes to the moving multitudes of ships, in language like the following:

"You are loosed from your moorings, and are free; I am fast in my chains, and am a slave! You move merrily before the gentle gale, and I sadly before the bloody whip! You are freedom's swift-winged angels, that fly round the world; I am confined in bands of iron! O that I were free! O that I were on one of your gallant decks, and under your protecting wings! Alas! betwixt me and you the turbid waters roll. Go on, go on. O that I could also go! Could I but swim! If I could fly! O, why was I born a man, of whom to make a brute! The glad ship is gone; she hides in the dim distance. I am left in the Hottest hell of unending slavery. O God, save me! God, deliver me! Let me be free! Is there any God? Why am I a slave? I will run away. I will not stand it. Get caught or get clear, I'll try it. I had as well, die with ague as the fever. I have only one life to lose. I had as well be killed running as die standing. Only think of it; one hundred miles straight north, and I am free! Try it? Yes! God helping me, I will. It cannot be that I shall live and die a slave. I will take to the water. This very bay shall yet bear me to freedom. The steamboats steer in a north-east course from North Point. I will do the same; and when I go to the head of the bay, I will turn my canoe adrift, and walk straight through Delaware to Pennsylvania. When I get there I shall not be required to have a pass. I can travel without being disturbed. Let but the first opportunity offer, and come what will, I am off. Meanwhile I will try to bear up under the yoke. I am not the only slave in the world. Why should I fret? I can bear as much as any of them. Besides, I am but a boy, and all boys are bound to someone. It may be that my misery in slavery will only increase my happiness when I get free. There is a better day coming."

Lloyd Garrison, in his preface to Douglass' narrative, from which we have taken the above, and the other quotations, says, "Who can read that passage and be insensible to its pathos and sublimity? Compressed into it is a whole Alexandrian library of thought, feeling, and sentiment--all that can, all that need, be urged in the form of expostulation, entreaty, rebuke, against the crime of crimes--making man the property of his fellow-men. O, how accursed is that system, which entombs the godlike mind of man, defaces the divine image, reduces those who, by creation, were crowned with glory and honor, to a level with four-footed beasts, and exalts the dealer in human flesh above what is called God."

"So profoundly ignorant of the nature of slavery are many persons, that they are stubbornly incredulous whenever they read or listen to any recital of the cruelties which are daily inflicted on its victims. They do not deny that the slaves are held as property; but that terrible fact seems to convey to their minds no idea of injustice, exposure, or outrage, or savage barbarity. Tell them of cruel scourging's, of mutilations and brandings, of scenes of pollution and blood, of the banishment of all light and knowledge, and they affect to be greatly indignant at such enormous exaggerations, such wholesale misstatements, such abominable libels on the character of the southern planters! As if all these direful outrages were not the natural results of slavery! As if it were less cruel to reduce a human being to the condition of a thing, than to give him a severe flagellation, or to deprive him of necessary food and clothing! As if whips, chains, thumbscrews, paddles, blood-hounds, overseers, drivers, patrols, were not all indispensable to keep the slaves down, and to give protection to their ruthless oppressors! As if, when the marriage institution is abolished, concubines, adultery, and incest, must not necessarily abound; when all the rights of humanity are annihilated, any barrier remains to protect the victim from the fury of the spoiler; when absolute power is assumed over life and liberty, it will not be wielded with destructive away."

But irresistibly destructive as slavery generally is in taming the mind, and rendering it comparatively contented with its fate, it did not, and could not, quench the spiritual fire in Douglass' nature. The wide expanse of Chesapeake Bay, the tumbling of its everlasting waves, whispering as they did of freedom, the memories of this former reading, and the teachings of nature fed within him the fire of hope and expectation. He was bent but not broken; and an opportunity soon presented itself for him to show that he had the will and the power to resist his oppressor. On one hot summer day, after working excessively hard, he was seized with a violent headache, attended with extreme dizziness. He trembled in every limb, and at last fell from sheet exhaustion. Mr. Covey seeing him down, came and asked him what was the matter. Douglass told him as well as he could, for he had scarce strength to speak. This only brought to him a savage kick. Douglass tried to get up; he again staggered and fell. While down in this situation, Covey took up "the hickory slat with which Hughes had been striking off the half-bushel measure," and gave him a heavy blow on the head, and made a large wound, from which the blood flowed freely. The loss of blood relieved his head; and as soon as he could rise, he resolved to go and tell his legal master, Mr. Auld, what had occurred; and after a journey of about seven miles, through bogs and briars, barefooted and bareheaded, he presented himself to this humane gentlemen. From his head to his feet he was covered in blood. His hair was clotted with dust and blood--his shirt was stiff with blood. He looked like a man who had just escaped by the skin of his teeth, a den of lions. But his tale and his pleadings availed nothing. He was told to go back to Mr. Covey, which he did the following morning. As soon as Covey saw him he ran after him with the cow-hide, and was about to lay it on "pretty slick," but Douglass made his escape into a corn-field; and as the corn was very high, it afford him the means of hiding. He spent the most of the day in the woods, having the alternative before him--to go home and be whipped to death, or stay in the wood and be starved to death, but the following day being Sunday he resolved to return. When he got home he met Mr. Covey in the gateway, who, instead of being angry, spoke kindly to him. He was told to drive the pigs from a lot nearby. This singular conduct impressed Douglass; he could not imagine what could have happened to have made his master so civil. All went on well till Monday. Long before morning he was told to go and rub, curry, and feed the horses, which he did with alacrity. But whilst this happened, Mr. Covey entered the stable with a long rope, and immediately caught hold of Douglass' legs and began tying them. But we will let Douglass speak for himself. "As soon as I knew what he was up to, I gave a sudden spring, and as I did so, he holding to my legs, I was brought sprawling on the stable floor. Mr. Covey seemed now to think he had me, and could do what he pleased; but at this moment, from whence came the spirit I don't know, I resolved to fight; and suiting my action to the resolution, I seized Covey hard by the throat; and as I did so, I rose. He held on to me, and I to him. My resistance was so entirely unexpected, that Covey seemed taken all aback. He trembled like a leaf. This gave me assurance, and I held him uneasy, causing the blood to run where I touched him with the ends of my fingers. Mr. Covey soon called out to Hughes for help. Hughes came, and, while Covey held me, attempted to tie my right hand. While he was in the act of doing so, I watched my chance, and gave him a heavy kick close under the ribs. This kick fairly sickened Hughes, so that he left me in the hands of Mr. Covey. This kick had the effect of not only weakening Hughes, but Covey also. When he saw Hughes bending over with pain, his courage quailed. He asked me if I meant to persist in my resistance? I told him I did, come what might; that he had used me like a brute for six months, and that I was determined to be used so no longer. With that he strove to drag me to a stick that was lying just out of the stable door. He meant to knock me down. But just as he was leaning over to get the stick, I seized him with both hands by his collar, and brought him by a sudden snatch to the ground. By this time, Bill came. Covey called upon him for assistance. Bill wanted to know what he could do. Covey said, 'Take hold of him! take hold of him!' Bill said, his master hired him out to work, and not to help to whip me; so he left Covey and myself to fight our own battle out. We were at it for nearly two hours. Covey at length let me go, puffing and blowing at a great rate, saying, that if I had not resisted, he would not have whipped me half so much. The truth was, that he had not whipped me at all. I considered him as getting entirely the worst end of the bargain; for he had drawn no blood from me, but I had from him. The whole six months afterwards, that I spent with Mr. Covey, he never laid the weight of his finger upon me in anger. He would occasionally say, he didn't want to get hold of me again. 'No,' thought I, 'you need not; for you will come off worse than you did before.'

"This battle with Mr. Covey was the turning point in my career as a slave. It kindled the few expiring embers of freedom, and revived within me a sense of my own manhood. It recalled the departed self-confidence, and inspired me again with a determination to be free. The gratification afforded by the triumph was a full compensation for whatever else might follow, even death itself. He only can understand the deep satisfaction which I experienced, who has himself repelled by force the bloody arm of slavery. I felt as I never felt before. It was a glorious resurrection from the tomb of slavery to the heaven of freedom. My long crushed spirit rose, cowardice departed, bold defiance took its place, and I now resolved that, however long I might remain a slave in form, the day had passed forever when I should be a slave in fact. I did not hesitate to let it be known of me that the white man who expected to succeed in whipping must also succeed in killing me."

Douglass fully expected that he would soon be taken by the constable to the whipping post, and he was surprised to find that Mr. Covey took no steps in that direction; and the only explanation he could give was, that had Mr. Covey done so to him--a boy about sixteen years of age--his reputation would have been lost, and so Douglass was unpunished. His term of service terminated with Covey on Christmas day, 1833. The days between Christmas day and New Year's day are allowed as holidays.

The holidays the slave enjoys are a part and parcel of the gross fraud of the system of slavery. They are professedly a custom established by the benevolence of the slaveholders. They generally consist in ball-playing, wrestling, running footraces, fiddling, dancing, and drinking whiskey: and this latter mode of spending the time is generally most agreeable to the master. It is deemed a disgrace not to get thoroughly drunk at Christmas; and he is regarded as lazy indeed, who does not provide himself during the year, with necessary means to get whiskey enough to last him through Christmas.

But why does the slaveholder promote those drunken orgies among his slaves? Because it is his interest to do so. The slaveholders like to have their slaves spend those days in such a manner as to make them as glad of their ending as of their beginning. Their object is to disgust their slaves with freedom. For instance, the slaveholders not only like when the slaves drink of their own accord, but will adopt various plans to make them drink more. One plan is, to make bets on the slaves, as to who can drink most whiskey without getting drunk; and in this way they succeed in getting whole multitudes to drink to excess. Thus, if the slave ask for freedom, the cunning master cheats him with a dose of vicious dissipation, willfully labeled with the name of liberty. But the slaves during the holidays having had a taste of liberty, and a bitter draught they get, are led to think there is but little to choose between liberty and slavery. So when the holidays end, they stagger from their filthy debaucheries to the field, and feel, on the whole, rather glad to go, from what their masters induce them to believe was freedom, back to the arms of slavery.

On the 1st of January, 1834, Douglass left Mr. Covey and went to live with a Mr. William Freeland, a much superior man to Mr. Covey. He, in fact, was the best master Douglass ever had until he became his own master. While with Freeland he had enough to eat, and what was equally valuable, time enough to eat it. From the description he gives of himself while in this establishment, it appears that he passed his time pretty comfortably, as he was only worked from sunrise to sunset. The small amount of spare time Douglass had at his command, he devoted to the very best account. He was not there long before he succeeded in creating in his companions a desire to read. This desire soon extended itself to other slaves in the neighborhood. They soon mustered up some old spelling-books, and nothing would satisfy them but Douglass meeting them on the Sunday to teach them. He agreed to do so, and accordingly devoted his Sundays to teaching his fellow-slaves to read. Not one of them knew even his letters when Douglass went there. This was all done in the greatest possible secrecy. It was necessary to keep their religious masters unacquainted with the fact; for these men would much rather see their slaves spending their Sabbaths in wrestling, boxing, and drinking whiskey, than trying to read the New Testament.

Here was a sight approaching the sublime--a sight that might be spoken of in story and chanted in song. Here was a poor slave, who had learnt to read himself, in spite of all the difficulties which were thrown in his way, now gathering around him his companions in bonds, and teaching them, in secret, how they might in some way soften their hard destiny by reading. But the fact got known, and one Sunday Messrs. Wright Fairbanks, and Garrison West, both class-teachers, with a great many others rushed in upon the teacher and his pupils, and with the aid of sticks, stones, and violence, broke up the Sabbath-school. Here were consistent followers of the meek and lowly Jesus dispelling by brutal force inoffensive men, and this too on the Sunday, who were guilty of no greater crime than trying to read the New Testament!

"I held my Sabbath-school," says he, "at the house of a free-colored man, whose name I deem it imprudent to mention; for should it be known, it might embarrass him greatly, though the crime of holding the school was committed ten years ago. I had at one time over forty scholars, and those of the right sort, ardently desiring to learn. They were of all ages, though mostly men and women. I look back to those Sundays with an amount of pleasure not to be expressed. They were great days to my soul. The work of instructing my dear fellow-slaves was the sweetest engagement with which I was ever blessed. We loved each other, and to leave them at the close of the Sabbath was a severe cross indeed. When I think that these precious souls are to-day shut up in the prison-house of slavery, my feelings overcome me, and I am almost ready to ask, 'Does a righteous God govern the universe? and for what does he hold the thunder in his right hand, if not to smite the oppressor, and deliver the spoiled out of the hand of the spoiler?" These dear souls came not to Sabbath-school, because it was popular to do so, nor did I teach them because it was reputable to be thus engaged. Every moment they spent in that school they were liable to be taken up and receive thirty-nine lashes. They came because they wished to learn. Their minds had been starved by their cruel masters. They had been shut up in mental darkness. I taught them, because it was the delight of my soul to be doing something that looked like the bettering the condition of my race. I kept up my school nearly the whole year I lived with Mr. Freeland; and, besides my Sabbath-school, I devoted three evenings in the week, during the winter, to teaching the slaves at home. And I have the happiness to know that several of those who came to the Sabbath-school learned how to read; and that one, at least, is now free through my agency."

The time flowed smoothly on while Douglass remained on Mr. Freeland's estate. The first year passed without his receiving a blow. He was not only blessed with a good master, but with generous companions. He loved them, and they loved him. They were linked and interlinked with each other. In speaking of them Douglass says, "I loved them with a love stronger than anything I have experienced since. It is sometimes said that we slaves do not love each other. In answer to this assertion, I can say, I never loved any. or confided in any people, more than my fellow-slaves, and especially those with whom I lived at Mr. Freeland's. I believe we would have died for each other. We never undertook to do anything of any importance, without a mutual consultation. We never moved separately. We were one; and as much so by the mutual hardships to which we were necessarily subjected by our condition as slaves."

Listen to this ye who prate about the inferiority of the negro race. Do you possess nobler feelings than these? If not, forever hold. your tongue in silence. Here were men shut out from the pale of civilization, robbed of their rights, debarred from all privileges of moral and mental improvement, yet yearning for knowledge, and acquiring it in fear of difficulty and bound together by a bond of brotherhood as strong and as sacred as ever united human beings.

This improved condition did not reconcile Douglass to his lot. He still panted for freedom; but he loved his brethren in bonds so much, that he would not-think of escaping without them. And having communicated to them what little he possessed in the way of learning, he began gradually to imbue their minds with a love of liberty. He in fact became a propagandist. He impressed on their minds the gross fraud and inhumanity of slavery. He ascertained their secret feelings, and found them all to possess generous, warm, and noble hearts. They often met and confidentially consulted over the idea of escaping; they recounted their difficulties; told their hopes and fears. At times they were almost disposed to give up, and try to content themselves with their lot; at others they were determined to go. But their path was beset with the greatest obstacles. They knew nothing of Canada. At every gate through which they were to pass, they saw a watchman--at every ferry, a guard--at every bridge, a sentinel--and in every wood, a patrol. They were hemmed in on every side. On the one hand, there stood slavery, a stern reality, glaring frightfully upon them,--its robes already crimsoned with the blood of millions, and even then feasting itself greedily upon their own vitals. On the other hand, away back in the dim distance, and under the flickering light of the north star, behind some craggy hill or snow-covered mountain, stood a doubtful freedom--half-frozen--beckoning them to come and share its hospitality. This, in itself, was sometimes enough to stagger them; but when they permitted themselves to survey the road, they were frequently appalled. Upon either side, they saw grim death, assuming the most horrid shapes. Now it was starvation, causing them to eat their own flesh; now they were contending with the waves, and were drowned; now they were overtaken, and torn to pieces by the fangs of the terrible bloodhound. They were stung by scorpions, chased by wild beasts, bitten by snakes, and, finally, after having nearly reached the desired spot,--after swimming rivers, encountering wild beasts, sleeping in the woods, suffering hunger and nakedness,--they were overtaken by their pursuers, and, in their resistance, they were shot dead upon the spot! We say, this picture sometimes appalled them, and made them

> "Rather bear the ills they had,
> Than fly to others that they knew not of."

In coming to a fixed determination to run away, they did more than Patrick Henry, when he resolved upon liberty or death. With them, it was doubtful liberty at most, and almost certain death if they failed.

Sandy, one of their number, gave up the notion, but still encouraged them. Their company then consisted of Henry Harris, John Harris, Henry Bailey, Charles Roberts, and Douglass. Henry Bailey was Douglass' uncle, and belonged to his master. Charles married his aunt; he belonged to his master's father-in-law, Mr. William Hamilton.

The plan they finally concluded upon was, to get a large canoe belonging to Mr. Hamilton, and upon the Saturday night previous to the Easter holidays, paddle directly up the Chesapeake Bay. On their arrival at the head of the bay, a distance of from seventy to eighty miles from where they then lived, they purposed turning their canoe adrift, and to follow the guidance of the north star, until they got beyond the limits of Maryland. Their reason for taking the water route was, they would be less liable to be suspected as runaways; they hoped to be regarded as fishermen; whereas, if they took the land route they would be subject to interruptions of almost every kind. Anyone having a white face, and being so disposed, could stop them, and subject them to examination.

The week before their intended start, Douglass wrote several protections, one for each of them, in nearly the following words:

"This is to certify that I, the undersigned, have given the bearer, my servant, full liberty to go to Baltimore, and spend the Easter holidays.

"Written with mine own hand, &c. 1835.

"WILLIAM HAMILTON.

"Near St. Michael's, in Talbot County, Maryland."

After preparing all their plans, they anxiously waited for the day when they were to start. They well sustained and fortified themselves in their resolution. Friday night previous to the eventful Saturday was a sleepless one for Douglass, as the whole of the responsibility of the enterprise rested on him. Early in the morning, they went as usual to the fields. With their hearts beating with high expectation; the horn was blown for breakfast. But just when they got to it, Douglass was seized by three constables, and without a word of explanation, his hands and feet were immediately tied; and one after another, the intended fugitives were all secured. Their intention by some means had got wind just on the eve of their contemplated flight, and all their bright hopes were blasted. Instead of freedom, they were all hurried off to prison. Their well-proposed scheme availed them nothing. And hearts, which were beating quickly in the morning with mingled hope, joy, and anxiety, were now thrown into confusion and shrouded with sorrow. And he to whom would be attributed all the glory if they succeeded, now had to bear the greatest share of the despair; but not from those who were in chains with him: they were all true to each other. There was no Judas among the lot--no one who would shift the responsibility on his brother's shoulders. Immediately on the arrest, Douglass managed to destroy his protection ticket; and as they were on their way to prison, the others asked Douglass what they should do with theirs. Having some biscuits with them he told them to eat the tickets with the biscuits, which they did. He also gave them a password, "Own nothing!" and "Own nothing," whispered they all. Firm to each other in misfortune, and undismayed in the hour of difficulty, they cared but little where they went as long as they went together, or what they suffered as long as they could share each other's sympathies. They were now more concerned about their separation than anything else. They dreaded that as much as death. They would have marched to the gallows with a martyr's spirit, and, if they were acquainted with the word, died with "excelsior" on their lips, rather than be false to each other.

They were told that the evidence against them was the testimony of one person, but who that was, their master would not tell them. When they arrived at the jail, they were delivered into the hands of the sheriff, who put them in different cells. They were not there more than twenty minutes, when a swarm of slave-traders, or agents for slave-masters, flocked into the jail to ascertain if they were for sale. "Such a set of beings," says Douglas, "I never saw before I felt myself surrounded by so many fiends from perdition. A band of pirates never looked more like their father the devil. And after taunting us in various ways they one by one went into an examination of us, with intent to ascertain our value."

Immediately after the holidays were over, Mr. Freeland came and gave all but Douglass a free pardon, and took him away with him. This no doubt was done because they were very much wanted at home, and besides as Douglass was the ringleader of the enterprise, and as the others would not in all likelihood, have made their escape, without his Instigation and encouragement.

Douglass was now left to his fate--all alone within the walls of a stone prison. Here he was left a week, when, to his surprise and astonishment, Captain Auld, his master, came and took him out, and instead of selling him, sent him back to Baltimore to learn a trade. No doubt, the chief reason why he was not sent away, was that he was a clever fellow; and his master saw that if well treated he could be turned to excellent account. In this unromantic manner ended, the grand project of escaping to the land of freedom, and Douglass was doomed to servitude a few years longer.

When he got to Baltimore, he was hired by a Mr. W. Gardner to learn how to caulk. It proved, however, a very unfavorable plan for the accomplishment of such an object; for, during the first eight months they were very busy, on account of some vessels which were to be launched during the coming summer, and Douglass being a general assistant, was claimed by everybody to do everything. He was placed at the back and call of seventy-four men, and was to regard them all as masters. "My situation," says he, "at times, was a most trying one. At times, I needed a dozen pair of hands. I was called a dozen ways in the space of a single minute. Three or four voices would strike my ear at the same moment. It was 'Fred, help me to cant this timber here.'--'Fred, come, carry this timber yonder.'--Fred, bring that roller here.'--'Fred, go fetch a fresh can of water.'--'Fred, come, help to saw off the end of this timber.'--'Fred, go quick, and get the crow-bar.'--'Fred, hold on the end of this fall.'--'Fred, go to the blacksmith's shop, and get a new punch.'--'Hurra, Fred, run and bring me a cold chisel.'--'I say, Fred, bear a hand, and get up a fire as quick as lightning under that steam-box.'--'Hallo, nigger! come turn this grindstone.'--'Come, come! move, move! and this timber forward.'--'I say, darky, why don't you heat up some pitch?'--'Hallo! hallo! hallo!' (three voices at the same time.)--'Come here!--go there!--Hold on where you are.-- * * * you, if you move, I'll knock your brains out!' "

This was my school for eight months; and I might have remained there longer; but for a most horrid fight I had with four of the white apprentices, in which my left eye was nearly knocked out, and I was horribly, mangled in other respects. The facts of the case were these. Until a very little while after I went there, white and black ship-carpenters worked side by side, and no one seemed to see any impropriety in it. All hands seemed to be very well satisfied. Many of the black carpenters were free men. Things seemed to be going on very well. All at once, the white carpenters knocked off, and said they would not work with free colored workmen. Their reason for this, as alleged, was that if free colored carpenters were encouraged, they would soon take the trade into their own hands, and poor white men would be thrown out of employment. They, therefore, felt called upon at once to put a stop to it. And taking advantage of Mr. Gardner's necessities, they broke off, swearing they would work no longer, unless he would discharge his black carpenters. Now, though this did not extend to me in form, it did reach me in fact. My fellow-apprentices very soon began to feel it degrading to them to work with me. They began to put on airs, and talk about the "niggers" taking the country, saying we all ought to be killed; and being encouraged by the journeymen, they commenced making my condition as hard as they could, by hectoring me around, and sometimes striking me. I, of course, kept the vow I made after the fight with Mr. Covey, and struck back again, regardless of consequences; and while I kept them from combining, I succeeded very well; for I could whip the whole of them, taking them separately. They, however, at length combined, and came upon me, armed with sticks, stones, and heavy handspikes. One came in front with a half brick. There was one at each side of me, and one behind me. While I was attending to those in front, and on either side, the one behind ran up with a handspike, and struck me a heavy blow upon the head. It stunned me. I fell, and with this they all ran upon me, and commenced beating me with their fists. I let them lay on for a while, gathering strength. In an instant, I gave a sudden surge, and rose to my hands and knees. Just as I did that, one of their number gave me, with his heavy boot, a powerful kick in the left eye. My eyeball seemed to have burst. When they saw my eye closed, and badly swollen, they left me. With this, I seized the handspike, and for a time pursued them. But here the carpenter interfered, and I thought I might as well give it up. It was impossible to lift my hand against so many. All this took place in sight of not less than fifty white ship-carpenters, and not one interposed a friendly word; but some cried, "Kill the • • • nigger! kill him! kill him! He struck a white person!" I found my only chance for life was in flight. I succeeded in getting away without an additional blow, and barely so; for to strike a white man is death by Lynch-law, and that was the law in Mr. Gardner's ship-yard; her is there much of any other out of Mr. Gardner's ship-yard, within the bounds of the Slave states."

After such brutal treatment, Douglass went to his master and told him his wrongs. Mr. Auld felt indignant that any one should treat his servant in such a manner, and immediately tried to get redress. He went to Mr. Gardner and tried to get redress, but could not, as no white man would testify to the brutal outrage. No warrant could be issued on Douglass' own word or on the word of any colored man. If he had been killed in the presence of a thousand colored persons, their united testimony would have been insufficient to have arrested one of the murderers. If any white man, out of sympathy, might have been induced to bear testimony in behalf of the slave, it would have required an unprecedented degree of courage, for at that time the slightest manifestation of humanity towards a colored man was denounced as "abolitionism," and that name subjected its bearer to frightful liabilities.

Douglass' master, finding he could get no redress, refused to let him return to Mr. Gardner, but kept him in his own house, while his wife dressed the wound, and tenderly treated him until he was restored to health. He was then taken to the shipyard of Mr. Walter Price, where he was set to work, and very soon learned the art of using his mallet and other tools. In the course of one year from the time he left Mr. Gardner's, as he was able to command the highest wages given to the most experienced caulker, he was now of some importance to his master, as he brought him eight or nine dollars per week--his wages being generally a dollar and a half a day. He soon made so much progress, and his master placed so much confidence in him, that he sought for his own employment, made his own contracts, and collected his money, which he regularly paid over to his master every week. He sometimes even enjoyed a little leisure, and when he did, those odd notions about freedom, about being his own master and realizing the blessings of his own industry, would steal over him and absorb his attention. While he was at Mr. Gardner's he was kept in such a perpetual whirl of excitement, that he could think of nothing but his own life, and in thinking of his life, he almost forgot his liberty. When the stream of life ran on more smoothly and comfortably, it did not increase his contentment, but made him more melancholy and miserable. He found to be a contented slave; it was necessary to be a thoughtless one. The moral and mental vision of the slave must be kept dark, and, as far as possible, his power of reason annihilated, or he will begin to think of his condition and get discontented. The saying of Napoleon, "The worse man the better soldier," may with propriety be applied to the slave.

It was reasonable that Douglass should feel unhappy. He was earning one dollar, fifty cents a day. He contracted for it, he earned it; the money was paid to him, and rightfully belonged to him, yet every Saturday night he paid over every cent to his master. Even the most ordinary slave could not but feel the injustice of such a condition of life; and to anyone who had really thought on the wrongfulness of slavery, and who had fanned in his breast hopes of freedom must of necessity have felt indignant when he paid over to another man that which rightfully belonged to himself.

The time had now come when he was determined to make another effort for freedom. In the early part of 1838, he became quite restless. He felt that his life was passing away without fulfilling its mission; that manhood had arrived, and he was still a slave.

Sometime after Douglass had been earning regularly his nine or ten dollars a-week, he induced his master to let him "hire his time"--that was to provide himself with tools, food, lodging and clothing, and carry his master so much every week. This sum he was compelled to make up or lose the privilege of hiring his time. Rain or shine, work or no work, at the end of each week the money must be forthcoming.

This arrangement was decidedly in his master's favor. It relieved him of all need of looking after Douglass. The master's money was sure. He received all the comforts of slaveholding without its evils, while Douglass, endured all the evils of, a slave, and suffered all the anxieties of a freeman. But, hard as it was, it was better than the general mode of slave life. It had the semblance of freedom. Even sham freedom was better than no freedom. This "hiring out" was a step towards freedom. It enabled him to bear and to feel the responsibilities of a freeman. But, better than all, it placed him in a position to make money by "overtime." But he had not gone on in this way long before he failed one Saturday to perform his engagement. This led to high words between the master and the slave. Words were on the point of coming to blows. Douglass, when alluding to this circumstance, says, "He raved and swore his determination to get hold of me. I did not allow myself a single word, but was resolved, if he laid the weight of his hand on me, it should be blow for blow. He did not strike me, but told me he would find me in constant employment in future. I thought the matter over during the next day (Sunday), and finally resolved upon the 3rd of September, as the day upon which I would make a second attempt to secure my freedom."

He says, "Things went on without very slowly indeed, but there was trouble within. It is impossible for me to describe my feelings as the time of my contemplated start drew near. I had a number of warm-hearted friends in Baltimore-- friends that I loved almost as I did my life--and the thought of being separated from them forever was painful beyond expression. It is my opinion that thousands would escape from slavery, who now remain, but for the strong cords of affection that bind them to their friends. The thought of leaving my friends was decidedly the most painful thought with which I had to contend. The love of them was my tender point, and shook my decision more than all things else. Besides the pain of separation, the dread and apprehension of a failure exceeded what I had experienced at my first attempt. The appalling defeat I then sustained returned to torment me. I felt assured that if I failed in this attempt my case would be a hopeless one--it would seal my fate as a slave forever. I could not hope to get off with anything less than the severest punishment, and being placed beyond the means of escape. It required no very vivid imagination to depict the most frightful scenes through which I should have to pass, in case I failed. The wretchedness of slavery, and the blessedness of, freedom were perpetually before me. It was life and death to me. But I remained firm, and, according to my resolution, on the 3rd day of September, 1838, I left my chains, and succeeded in reaching New York without the slightest interruption of any kind." How he did so, what means he adopted, in what direction he travelled, and by what mode of conveyance, he leaves unexplained, as he considers it very injudicious to publish to the world the manner in which slaves escape, because it only puts masters more on their guard, and renders it more difficult for the slaves to get away.

When speaking on this point, Mr. Douglass says, "I deeply regret the necessity which impels me, to suppress anything of importance connected with my experience with slavery. It would afford me great pleasure indeed, as well as materially add to the interest of my narrative, were I at liberty to gratify a curiosity, which I know exists in the minds of many, by an accurate statement of all the facts pertaining to my most fortunate escape. But I must deprive myself of this pleasure, and the curious the gratification such a statement would afford. I would allow myself to suffer under the greatest imputations which evil-minded men might suggest, rather than exculpate myself, and thereby run the hazard of closing the slightest avenue by which a brother-slave might clear himself of the chains and fetters of slavery." In this Mr. Douglass acts wisely and well. As a statement of the means of escape would do nothing to enlighten the slave, whilst it would enlighten the master. It stimulates him to greater watchfulness, and enhances his power to capture the runaway. "I would keep the merciless slaveholder," says Douglass, "profoundly ignorant of the means of flight adopted by slaves. I would leave him to imagine himself surrounded by myriads of invisible tormenters, ever ready to snatch from his infernal grasp his trembling prey. Let him be left to feel his way in the dark; let darkness commensurate with his crime hover over him. And let him feel at every step he takes in pursuit of the flying bondsman, he is running the risk of having his hot brains dashed out by an invisible agency. Let us render the tyrant no aid; let us not hold the light by which he can trace the footsteps of our flying brethren.

"I have been frequently asked," says he, "how I felt when I found myself in a Free State. I have never been able to answer the question with any satisfaction to myself. It was a moment of the highest excitement I ever experienced. I suppose I felt as one may imagine the unarmed mariner to feel, when he is rescued by a friendly man-of-war from the pursuit of a pirate. In writing to a dear friend, immediately after my arrival at New York, I said I felt like one who had escaped a den of hungry lions. This state of mind, however, very soon subsided; and I was again seized with a feeling of great insecurity and loneliness. I was yet liable to be taken back, and subjected to all the tortures of slavery. This in itself was enough to damp the ardor of my enthusiasm. But the loneliness overcame me. There I was in the midst of thousands, and yet a perfect stranger; without home and without friends, in the midst of thousands of my own brethren--children of a common Father, and yet I dared not unfold to any one of them my sad condition. I was afraid to speak to any one, for fear of speaking to the wrong one, and thereby fall into the hands of money-loving kidnappers, whose business it was to lie in wait for the panting fugitive, as the ferocious beasts of the forest lie in wait for their prey. The motto, which I adopted when I started from slavery, was this--"Trust no man!" I saw in every white man an enemy, and in almost every colored man cause for distrust. It was a most painful situation; and, to understand it, one must needs experience it, or imagine himself in similar circumstances. Let him be a fugitive slave in a strange land--a land given up to be the hunting-ground for slaveholders--whose inhabitants are legalized kidnappers--where he is every moment subjected to the terrible liability of being seized upon by his fellow-men, as the hideous crocodile seizes upon his prey! I say, let him place himself in my situation--without home or friends--without money or credit--wanting shelter, and no one to give it--wanting bread, and no money to buy it, and at the same time, let him feel that he is pursued by merciless men-hunters, and in total darkness as to what to do, where to go, or where to stay--perfectly helpless both as to the means of defense and as a means of escape--in the midst of plenty, yet suffering the terrible gnawing's of hunger--in the midst of houses, yet having no home--among fellow-men, yet feeling as if in the midst of wild beasts, whose greediness to swallow up the trembling and half-famished fugitive is only equaled by that with which the monsters of the deep swallow up the helpless fish upon which they subsist--I say, let him be placed in this most trying situation--the situation in which I was placed--then, and not till then, will he fully appreciate the hardships of, and know how to sympathize with the toil-worn and whip-scarred fugitive slave.

Fortunately, Douglass did not remain long in this situation. He was found out and relieved by Mr. David Ruggles, a man well known for his philanthropy. He told Douglass it would be better for him not to remain in New York, but to remove to New Bedford. This Douglass consented to do; but before he left, he resolved to fulfill an engagement, which would materially add to his happiness or misery.

Long before he escaped from Baltimore, he formed an attachment to a free negro woman, whom he resolved to marry when he became free too. While in bondage, he had therefore a double inducement to gain his freedom. He wished it not only for himself, but for the sake of her who was as dear to him as his own life. And his ambition was to obtain his freedom, so that he might show his intense love by his acts, and consecrate the fruits of his free labor to her benefit. We have seen before how capable Douglass was of loving his companions in slavery, and we may imagine how deep and devoted was his passion for her who afterwards became his wife.

He had not been in New York long, before he wrote to her, telling her to follow him immediately. Though he told her of his houseless, homeless condition, she obeyed the affectionate summons, and in a few days was by his side. And a few days after her arrival, they were married by a colored minister, Mr. J. W. C. Pennington, another fugitive slave.

> "Woolly locks and dark complexion
> Cannot alter nature's claim,

Skins may differ, but affection
Dwells in white and black the same."

Almost immediately after their marriage, they proceeded to New Bedford. When they arrived, they went to the house of Mr. Nathan Johnson, to whom they were introduced by Mr. Ruggles. They now felt a sense of security, and began to prepare themselves for the duties and responsibilities of a life of freedom. On the morning after their arrival, while at the breakfast-table, the question arose as to the name, Douglass should be called by in future. The name given him by his mother was "Frederick Augustus Washington Bailey." He had, however, long dispensed with the two middle names, and was known at Baltimore by the name of Frederick Bailey. He, however, started from that town bearing the assumed name of Stanley. When he got to New York, he again changed his name to Frederick Johnson, and was married with that name. But when he got to New Bedford, he found that there were so many Johnsons that he thought it necessary to again change his name. He gave Mr. Johnson, with whom he was staying, the privilege of choosing him a name, but told him he must not drop the name of Frederick, as he wished to hold it to preserve a sense of his identity. Mr. Johnson had just been reading the "Lady of the Lake," and at once suggested that his name should be "Douglass," and from that time to the present he has been known by the name of Frederick Douglass.

The third day after his arrival at New Bedford he found employment, that of stowing a sloop with a load of oil. It was new, hard and dirty work, but he went to it in earnest, with a glad heart and willing hand. He felt the consciousness of his freedom. He was now in that condition, after which he had so ardently longed, and for which he had braved so many difficulties. The goal of his hopes was now reached, and the yearnings of his ambition realized. He was now his own master. It was a happy moment; the rapture of which can be understood only by those who have been slaves. It was the first work, the reward of which was to be entirely his own. There was no Master Auld standing ready, the moment he earned his money, to take it from him. He worked the first day with a pleasure he never before experienced. It was the starting part of a new existence. The reality of life appeared like a golden dream, too beautiful to be true, and too enchanting to endure. It would be impossible for anyone who has not actually been a slave, and into whose flesh the cord of oppression has not eaten, to imagine the flood of joy which must have streamed through the soul of such a man as Frederick Douglass when he felt the consciousness of freedom, and when he was not only working for himself, but for his newly married wife.

After he finished his engagement, he went in pursuit of a job of caulking; but such was the prejudice against color, among the white caulkers, that they refused to work with him, and consequently he could get no employment. He now prepared himself to do any kind of work he could get to do. He says, "There was no work too hard--none too dirty. I was ready to saw wood, shovel coal, carry the hod, sweep the chimney, or roll out casks, all of which I did for nearly three years in New Bedford."

In about four months after he went to New Bedford, a young man called on him, and inquired if he did not wish to take the "Liberator," an anti-slavery paper. Douglass said, he should, but being very poor, he said he was unable to pay for it. He, however, finally became a subscriber to the paper, and, week after week, he read it with feelings of intense delight. The paper became his meat and his drink. It set all his soul on fire. Its sympathy for his brethren in bonds--its scathing denunciation of slaveholders, its faithful exposure of slavery, and its powerful attacks upon the upholders of the institution, sent a thrill of joy through his soul such as he never felt before. He soon became impregnated with the anti-slavery spirit, and grew ambitious to serve the cause. He never felt happier than at an anti-slavery meeting. He felt his very existence was more or less wrapped up with those who were less fortunate than himself, and was determined to do his best to render them all his assistance. He accordingly spoke at their meetings, but what he said was said diffidently. But while attending an anti-slavery convention at Nantucket, on the 11th of August, 1841, he felt a strong desire to speak, and being at the same time urged to do so, by Mr. W. C. Coffin, a gentleman who had heard him speak at the colored peoples' meeting at New Bedford. He got on his legs and commenced in a hesitating tone. He felt even then that he was a slave, and could say but little to edify educated white men. But he was encouraged to proceed, and he had only spoken a few minutes, when he felt a degree of freedom, and said what he desired with considerable case. The impression he made at the meeting has already been described at the opening of this sketch.

From that time to the present, he has been engaged in pleading the cause of his brethren in bonds, and his success has been almost unparalleled. He became almost immediately a popular man in his native country. Wherever he went he gathered round him very large audiences. These audiences he filled with enthusiasm. The anti-slavery party in the Northern States found that they had brought out no common man; but one who, if no social and political obstacles were in his way, would reflect enduring luster on his race.

His fame soon reached this country, and here he came, four years after he gave his inaugural address in Nantucket. He produced a similar sensation wherever he went in England as he did in America. He addressed large meetings in all our principal cities and towns, and stirred up a feeling in England against slavery in America as was never done by any other man. He remained with us about twelve months. But as he was liable, as soon as he returned to be snatched back to slavery, some of the most benevolent of our countrymen--among whom of course figured

Quakers--subscribed sufficient money to purchase his freedom. And before he reached his country, his legal master was paid the worth of his property in gold subscribed by British benevolence.

His friends were not satisfied with merely rendering him free and independent as soon as he reached home, but they desired that his extraordinary abilities should be turned to the best account. The result was the 500l. more were subscribed to enable him to commence an anti-slavery paper when he got back.

Frederick Douglass came to this country a little after the Scottish Free Church had sent a deputation to America to solicit subscriptions to build new churches and chapels. That deputation perpetrated the blunder of going to the slave-holding States, and collecting money from slaveholders to build free churches in Scotland. By doing this, they tarnished their otherwise bright reputation, and brought upon themselves everlasting dishonor. And never will they drive away the deep disgrace until they "send back the money." This they were and are too blind or too obstinate, or perhaps the both combined, to do, and consequently, they render themselves liable to be condemned by the Christian world as having performed an act which, while it encouraged the slave-holder in his internal baseness, culminates into a crime before high Heaven. Even now, it is not too late to "send back the money." Frederick Douglass, while he was with us, as may be seen in the speech of his which we give in the Appendix, showed the infamy of this transaction of the Scottish Free Church, and in doing so, deserved well of his race.

After he performed his mission here, he prepared to start for America. He went to Liverpool, and paid his passage-money as saloon passenger. He no sooner went on board than he found the American prejudice against color. The Yankees on board, true to their ignorance and their prejudices, refused to be put on an equality with a black man.

When Douglass arrived in America, he was warmly welcomed by his friends and others who were aware of the reputation he gained in this country; and the anti-slavery convention of New England, which was held a short time after, placed sufficient confidence in his character and abilities, that they elected him the president of the convention. If the slaveholders had minds and hearts as impressible as men ordinarily, they would have felt humiliated when they saw one who was so short a time before in bondage, elevated to such a distinguished position.

Almost, immediately after Douglass started the "North Star," an uncompromising anti-slavery paper, which has flourished ever since, though it is now called Frederick Douglass' Paper. This paper is taken in by many families in this country Besides writing in this and other papers and magazines, he employs himself in lecturing and attending conventions, and in every other way in his power consecrating his great abilities to the deliverance of his race.

JAMES PENNINGTON, THE FUGITIVE BLACKSMITH.
CHAPTER I.
THE MASTER AND HIS SLAVES.

In a fertile valley, bounded in the cast by the primeval forest, which rose by successive platforms to the summit of a mountain ridge; and on the other by a continuous, though abrupt slope of the greenest sward, was situated an extensive tobacco and sheep farm, where industry plied her numerous arts, and nature favored man's intentions. It was in the State of Maryland, in North America, not far removed from the eastern shore. The farm was one of the finest in the State, its master was wealthy and enterprising, the land fruitful and the climate favorable to agriculture and as on every hand the conquest of the soil proceeded, the welcome bounty fell before the hand of the reaper. In other lands, the labor of the fields begets associations of rural beauty and simplicity, and the liveliest of nature's impulses spring from the green of the grass blades and the music of the rustling corn. Rustic fetes, ceremonies, greetings, and songs, render still more cheering the story of the tillers' lifetime, and invest with human sympathies the commonest fact in nature.

In 'other lands' we said, the tillage of the soil is among the noblest occupations: here it is full of hateful symbols, of disgusting pictures of degradation and tyranny. The song of the laborer is not heard, but the cries of the tortured slave instead; the hedgerows echo not laughter nor strong speech, but the curses of the taskmaster, and the prayers of the dejected slave, instead. The domestic peace, the social security which in free lands springs from the bond which unites the peasant and the lord are wanting here, for there are no such bonds, but in their place a fierce hate, an eternal disparity, and a keen longing on the part of the oppressed, for implacable and summary revenge. This Maryland is in fact, one of the slave States of the American Union, and like all Slave States lies under the ban of a great social blight, meriting only the curse and the pestilence.

In the valley mentioned, Colonel Gordon owned an extensive farm, the tillage of which was performed by slaves. The Colonel was reputed a good man: he was a member of an Episcopalian congregation, and was said to be a kind master to his slaves. Some ten miles to the west was another farm, owned by a Mr. Whyte, who also carried on his farm business by aid of slave labor. Among the slaves on Colonel Gordon's farm, was a middle-aged woman, the mother of two children, whose husband was a slave of the farm of Mr. Whyte. Such family separations are common, husbands, wives, and children, being subject to sale at any moment, and having no remedy against the caprices, or changing fortunes of their masters. The second of these children was named James, and forms the subject of the present narrative. Born in slavery, though what is termed its milder form, he inherited from birth the ban of an unjust bondage, and came into the world simply as an article of property. Notwithstanding that slave breeding is carried on in Maryland and elsewhere as a profitable enterprise, and that marriages, whether extemporaneous or by religious bonds, are encouraged among the negroes; it is found that the higher sentiments of human nature animate these negro breasts, and tears flow even from their eyes when heartless separations between parents and offspring, husbands and wives are compelled, to please cruelty or convenience. Hence young Pennington made his first acquaintance with suffering under the rigorous exaction of his owner's will, which sent his mother to the south with two babes in her arms, and left his father two hundred miles distant to weep for his partner's loss. It happening however, that his original master found it to his convenience to repurchase these slaves, the family were again united. "About this time," he says, "I began to feel another evil of slavery--I mean the want of parental care and attention. My parents were not able to give any attention to their children during the day. I often suffered much from hunger and other similar causes. To estimate the sad state of a slave child, you must look at it as a helpless human being, thrown upon the world without the benefit of natural guardians. It is thrown into the world without a social circle to flee to for hope, comforts, or instruction. The social circle, with all its heaven-ordained blessings, is of the utmost importance to the tradeoff this the slave child, however tender and is robbed."

    Submitting to the tyrannical authority of his young masters--who imitated the older ones in the treatment of slaves--and suffering frequently from the cruelty of overseers, young Pennington grew up, and while still in tender years, was drafted to the severe labor of the fields. As the capacities of the mind were opening, and the natural acuteness of the boy beginning to manifest itself, he saw with a quick eye the abject condition of his parents and the degraded portion of his race. Sometimes crouching in a ditch or behind a fence to evade the fury of the overseer, who delighted in torturing young slaves with a hickory whip, which he carried constantly in his hand, and at other times pleading with tears for mercy from his younger masters, he was at last sent to labor for a stonemason, who hired him of his master when he was but nine years of age. He remained with this stonemason for two years, and then was separated from an older brother who had been placed out near him, and brought home to be placed under a negro blacksmith, one of his master's slaves. In this occupation, he soon acquired skill, and became noted as a "first-rate blacksmith." Now he entered into the full routine of slave-life, and submitted to the tasks and insults incident to his condition. But he possessed a natural genius; and a few sparks of independent feeling, which slave ancestry and slave birth had not entirely quenched, still burned in his breast. The first thoughts of freedom flashed upon him under the prompting of this relic of his nobleness, when an incident in the slave routine gave it its necessary impulse.

It is customary on slave farms for the men to go on Saturday evenings to see their families, and to return on Monday mornings, half an hour after sunrise. On one occasion two men who had families, and two unmarried youths, had not returned at their proper time to Colonel Gordon's farm; and the tyrannical slave owner walked about with a rope in his pocket, and a cowhide in his hand, determined, as he said, to have "a general whipping match among them." Among other duties discharged by Pennington's father, was that of shepherd to a flock of merino sheep, which he tended with the most assiduous care. This Monday morning, the old man was engaged in the tenderest of a shepherd's duties: a little lamb, not able to go alone had lost its mother and he was feeding it by hand. As he stooped over it in the yard, with a vessel of milk he had, obtained for the purpose of feeding it, the master came along, his face purpled by anger at the absence of the men and boys, and his hand prepared with the cowhide for their reception.

"Have you fed the flock, Basil?" he cried.

"Yes, sir," replied the slave.

"Were you away yesterday?"

"No, sir."

"Do you know why these boys have not got home this morning yet?"

"No, sir, I have not seen any of them since Saturday night."

"By the * * *, I'll make them know their name. The fact is, I have too many of you; my people are getting to be the most careless, lazy, and worthless in the country."

"Master," said the old man, with tears in his eyes, "I am always at my post: Monday morning never finds me off the plantation."

"Hold your tongue, sir. I shall have to sell some of you, and then the rest will have work enough. I haven't enough to work you up there are more mouths at work than hands at work."

This was said in an angry, threatening tone, and with an intention of insult. While he spoke, Colonel Gordon twirled the cowhide about, as if determined to use it by some means. But the old slave had a shadow of the man in him, and the insult cut him to the core. "If I am one too many, sir," said he, in answer to the last expression, "give me a chance to find a purchaser, and I am willing to be sold when it may suit you."

"Basil," cried the other, seizing the opportunity for which he had been waiting to give full vent to his pent-up anger--"Basil, I told you to hold your tongue;" and at the same moment he drew forth the cow-hide, and dancing over the poor old shepherd as he fed the lamb, inflicted fifteen or twenty stripes with all his strength; and as he rose on the tips of his toes to give full effect to the last stroke, he cried-- "By the * * *, I will make you know that I am master of your tongue, as well as of your time!"

The son saw this--he saw the stripes and heard the words, and from that moment, he was in his heart a free man. It was not Saxon but negro blood that felt the insult; and from an infancy of youth and slavery, he suddenly broke forth and became a freeman. The whole family were insulted in this insult to its head, and the oppressor saw in their melancholy aspect, the deep hate which had possessed them against him. Contrast the employments of the two--the black man was feeding a motherless lamb, but the white man flogged the shepherd.

Insults such as these were repeated, and each served to widen the breach already made between master and slave. On one occasion, an old man, a pious and exemplary slave, had had a misunderstanding with the overseer, who immediately attempted to flog him. The slave fled to the woods, but returned next morning and resumed his work, and the master went with one of his sons, and a rope and a cow-hide, and tied the old man to a post in the stable, and there ordered the son to lay on thirty-nine lashes, which he did, making the keen end of the cow-hide lap round and strike the culprit in the tenderest part of the side, till the blood sped out us if a lance had been used. As he stood thus receiving the lash, he was heard articulating in a low voice, and the fellow-slave who listened trembling, heard between the stripes that the old man was praying! His weeping child was at the barn door, beseeching mercy for her father; she was driven away with the whip, and soon after sold to the traders, and removed from the old man forever.

In another case, a young man had a dispute with the overseer, when the latter made at him with a hickory club. The slave took to his heels and ran to the woods; as he crossed the yard, the overseer snatched up his gun and fired at the fugitive, putting several shots into the calf of his leg. The poor fellow got to the woods, but was in so much pain that he was compelled to return. He was tied to the post and flogged, the shots taken out of his leg, and then with threats and insults sent to the hoe. But there was one case still more terrible, which wrung the heart of the young blacksmith, and caused tears of anguish to dim the eyes of every slave upon the farm. Amongst the farm servants, there was a beautiful girl of twenty-four years of age. She was her mother's darling child, and had been reared with every care, so that she possessed a warm affectionate nature in addition to her beauty. She was purchased for a nurse, and after discharging this duty with an almost maternal tenderness for a year, one of the master's sons became attached to her, but for no honorable purposes. This son won the hatred of the slaves, and the contempt of his own brothers and sisters by the same lying hypocrisy by which he robbed the beautiful girl of her virtue. To get rid of the annoyance, the Colonel determined to sell her, and Rachel was carried immediately to the town where her parents lived, and sold with her disgrace upon her, before their weeping eyes. But worse, that same son, who might be supposed to possess even a lingering affection for her to whom he professed so much, and whom he had thus degraded in the presence of her kindred; that same son, whom in any other case we should call her lover, acted as salesman of her body; so that from before his own eyes, and out of his very hands, she proceeded to the South--bought expressly for prostitution!

Upon this farm of Colonel Gordon's, slavery was seen in one of its mildest forms, and such incidents as we have just described, were but the legitimate consequences of this milder form of bondage. Under the same lenient system, children of tenderest years are sent in chain gangs from Washington to Louisiana, and away still further to the South, to till cotton and rice fields, and to die before manhood, after suffering every species of torture, victims of the marsh pestilence. Under the same "mild system" women are flogged before their own sons and daughters by white men--descendants of Englishmen--who know no bounds to their cruelty, who scruple at nothing which may degrade and dishonor the slave, and who are not only lost to common decency, but outrage every tender tie, and forget in their savage spite the very mothers who bore them. And if there are none of these things, the slave is still the property of another; he rises with his master's pride, falls with his master's poverty, and may be sold at last to the completed horrors of the Southern States to relieve that master from a state of insolvency. If such things happen under the milder forms, what must be the case of the slave where the terms are acknowledged to be harsh?

CHAPTER II
LIFE STAKED FOR LIBERTY.

PENNINGTON had nursed the idea of flight and though he still wore the shackles of the slave in his soul, he was no longer a bondman, but breathed the air of freedom and felt himself a man. A wretched Irishman employed as a spy amongst the slaves, helped to break still wider the breach already made by slanderous reports and accusations, and the whole of this family were charged with disaffection, the mother being threatened with the whip. It was Saturday night, and the young blacksmith, keeping his intention secret, prepared for flight on the morrow. Tying up a little bundle of clothing, he went to a cave not far off and secreted it, and then went to his workshop to reflect upon his means of flight.

There was a father and mother whom he loved, there were six brothers and sisters on the plantation. Not one of them must know of his intention, not one must give him counsel, and not one say, farewell. By strict secrecy only could he succeed, and even then he might entail upon his kindred in bondage innumerable pangs, for it is the custom to break a disaffected family asunder and sell each to a different dealer in a different place, to prevent their ever meeting again. But above all these solemn thoughts, came a presentiment which the uneducated slave could not resist, that if he did not escape there and then, he would be self-doomed, and his ear nailed to the doorpost forever. But the hour was come, and turning his back on mother, father, and friends, and facing the difficulties of the way, the reward that would be offered for his capture, the blood-hounds that would be set upon his track, the weariness, the hunger, and the unknown world wherein every man was the slave's enemy, he set forth on the Sabbath afternoon with his bundle of clothes in one hand, and half a pound of corn-bread in the other.

He had a brother living in a town six miles away. To him he intended first to repair, to give him tidings of his flight and take his counsel upon it. He reached the town at dusk, and then determined not to see his brother for fear of implicating him in his flight. Darkness came, and he passed out of the town into the open country. He was in the heart of a slave country, where every man whom he met would look upon him with suspicion. He was wholly untaught, excepting the handicrafts which the master had found profitable; he knew not how to read or write, had never heard of the Gospel, and was held onward only by a wild hope, that he would somehow gain his liberty by following the direction of the North Star. Think of this solitary black man making his midnight journeys towards a land of freedom--a land which he has only heard by name, and of the position of which he only knows that it is northward. He is in the midst of slave institutions and slave captors, with thirteen Slave States lying behind and around him. He has to wade through bogs and marshes, to cross rivers, and to thread his way through forests, all of which he has never seen before; and for this task he has nothing to stimulate him but his newly-awakened passion--freedom nothing to sustain him but half a pound of bread. But Providence watched him, and he went on.

After the first night's travel, he found himself at the dawn of daylight in the midst of an open country, and with no shelter but a corn shock, into which he crept to pass the day. Night came again, and he rose to pursue his journey, but his strength failed, and his star was not visible. Overcome with hunger and fatigue he crept into a small archway and passed the second day in ambush. At nightfall, he came forth again, conscious that he could not pass another twenty-four hours without food. He made but little progress, and sat down several times and slept for fifteen or twenty minutes. In the morning he came to a turnpike, and met a lad who told him he was eighteen miles from Baltimore--he had travelled nearly sixty-two miles.

He now struck into the road to Philadelphia, and after walking, a mile in the daylight was warned by a young man not to pursue his course by daylight for fear of capture. Alarmed at his position, and vexed at having travelled so far out of his way, he turned aside into a wood; but it being a busy hour, and many persons about, he felt greater safety in keeping to the open road, so as not to excite suspicion. He had scarcely regained the road than a voice came from a lot on the roadside--"Halloo!" It came from a man digging potatoes. Pennington answered him politely, when the following occurred--

"Who do you belong to?"

"I am free, sir."

"Have you got papers?"

"No, sir."

"Well, you must stop here."

"My business is onward, sir, and I do not wish to stop."

"I will see if you don't though, you black rascal."

The fugitive walked on, and then ran, determined not to surrender without a struggle; the other followed and a second pursuer coming to his aid, the slave was caught! He was now surrounded by a body of white republicans, and dragged by force into the bar-room of a tavern near at hand. A crowd came round the "nigger" and the yard was soon crowded with gossipers. The first who spoke was a man dressed in black with a white kerchief, evidently a preacher of the Gospel. He did not say in the words of Scripture--"Blessed are the merciful for they shall obtain mercy," but--"That fellow is a runaway I know; put him in jail a few days, and you will soon hear where he comes from:" then fixing a fiendish look on the victim of his pious intentions, he continued--"If I lived on this road, you fellows would not find such clear running as you do, I'd trap more of you."

But here comes the pinch of the case. Is he to acknowledge to these human bloodhounds the facts of the case, and be immediately enslaved forever, and after receiving a hundred lashes sent to the South to experience the extremist torments? or are the facts his own, bound up with his liberty; to either of which no man has a claim? He must do one of three things, he must tell the truth, or lie, or say nothing. The untutored slave, who has been bred without morel teaching, and with examples of tyranny and hypocrisy always before him, prefers the course which savors of safety, and boldly asserts that he is free.

He is dragged over fences and across fields to the house of a neighboring magistrate; but the magistrate is not at home, and he is dragged back to the tavern. On the way he determines once more to escape, and suddenly sweeping the legs of one of his captors from under him, leaves one standing on his head and the other gaping in astonishment, and takes to his heels. Pursued and overtaken he is at last brought to the tavern. Here they cool down, and try to draw from him some confession. "If you will not put me in jail," says he, "I will tell you where I came from." They promised. "Well," said he, "a few weeks ago I was sold from the eastern shore to a slave-trader, who had a large gang, and set out for Georgia, but when he got to a town in Virginia he was taken sick and died with the small-pox. Several of his gang also died with it, so that the people in the town became alarmed, and did not wish to have anything to do with us. I left the rest, and thought I would go somewhere and get work!"

This was believed by all present, and several who had clustered very near gradually moved off, and gave the supposed small-pox patient-breathing-room. Some cleared off entirely, and said--"better let the small-pox nigger go." He was now kept with the man who had first captured him; and this one made a proposal to employ him, to which Pennington assented. "Well," said he, "take something to eat, and I will go with you."

It was Wednesday, four o'clock; he had had no regular meal since Sunday. This over, he set out with his captor, determined never to reach the town alive. They would presently have to pass a wood, and the slave determined there to free himself or die in his adversary's arms. He was within six rods of the spot, when a gentleman turned the cover meeting them on horseback. His captor held a parley with the new comer, but as they conversed in Dutch, the captive gathered nothing from it. Then turning to Pennington, the horseman (who was a magistrate) put on a stern countenance and interrogated him closely. He repeated the story he had already told, and it was agreed that he should go back to the tavern, and from thence proceed to the house of the interrogator and assist at the farm for twenty-five cents a day. Arriving at the tavern he was left in the charge of a little boy, while the horseman went his way, and the man who captured him attended his team close by. For one moment while the man tended his horses there was an opportunity of escape, and away he went across the fields to a wood close at hand, and found temporary refuge in a matting of wet underwood. He was out of the hands of the slave-hunters, but he was alone again without friends, money, shelter or food; the North Star too being hidden by thick banks of clouds. He went in fear, knowing not what ravenous beasts might be hidden in the wood, nor what waters or precipices were concealed within its bounds, his clothes soaked through to the skin, and his whole frame shivering with cold and fright. At last he came to a road, and walked on at random, knowing not whether it would lead him. The day dawned, when he was near a barn and into this he crept for shelter. It happened that the barn was filled with fodder, and as he crept into this, the crackling around awakened a yelping dog, which commenced a fierce barking immediately. He crouched down among the fodder and trusted once more to Providence. He soon began to think how he could pass the day without food, having had but one meal since Sunday, and that one in the midst of great agitation and suffering. He was awakened from such contemplations by the tramp of horses and the voices of men and his heart sunk within as he discovered that his pursuers were upon his track. One said, "The only liberty such a fellow should have would be ten feet of rope," another said, "I reckon he is in that wood now," and another, "who would have thought the rascal was so 'cute." Then they interrogated the cottager, and concluded by affirming with oaths that, "he is a blacksmith, and a stiff reward is out for him--two hundred dollars." All this while the dog was barking at the crouching fugitive, occasionally giving fresh piquancy to his anguish by dancing out into the road and back again in the endeavor to attract some one to the mow in which he lay.

Night came, and he sped on, wading across marshy fields, dragging through woods where there were no paths, wet to the skin, shivering and expecting to fall from extreme exhaustion. At last he came to a corn-field covered with shocks of Indian corn, and creeping into one of these he began the operation of grinding a few cars with his teeth for nourishment. The operation was more than he could sustain, and he fell asleep, and slept till broad daylight. Again he ground away with his teeth, and got a little nourishment, until a party of gunners approached, and threw him into a fresh panic. Night came again without a renewal of dangers, and considerably refreshed by sleep and raw corn, he sallied forth in high spirits, and ran clapping his hands, and talking in a half delirious joy to himself. Then the gloom came back. "Where are you going? What will you do? Where will you find father, mother, and kindred? If you ever get your freedom, what will you do in a world where you have not one friend?" Saturday morning came, and hunger fiercer than ever came with the daylight. Let it be noted here, that he set out unarmed, and never once sought to obtain weapons, so that to harm any man, much less to take life, was no part of his plan for freedom.

CHAPTER III.
HOPE SUPPORTS, AND FREEDOM AWAITS HIM.

THE morning dawned, and the shivering slave sped on, facing the daylight now, and feeling in the renewed confidence which hope gave him, that he was nearing free soil, and that his North Star had guided him rightly. There was a tollgate at hand, and an elderly woman stood at the door of the toll-house. He had hitherto been flying from the savagery of men, now he would try the heart of a woman. Fortune rewarded his faith in the gentler sex, and the dame pointed him towards the house of a good Quaker, W. W., who lived three miles away, who she said, would take an interest in him.

In half an hour he stood trembling at the Quaker's door. The door opened, and displayed a table spread with a comfortable breakfast. Pennington asked for employ, and still stood at the door in agitation, at the thought that he might be recaptured. But he was met by no harsh man-eater, but with the gentle words of a true disciple of Jesus--"Come in and take thy breakfast, and get warm, and we will talk about it; thee must be cold without thy coat." It was too much for the hunted slave, who stood at the threshold fainting with fear; and the big drops started from his eyes, as he fell on his knees before his benefactor, and blessed him with his negro tongue--his human heart. It was his last hope, for he must have perished had not this man's threshold stood between him and the realization of his despair. There are but few white men in America who do this, but these few stand out like Abrahams and Lots, to stay the coming judgment of that bloodstained soil, that Ichabod of white man's villainy.

Under the care and guidance of this pious man, Pennington stayed six months, the whole time in a state of concealment. Arriving without any other recommendation than his own representations of his pitiable case, and the demands upon humanity, wherever the Christian doctrine is practiced as well as preached, to set free the slave, and to give comfort to the weary, he here found a hospitable home, and secular and religious instruction. It is cheering to note the progress which this negro made under the kind tuition of his benefactor. He was twenty-one years of age, and as ignorant as a child of five. He had once seen the New Testament; the entire Bible he had never seen; neither had he ever heard mention of the Patriarchs, or of the Savior Jesus. His state was that of mental and spiritual darkness, and when he became conscious of his terrible position, a man in years, an infant in knowledge, ignorant even of the only means of grace, and of the redemption necessary for the sinner, he sunk under the load, and could scarcely hope ever to be happy, or useful to his fellow-beings. But let it not be said that negro blood needs the stimulus of regular instruction, and favorable circumstances to develop a love of mental and moral acquirements. Amongst these degraded slaves on rice and tobacco farms, are many who have taught themselves, in secret, to read and write; who have made acquaintance with the Scriptures, and become exhorters to the negro youths around them, and even in the abject condition of slavery--having existence only as articles of property--have achieved moral and religious conquests, such as shame the white man who makes profession of piety while enslaving and oppressing them.

Pennington had himself made laudable efforts at self-instruction, and had spent whole Sabbaths in looking over the overseer's book in the blacksmith's shop, and endeavoring, by means of a stray feather, and ink made of berries, to copy the names there inserted. It was while engaged in these rude attempts at self-culture that finding his stray quills too soft for the purpose, he endeavored to fashion a steel pen, which by his skill as a blacksmith, he accomplished, and learnt thereby to make a few letters. This was in 1822, when Pennington was thirteen years of age. But self-culture is not allowed the slave: knowledge is kept from him by every possible means, and the light of the mind jealously barred out. No parent dare instruct his infancy; his youth has no teacher but the driver, who breaks him by the whip to the most servile tasks. He is not even cast on himself, that his natural impulses may grow in communion with wild nature; but he is fed and clothed like a child, doomed forever to monotonous toil, kept brutally unconscious of his own spiritual nature, his body lacerated with stripes, and his soul crushed out by the harshest terms of bondage. Not even benevolence dare tread upon the slave farm--no pious pilgrim give free instruction there. The slaves are chattels at the disposal of their owner, who tortures them as long as they live, and shoots them dead with bullets if they attempt to escape.

The six months spent with Mr. W., the earthly savior of the slave, was varied by occasional fears and by reports of strenuous efforts on the part of Colonel Gordon to recapture the skillful blacksmith, whom he valued at a thousand dollars. On leaving his benefactor, Pennington proceeded to Philadelphia, and found shelter and employ in another Quaker family, where he made still further advances in moral and religious instruction. After his labor on the farm, he occupied his evenings by making rude maps of the solar system, or by committing hymns and passages of Scripture to memory. After seven months he went to Long Island, bearing with him letters of recommendation, and testimonials of exemplary conduct, and soon obtained work again. Here he pursued his studies with ardor, and by the help of evening schools and private tuition, made such progress in his studies, that in five years from his escape out of bondage, he was engaged as a teacher in a school at a salary of two hundred dollars. He was now a master of the English language, and had purged his tongue of the abominable patois of slavery. He had studied the Greek Testament, logic, rhetoric, and composition, and to these acquirements he had added a knowledge of the ways of grace and the salvation provided for the sinner.

It remains to add that Mr. James W. C. Pennington became, not long after his conversion, the pastor of a Presbyterian Church at New York, where he distinguished himself by his intelligence and simplicity of mind, his piety and benevolence, and by his zeal in the efforts then and since made for the relief of his enslaved kindred. His family he had left behind, and after leaving the family of Mr. W. he ventured to write to one of his brothers informing him how he had fared in his escape. The letter was directed to the care of a white man who professed a warm friendship for the family; but instead of acting in good faith, this wretched hypocrite--who we blush to say was an Englishman--handed the letter to the master, and thereby entailed on the family innumerable sufferings. The family were divided, and the parents with some of the children sent to New Orleans. From thence they were brought back to Virginia, and by virtue of a law of that state became entitled to freedom. But before justice could have its way they were brought buck to Maryland and doomed again to bondage; and in order to defeat a law of Maryland which gave them another claim to freedom, Colonel Gordon obtained a special act of the Senate to retain them in captivity. But the hand of God was heavy on this villainous perpetrator of the mildest form of slavery, and in a few years he became insolvent. Pennington wrote immediately inquiring on what terms he would release his parents, and received back an insulting and evasive answer, which implied the willingness of the Colonel to receive five hundred and fifty dollars for the liberation of the runaway. To this gracious proposal Pennington wrote again, stating that no proposition would be acceded to which did not include his parents, to which the other maintained a dignified silence. By his unwearied exertions, however, on behalf of his beloved parents, his father and two brothers were got away to Canada, and are now freemen. His mother, after being sold a second time south, passed into freedom by the aid of death, to meet her tyrant master at the bar of judgment, for he passed into captivity by the same impartial hand. Several of his sisters married free men who purchased their liberty; while he was enabled to render efficient service to the children of his oppressor, who were in extreme want, by the purchase of the remaining members of his family.

Mr. Pennington has been four times appointed to a seat in the General Convention for the Improvement of the Free Coloured People. In 1843 he was elected by Connecticut State to attend the World's Anti-slavery Convention; also by the American Peace Society to represent them in the World's Peace Convention: both of these meetings were held in London the same year. He addressed the Anti-slavery Convention at great length. The speech was an eloquent and impressive one. During his visit in this country in 1841, he preached in many of the principle of the independents and other Dissenters; and wherever he went he moved on a footing of social and intellectual equality with ministers and congregations. He was, in fact, owing to his abilities as a preacher, sought out to supply the pulpits of some of the most popular ministers of the day. On his return to America he was received with much favor, and exchanged pulpits with several of the leading ministers of

Connecticut. He is a member of the Hartford Central Association of Congregational Ministers, which consists of a large number of the leading ministers of that denomination in the State. He has been twice elected president of this association, in which capacity he presided over assemblies composed entirely of whites. At a meeting, a few years since, two young men presented themselves for licenses to preach. They were examined by the president in the most satisfactory manner; and the white candidates were both licensed, and the certificates were signed by the black president. At the same meeting Mr. Pennington was appointed as a deputation to the General Conference of Congregational Ministers of the State of Maine. He is also a member of the American Tract Society.

Mr. Pennington has for some years been the settled minister of the first colored Presbyterian Church in New York, and was a member of the Presbytery.

In 1851 he was deputed to attend the Paris Peace Congress, where he delivered a beautiful and impressive speech. It was on the evening of the third day of the sittings of this important assembly; and when almost everyone was wearied with sitting, listening, and cheering, this member of the negro race arose and spoke words wise, gentle, eloquent, and touching; and when he resumed his seat, the enthusiasm of the meeting broke out afresh.

And, reader, will you believe it; this man, who, in the face of difficulty and danger, has vindicated, by the beauty and nobility of his life, the capabilities of his race and the glory of his kind, is now in this country, afraid to return to his own; as, since the passing of the Fugitive Slave Bill, he is subjected to the liability of being at any moment pounced upon by the man-stealer, and delivered into the hands of his cruel master? Such is American slavery!

This narrative gives but a faint picture of the minor horrors of slavery. Pennington was reared under one of its milder forms, and hence his experiences were less painful than would have been the case farther south. Yet this milder form, how frightful is it? These slave-owners how diabolical! Is it right any longer to recognize these slave-driving, whipping, maiming, and shooting fiends as members of human society? Is it right that we should call them citizens, and look westward with any other hope than that the heaviest curse may light upon their lands, the heaviest blight upon their heads and hearts, that eternal justice may assert itself by the infliction of a terrible doom from which not one slaveholder shall escape. How is it that free states and slave states have held together so long? How is it that these cannibals, who torture and barter, without regard to age, sex, or condition, the slave whose labor feeds them, how is it that these are recognized in the world as men worthy of political and social protection? How is it that every door is not shut in their faces, every hearth denied their presence, every assembly closed against them?

Common dignity must be elastic indeed, else the whole world of civilized and free men would be ready at any moment to treat them with ignominy, to cease traffic with them, and in every sense to deal with them as fiends in human shape, too devilish in nature to mix with any other communities except the slave-traders of Spain and Portugal, and the slave capturers of Dahomey, where the king sits on a throne of skulls, and bloodshed is the only occupation of both men and women. Cast down your eyes, you slave-dealing, man-eating monster, and bury your face in shame before this holy man, whose existence you would long since have terminated, rather than he should have been free, but who, by the blessing of God, has escaped your fangs to do an useful and an honorable work.

This is the man whom you stigmatize (not humorously, but spitefully) as a "nigger," whom you shut out (not by fair arguments or for fair purposes, but by a pompous insolence) from all civil rights and legal protection, and to whom you deny political and religious existence. This is the man who has no name amongst you, who is no citizen, and, as far as your wishes go, never will be. In whom you recognize neither birthright, nor filial, nor parental ties, nor brotherly love, nor care for his kindred; whom you refuse to meet on equal terms anywhere, unless he previously pays you for his own freedom in thousands of round dollars, and whom you estimate as so many pounds weight of body, capable of so many pounds weight of labor, and worth (climax of the curse) so many pounds weight of gold or silver. This is the man whom you buy and sell without consent, whom you register as farmer's stock in the same catalogue with horses, dogs, and swine, and against whose body and soul you wage a war, sufficiently wicked, but too paltry for Satan. This is the man--preaching, teaching, doing good; erect in his manhood, looking down on you--"Hyperion to a satyr"--but whose grey-haired father you kick and insult before his face, whose mother you flog and manacle, while she is still suckling the babe that is your property, whose brother you send to die in the hot pestilence of the rice-fields in the south, whose sister you debauch, and compel to prostitution, that you may sell her to the heartless libertine--treading out of existence him and his race, as if they were worms, and offering as a plea, the fact that he differs from you in the color of his skin! Is not this enough to make us ashamed of our color? Is it not enough to make us suspect that the white man has become white from a very shame of his own infamy?

This is James Pennington, whose manly heart revolts at the indignities offered to his race, who flies from your snake-like embraces, and, in spite of the shame and ignorance, and moral darkness in which you have reared him, becomes the purchaser of his own body, and under the grace of God, the saver of his own soul, a light to the benighted of the world, a father of his race and people! This is him whom Herod-like you tear from his mother's breast, over whom, like Nero, but with less honor, like Caligula but with less pride, you tyrannize and usurp, and on whose flesh and blood, ghoul-like, you feed and fatten--drawing your choicest luxuries from his unceasing toil--toil which you enforce with stripes, and insult, and bloodshed--toil which feeds and clothes you, that you may carry bloated bodies into early graves. What special charter has the God of heaven given you to make a property in this man's body, to brand him with irons, to torture him with whips, to call him "slave!" or, if he escapes, to pursue him with bloodhounds, to shoot him as he flies, or to flog him to death if your hell-kites overtake him? And you are white men too, with Saxon blood in your arteries; you think yourself civilized, guard your interests, defend your political rights; you convene meetings, and inaugurate movements for the advancement of your liberty, and under the banner of that liberty, make laws from the purchase, sale, and degradation of the slave! Know you that the eyes of Europe look westward with abhorrence, to know that a people, calling themselves free, subsist daily on the flesh and blood of Africans? Know you that Britain, whose sons you are, spurns you as base sons, unworthy of maternal acknowledgment? and that before the world you stand as monsters too hideous for the form of humanity, too lying and cannibalish for the services of religion, and fit only for that place of darkness to which, in your blind obesity of ill-got gains, you are sinking like plummets in the ocean.

JOSIAH HENSON.

IT is often said, that truth is stranger than fiction, but it would be wiser to say, that there is no fiction. That which we call fiction, is a new embodiment or new arrangement of some few truths, already sufficiently well-known and accepted, as to warrant their adoption, and for this very reason, it is that fiction (so-called) is less wonderful than truth. The selection of incidents, which the novelist makes, is always bounded by the plan and moral of the world; but fate has no such bounds or limits, and flings men and women into positions and circumstances so varied and opposite as to surpass, in all cases, which are suited for comparison, the changing fortunes of the romancist's hero. The merest tailor, shoemaker, or grocer's errand boy, passes through circumstances, and endures emotions, such as (if they could be written) would outdo in interest the finest romance or epic ever penned; but when we deal with an exceptional character, we expect exceptional incidents; and these, from their novelty and juxtaposition usually prove sufficiently attractive to need no extraneous embellishments. The life of a slave, especially of one who becomes a free man by his own efforts, is a case in point. The necessities of such a life ensure a variety of striking incidents, and of many dramatic pictures, and the movement of the story itself--by virtue of its primal elements, the oppressor striving to enslave--the enslaved struggling to be free--is always striking and instructive. For such a reason it is that we introduce into this work nothing which may be deemed fictitious, and give the pen no license beyond a sufficiently graphic narration of facts; and of all things in the world, which need illustration and description, the truth, is sufficiently vivid in the case of slavery.

JOSIAH HENSON was born on the loth of June, 1789, in Charles County, Maryland, on a farm belonging to Mr. Francis Newman, about a mile from Port Tobacco. Born an article of property, he soon became aware of the value of existence, which, in his case, was represented by a certain number of dollars. However intelligent horses and dogs may be, it is generally believed that they have no ideas of commercial value as attached to themselves; and it can scarcely be considered pleasant for an individual to acquire by degrees a distinct idea, that he is worth so much to somebody else, and that all his thoughts and actions must through life have reference to his own price in the market. Such is the condition of the slave, and Josiah Henson came into the world by what his master would regard as a special providence in his own behalf. His mother was the property of Dr. McPherson, but was hired out by a Mr. Newman, to whom his father belonged.

His first experiences were of a nature peculiar to slavery. The slave owners seem determined that the slaves shall feel no surprise as to the bondage in which they are held, for they exhibit so much debasement of mind, such disgusting brutality in all their actions, that no slave can reasonably wonder that such men keep them in bondage. The overseer attempted an assault upon his mother while she was at labor in the fields. She informed her husband, and on the same treatment being repeated on a subsequent occasion, the sturdy slave, stung to madness by the insult (which slaves are supposed not to feel) flew upon the white man, and would have killed him on the spot, had not he begged for his life by promising never to divulge the fact that the slave had struck him. There never was an overseer yet who was not a liar, and this adulterous wretch, when he knew his life was safe, accused the slave, and procured the sentence of a hundred lashes.

But the nature of the slave was changed, when his blood oozed from his body, his goodness was also flogged out of his heart; and from being an amiable, kind-hearted man, he became morose, disobedient, and untractable, so that he was soon sold to his master's son, and sent to Alabama; and neither wife nor child heard of him more.

Young Henson, a jet black, well-built lad, with bright eyes and white teeth, was rather lucky in his youth in being propertied by a kind master; so much so that he was neither shot at nor hanged, though some other casualties happened, to be described in their places. His master was really a kind man, and was so reputed by his neighbors; he was also very jovial, or, to speak plainly, very fond of dissolute companions, late hours, and strong drinks. He was more than usually fortunate too in another particular; his mother possessed some amount of religious knowledge, and taught her son to pray. Her prayers were little else than a series of ejaculations, and were rather the expression of an earnest heart wishing to pray, than the full breathing of its simple piety. But the scene was soon changed by one of those incidents common to the milder forms of slavery. The master was returning one evening from a debauch, when, in crossing a little stream, he fell from his horse, and was too intoxicated to save himself from drowning. The estate was broken up, and the slaves sold. The mother was bought by one man--the child by another. The mother fell on her knees before the man who had purchased her, and implored him to purchase her baby too, that one of her little ones might be spared her. She was immediately kicked away, and bodily suffering added to the anguish of a breaking heart. The boy sickened, and his master soon afterwards sold him to the mother's master, and thus restored to maternal tending he soon grew to be a vigorous and healthy lad.

The man who owned both mother and child was named Riley. He was a coarse, vulgar, low-bred tyrant--a sort of Caliban in power, licentious and dissolute. His slaves were equally cringing, treacherous, and false, and the farm was hence a pandemonium wherein the worst passions of despots and slaves were let loose. The fare of the slaves was the most scanty; the meals only two a-day--the first at twelve o'clock, after laboring from daylight; the second when the work was over. Corn meal, salt herrings, and occasionally a little buttermilk, or a few vegetables grown on a "truck patch" by assiduous labor after the regular work was done. The clothing for children and youths consisted of a single dress of tow cloth, something like a shirt; but the older slaves were decorated with pantaloons or gowns according to sex; and to this thin wardrobe was added a pair of shoes once a year, and a wool hat in two or three years. The lodging was in log huts, or a single small room, with no other floor than the trodden earth, and with neither beds nor furniture, in which ten or a dozen persons--men, women, and children--might sleep pell-mell, altogether irrespective of chastity or cleanliness, and with no other covering than a single blanket. In these hovels, the slaves were penned by night, and fed by day; here were the children born, and the sick neglected--and yet this was not the severest form of slavery.

In spite of these untoward influences, the young negro soon became a portly fellow. He became ambitious--he hoed, dug and reaped, with uncommon ardor, and now and then looked up (but humbly, as a dog does) to catch an approving smile from his brutal master. The snow-water has worn furrows in mountain sides, but the heart of a slave owner is harder than granite, and the exertions of the slave make no impression. The reward of such faithful service was not a kind word, but a cool calculation of the slave's increase in value.

Under this repulsion, he suddenly woke up to a perception of his condition, and felt a lively sympathy for his companions in bondage. The condition of the male slave was bad enough; but that of the female, compelled to perform unfit labor, sick, suffering, and bearing the burdens of her own sex un-pitied and unaided, as well as the toils which belonged to the other, often oppressed him with a load of anguish, and he determined to do something in their relief. Proper food none of them had, and Henson, spurring them on to greater industry by the force of an irresistible persuasion, also provided for them a supply of fat sheep and pigs by occasionally selecting one from the stock, and driving it a mile or two into the woods, where it was cut up and distributed, and was at once food and medicine and luxury to the poor starving creatures. Slave owners would call this dishonest, but slaves are not educated in moral philosophy, and moreover they have a habit of being hungry when compelled to excessive toil on small rations.

There are cases in which falsehood assumes the character of a virtue, and this case of theft (if it is necessary to call it such) became a blessing to the legal owner of the goods. The slaves grew more lusty as their appetites were appeased; and they became so attached to Henson that his persuasives induced them to more willing services; and by the victualing process which he conducted the farm soon became noted for efficient culture and the alacrity of the slaves. Just then, the overseer was detected in robbing his employer, for selfish not social ends, and was discharged. Henson, the favorite of the negros and the confidant of the master, being appointed in his stead. This change effected a complete reform in the farm; the crops were more than doubled, and the labor was performed with a willingness unprecedented.

At this time a pious baker, living near, who was noted for his benevolence and detestation of slavery, was in the habit of preaching the Gospel to such few as would hear him, and Henson's mother persuaded her son to ask leave to attend one of the services; he asked, and got leave, though with a pious promise of a few lashes if he was not home as soon as it terminated. He was eighteen years of age, and had never yet heard a sermon or any discourse upon religion. The text was from Hebrews i. 9, "That he, by the grace of God, should taste of death for every man." The solemn hush, the earnest attention to the preacher, and the fervent prayer which closed the service, made a deep impression on the mind of the slave, and when the pastor dwelt with force on the words, "For every man;" the despised slave, who had been taught to believe himself created only for the degradation to which he was reduced, now awakened to the consciousness that even he had a soul capable of immortality, though the white man had claimed even that, and had done his best to damn it forever.

One of the duties which devolved upon him as overseer was that of fetching his master every night from the tavern, a task usually performed by manual strength, rather than persuasion--whiskey predominating in the one, and muscular strength in the other. It is the fashion, indeed, of these southern gentry to assemble on Saturdays and Sundays, for gambling, horse-racing, cock-fighting, and political talk (for they are citizens of a great republic) and at these reunions quarrels and duels are frequent--glasses being thrown, dirks drawn, bowies and pistols brought into active use. But, however desperate the melee, or however infuriated the combatants, there is one duty charged upon the slave, which is to rush in, and at every risk to secure his master's safety by carrying him off, a stray bullet in the slave's hide being of little moment, but a scratch on the skin of the master a sufficient justification for the administration of a whipping. On one of these occasions Henson had called for his master as usual, but found him engaged in a desperate combat. It was his duty to save his master, no matter what the danger to himself, and forthwith he rushed into the midst and bore him off, having the misfortune to complete the prostration of a man who was already at an angle of forty-five from a tendency of whiskey to the head. This man was Bryce Lytton, overseer to Mr. Riley, the brother of Henson's master. He gave Henson, instead of the whiskey, the full credit of destroying the poise of his equilibrium, and promised him a complete reward on a favorable opportunity. The opportunity came--the stalwart slave passed along on horseback with some letters, and Lytton made preparations for his return. Three strong slaves were placed in ambush, and Lytton sat on the fence. As Henson returned, Lytton called him to dismount, and at the same moment seized the bridle of the horse.

"What for shall I get down, massa?"

"To take the cursedest flogging you ever had in your life. You * * * black scoundrel."

"But what am I to be flogged for, Mr. Lytton?"

"Hold your tongue, you devil's imp, and take off your jacket."

The three slaves leaped from ambush, and Henson was enclosed. He leaped off the horse on the side opposite his assailant, who immediately flew at him with a stick, and so startled the horse that it broke away and ran home, leaving the besieged in a corner with no chance of escape.

"Take off your shirt," cried the overseer, ordering the slaves to seize him. The repute of Henson's physical power was such, that the slaves were slow to obey. At last they approached him, and he knocked each down in succession; the last, who tried to trip up his feet, when he was down, receiving for his pains a kick which knocked out all his front teeth, and sent him away groaning and grinning. In the meantime, the overseer labored at his head with a stick, but had not strength to knock him down, though he drew blood freely. Then, suddenly seizing a stake of seven feet long, he summoned all his strength, and struck the enemy to the ground. Henson fell with a broken arm; and, when on the ground, received a series of kicks and blows which broke both his shoulder-blades, and was then left weltering in his blood. The arrival of the horse without a rider caused an alarm at the farm, and assistance was dispatched to convey the victim home. He was found in a helpless condition, and carried home in extreme agony, the shoulder-blades grating against each other, and the agony of his splintered arm taking away his breath. As a special act of mercy, the sister of Riley, who enjoyed the most perfect immunity from a knowledge of anatomy and surgery, was called in to tie up the slave's wounds, and, with some tow round his shoulders, and a bandage on his arm, and a little brown paper and vinegar, this female Aesculapius left him to the care of nature. In five months he was able to leave his earthen floor (slaves never have beds) and proceed to the field. The first work he was ordered to was ploughing; and a hard knock of the coulter against a stone, shattered his shoulder-blades again, and gave him greater agony than before. From that day to this he has been unable to raise his hands to his head. There he is, all of a lump, his arms twisted behind him, and his hands twirled round like the paddles of a seal, while his shoulders are sufficiently elevated to look down right and left upon his head; and this for accidentally changing the position of a drunken scoundrel from a slant of forty-five degrees to a prostration of a hundred and eighty. In such cases, the law affords no compensation. Lytton stated before a magistrate, without being put on oath, that he had acted in self-defense, and was freed from all liability.

The crippled slave was still retained on the farm in consequence of his skillful management of cattle and crops, and the increased industry of the slaves under his direction. Here he acted honorably, and won the favor of his master. At twenty-two years of age, he fell in love with a pretty negro girl whom he met at the chapel-- which he still continued to attend. She was frugal, industrious, cleanly, and pious, and of rather a higher mental stamp than slaves are generally. He met her in the evenings when the work was done, and the simple but earnest courtship terminated in a happy marriage, she loving him none the less for his fin-shaped hands and elevated shoulders. Sometime after, his master married a very economic girl who carried out the starving system, in regard to the pigs and the poultry, as well as the slaves. But what she saved by her system of corn and meat-preserving, the husband wasted by excessive drinking, and Henson soon learnt from his master's own lips, that he was ruined.

"Si," said he, in a more than usually conciliating tone, "Si, I'm a ruined man; but there is one resource for me, and that depends on you."

"How can that be, master?" said the other in astonishment.

"Well, you must first promise to do whatever I ask you, Si."

"You might ask me to do more than is possible, or more than my duty to God will permit; you might ask me to do something which may bind the yoke tighter round the necks of my fellow-slaves; in which case, master--"

"Not a word, Si. For heaven's sake promise, or I shall be stripped of everything, and lose every hope of getting even bread."

Thus he pressed his faithful servant, and by entreaties and tears wrung from him the promise he desired. He was then told to take all the slaves to Riley's brother in Kentucky; and, accordingly, in February, 1825, he set out in the midst of heavy snows on a journey of a thousand miles, with eighteen slaves in his command. In passing through Ohio and Cincinnati, they were told that they were free, if they chose to be so, and frequently urged to quit their master. Now was the time for Henson to realize the dreams of his life--personal liberty towards which he had hitherto treasured every dollar--he could call his own, that he might, at some future day, purchase his freedom. Himself, his family, and his eighteen partners in bondage, could now shake off the yoke of a man whom none of them loved, and who had been guilty of every cruelty and oppression. He hesitated between the boon offered, and the word he had pledged, and struck the balance in favor of the latter. White men have been known to abscond with property, and to defraud, and even murder those to whom they had promised help; but the uneducated slave, the "nigger," had sentiments of honor which even the disposal of his own person could not shake or alter.

In April, 1825, the party arrived in Kentucky, and Henson delivered his charge to Amos Riley, the brother of his master, who lived five miles south of Ohio River, on Big Blackford's Creek. Here he remained three years employed upon the farm, his services valued by his new master, and the condition of himself and fellow-bondsmen considerably improved. His post of superintendent enabled him to attend more regularly than before the meetings for religious purposes, and so rapidly did his mind become enlightened, and his heart opened to the influences of Christianity, that he became in a short time a preacher of the Gospel, esteemed by the neighbors of both colors, and admitted by a Conference of the Methodist Episcopal Church. At this time news arrived from his master in Maryland, who was unable to induce his wife to proceed to Kentucky, and sent orders to his brother to sell all the slaves except Henson and his family. Now occurred one of those heart-rending scenes so common in slave countries, the separation of wives and husbands, sisters and brothers, who are torn asunder with stripes and kicks, and sold, some to the north to be starved, some to the south to be destroyed by marsh plague, all scattered abroad for ever, to suit the caprice of one owner, or serve the necessities of another. Soon after the sale, Henson made acquaintance with a Methodist preacher of some reputation in Kentucky, and this man urged the slave to acquire his freedom, and promised to bring about the means of his purchase. The plan was for him to obtain leave to visit his master in Maryland, by permission of his present master, and, on his way, to raise subscriptions towards the fund he required. With a letter of recommendation from his friend, he started in September, 1828, for Maryland. On the road, he had opportunities of preaching in several pulpits, where he stated the object he had in view, and when he arrived at his master's house, he was possessed of a suit of clothes, a horse, and two hundred and seventy-five dollars. The master was astonished to see him in this trim, and still more so to hear his plans for obtaining freedom. He asked him for his pass, and, seeing that it authorized his return to Kentucky, coolly put it into his desk. Henson understood this maneuver, and determined to maneuver too. At night he was sent to his accustomed burrow, with its earth floor, its filth, and its crowd of crouching occupants. During his absence, his mother had died: every tie which connected him with the place was broken, and strangers were around him on every hand. Obtaining his pass, by a ruse, from Riley's wife, he set off to visit the wife's brother at Washington, to whom, as an old friend, he confided his plan, and obtained promises of assistance. This brother soon after persuaded Riley to suffer Henson to buy himself, urging that he had his pass, and could return back to Kentucky unless the other seized the opportunity to profit by his determination. A bargain was struck, and the price of the cripple fixed at four hundred and fifty dollars, three hundred and fifty of which were to be paid down. On the 9th of March, 1829, the manumission papers, certifying his freedom, were handed to him, and he was prepared to start for Kentucky.

"What do you mean to do with your freedom-certificate, Si," said his master, "in the event of anybody asking you to show it?"

"I shall open it, and let them see that I am free, master."

"Ah, then you'll be robbed of it in a day or two, and then thrown into prison, as a runaway, and sold to pay the gaol fees; and then, how the devil will you buy yourself again? Now, you can go back to Kentucky with your pass, and if I seal up your certificate, and direct it to Amos, nobody dare molest you. To break a seal, you know, is a State prison job."

"Then seal it up, master, and I'll be grateful to you forever."

The document was sealed: and, so far, the trick of the wily trader was complete. The slave himself dare not now break the seal, and was at the mercy of the man to whom the packet was directed.

Reaching the brother's farm at dusk, Henson went straight to his cabin, and found his wife and little ones in ecstasy to see him. Now he heard that letters had reached the house, telling of what he had been doing, and his wife Charlotte asked him how he expected to get the remainder of the thousand dollars? He saw the trick that had been played. Since the agreement and the signing of the manumission-papers, his price had been increased five hundred and fifty dollars, and, instead of a hundred dollars, he had now to pay six hundred and fifty, besides which, his own certificate was under seal addressed to another, and he dare not touch it. Tricked at every turn by these designing scoundrels, members of a superior race of mortals, he now tricked in his turn, and begged his wife to hide the packet so that he might not know where it was, and then, on the interrogations of his master's brother, and the confirmation of the report concerning the price he had agreed to pay, he assumed to have lost the packet. But there was another net preparing for him. Amos Riley, taking advantage of the supposed loss of the certificate, and annoyed at the prospect of losing the services of so valuable a slave, determined to sell Henson immediately, and ordered him to prepare for a voyage with his son to New Orleans.

> He who takes hold upon a slippery place
> Makes use of no vile hold to stay him up.

The heart of the disappointed man sunk within him as the truth flashed upon his mind; but there was no alternative but submission. Bidding farewell to his wife and babes, he got on board, and took his station at the helm. On the voyage down the river the captain fell blind, and Henson was left to the guidance of the boat. Night came, and he paced the deck alone. He knew that he was being carried without warning or consent to be sold in the public market. All that he had done for these two faithless masters was to end in this--separation forever from those most dear; a life of suffering and toil in the south among strangers; liberty lost irretrievably and forever, and a speedy death among the sugar swamps. His blood turned to gall and wormwood as he looked forward at his fate, and, from being a kind-hearted Christian man, he suddenly became a savage and a dangerous slave. Should he go like a lamb to the slaughter, or now seize the only opportunity that might ever occur, and free himself from their shackles at any price? He had met some of his acquaintance on the river who had been sold into this region, and, as the haggard looks and crushed hopes of these now came to his mind, he determined to shed blood rather than fall a helpless victim, and to free himself at once by a decisive blow.

There were four men sleeping below, two of them white servants, the others the blind captain and young Amos. He resolved to kill them all, to scuttle the craft, and escape to the north, with what money was in the boat. The hour had come; and with a maddened resolution he crept down the cabin and lifted up an axe above the head of Amos--one blow and he breathes no more--one blow and four murders must be done to-night, and none see me but the stars--stay, none but the stars--yes, God sees me and I am a murderer, though I thought I was a Christian. Conscience broke in like sunlight through a thunder-cloud, and a voice whispered--just like the whisper of his Charlotte, and he turned his head to listen. He shrunk back, laid down the axe, crept on deck again, and on his knees in the black midnight he thanked God for this deliverance.

Not a few slave-owners have been as near death during sleep as Amos Riley.

In a few days the crisis came, and the boat touched at New Orleans. Amos sold the cargo, and the men were discharged, and there was no longer any secret about selling Henson. Several planters came to look at him, and he was sent on several hasty errands in order that they might see how he could run. In fact he was trotted to and fro, poked in the ribs, punched in the back, and pinched from head to foot to test his value. As yet he was not sold, but expected to go off every hour, a strange consciousness and expectancy which horses and dogs are happily spared. But now Amos fell ill and became rapidly worse, for the river fever had seized him, and death seemed in no need of an invitation by a hatchet. He was far from home, and with none to trust to but the faithful slave, and he lay helpless as a child with his head in the negro's lap, begging him to do something to mitigate his anguish. Henson immediately sold the boat and got his young master on board a steamer, and by twelve the next day he was on the voyage homewards. He grew worse, and expected every moment to breathe his last, and begged, with tears in his eyes, that if he should die on board Henson would not suffer his body to be thrown into the river. His strength was gone and his voice was failing, yet the slave took no advantage of his weakness, made no effort now to obtain his liberty, but nursed him as if he were a babe, and saved his life by ceaseless care and watching.

Twelve days after Amos and Henson arrived at home, and it was said that Henson had acted very well for a slave, and there ended all acknowledgment of the saving of the young man's life, gratitude for such a service being a dream which never disturbs the mind of a planter. But now it was time for Henson to think seriously of escape; for two designing men were plotting against his life and liberty, and he was literally kidnapped after paying three-fourths of the market value for himself. He had heard of Canada as a land whereon no slave could tread; free men only were to be found there, and once place his foot on that soil, he, the despised and cheated, would be a free man too. At first Charlotte refused, dreading the danger of escape and the risk of capture. At last she consented, and preparations were at once made for their departure. He made a pack for his back large enough to hold his two youngest children, and after the day's labor was performed he trotted round the cabin with his burden on his back, in order to accustom himself to carry it through the wilderness. Saturday night came, the night on which fugitive slaves invariably commence their flight, in order to get clear of the neighborhood before being missed on Monday morning. A faithful slave rowed him and his family across the Ohio

River, though it was at the risk of his life he did so. Landed on the Indiana shore he set forth with a cheerful heart to make his pilgrimage to freedom. As fast as the darkness would allow they trudged on, and the hearts of the happy six beat high with hope, and they felt themselves already the inheritors of liberty.

In a fortnight they reached Cincinnati; their provisions were now used up, and the cry of hunger resounded in the camp. He must face the danger now or all must starve in the woods; so he steps boldly from his ambush, and walking southward to prevent suspicion, approaches a house and asks if they will sell him some bread and meat. No! they have nothing to sell to niggers. At the next house he made a purchase, the man not refusing his tendered money, but giving as little as possible for it, for the same reason that the other would give him none. From Cincinnati they fared better, and got a lift in a wagon for thirty miles. Here they made night journeys again, and arrived at the Scioto, in the heart of a wild country, and struck out into an open road roughly cut in the woods.

Now he might travel by day as well as by night, for civilization had not reached these wilds, and the native wolves were less to be dreaded because less ferocious than men. Still there were many fears to trouble the little band, and danger thickened as they sped onward deeper and deeper into the savage wood. Hunger now came in terrible reality; and a small piece of dry beef was all that they possessed. This was divided, and another day's toil commenced. The road was rough, covered with logs and brushwood, and there were few marks to betoken the track. Now the wife fell from exhaustion, and the children clung around her sobbing, "Mother, mother, do not die and leave us here." A little rest and the last piece of dry beef were all the poor slave could give his exhausted partner; and in a few hours they set out again. After some time there were sounds of footsteps, and in an instant the little party flew to ambush. Looking out, Henson saw that it was a band of Indian hunters, and the moment the Indians caught sight of him they set up a fearful howl and scampered away, believing they had seen the Mah-je-mah-ne-doo. Presently they came upon the wigwams of these Indians, and the whole party fled from the camp terrified. At last they saw the chief standing with a dignified air waiting for their approach. As the black visitors did not eat up the chief, or commit any acts of a particularly diabolical nature, the Indians were reassured and returned to the wigwams, and began to examine the party, to be assured if they were human; poking their fingers into the eyes of the children, and pinching little bits of flesh from the father's nose, in order to be satisfied of their "sensibility." Surprise over, they became hospitable, and gave the fugitives abundance of food, a good night's rest, and full directions, by signs, as to their future progress northwards.

Now they came to Sandusky city, and approached a wharf where a number of white men were loading a vessel with corn. Hiding his family, Henson pushed forward, and was hailed by one, who asked him if he wanted work. He said yes, and the next instant was running with a bag of corn in his hand like the rest, and although he was wasted by travel and privation, and his back thoroughly skinned by the scratching of the knapsack, the first taste of voluntary labor was so sweet, that he ran to and fro faster than any of them. The captain got a hint of the errand he was on, and Henson at once confessed the truth, to which the captain responded, by offering to carry him and his family free of charge to Buffalo. "But keep out of the way," said he, "for this place is full of Kentucky spies, and you may be kidnapped, and sold in less than two hours, unless you are careful." The sails were hoisted, and the vessel got off, and at dusk the captain put off a boat for the fugitives, and they were brought on board, and landed at Buffalo, on the second morning from their departure from Sandusky. The captain then put them on board a steamer for Waterloo, paid their passage-money, and gave Henson a dollar at parting. This captain's name was Burnham, and he was a native of Scotland. The names of such men should be remembered, for they preserve society from putrefaction.

At last he landed on the Canada shore, and no sooner touched the soil with his feet, than he fell into a transport of joy. He laughed, then cried, twirled his legs about like a tortured spider, and took leaps like a gigantic flea. Then he rolled on the ground, shouting and laughing all the while, and then leaped up and spun round and round, till he rolled over from giddiness, and nearly crushed his own children into a jelly, by tumbling pell-mell into their midst. A gentleman seeing these antics, rushed toward him with arms extended, crying, "Poor fellow, he's in a fit!" whereat Henson leaped to his feet, his mouth stretched into an almost inconceivable shape by laughter, and his face greasy with his tears, and cried out, "I'm free! I'm free!" Then Colonel Warren laughed too, and looked on with pleasure, as the liberated slave kissed his children all round, and then his wife, and then sprang to kiss the Colonel, but changing his mind, kissed his little ones again, still shouting, "I'm free! I'm free!"

Now came facts again, and romance began to fade. He was in a strange land without money, without a home, and the means of subsistence he must earn by labor. He got into the employ of a Mr. Hibbard, who gave him a two-story shanty, which had been used by the pigs as a house of call, and into this he and his troop entered, calling it at once, "our house;" and so touched with pride at having a house, that they felt inclined to look condescendingly on the world, at which, as from a castle, they might peep through a hole the pigs had made. Straw was got, and the pigs expelled, for men only sleep with cattle when they are called "slaves." Mops, hoes, and brooms were brought to work and in a few hours the shanty equaled any in the country, and was as good in every respect as an Irishman's.

Now Mr. Hibbard, the employer, found, as the Rileys had found before, that Henson's labor was worth more than he was accustomed to, and instead of tightening the bonds of labor, they were relaxed, and comfort added to comfort, till Henson found himself the joyful possessor of some pigs, a cow, and a horse. Your nigger can do something better than lie and cheat when he has a chance, you see, most detestable cannibal fiends. While you despise him, and whip him, and starve him, and make him a beast of burden, and call him "slave," his hopes are crushed, his body bent by labor, and his soul trodden out by the heels of your shoes; but call him "man," and let him work as other men work, by his own will, and not by compulsion, and his industry, sobriety, and intelligence, shame you and your boasted civilization. Civilization--pshaw! nothing of the sort; you are degenerating back to barbarism, and unless you stir up the last relic of manhood which lives in you, you will sink so fast and so sure, as soon to be a beast of burden yourself.

Now came a trial for Henson. His eldest boy had been put to school by Mr. Hibbard, and an old friend, who had arrived from Maryland, had spread abroad Henson's former reputation as a preacher. He was willing to preach as before, though he had himself said nothing about it; but he could not read, he knew nothing of theology, not even of the Scriptures. Slavery had robbed him of his manhood, because it entailed an ignorance which sealed his manly dignity. One beautiful Sabbath morning, when he was preparing his mind for the performance of his sacred duties, he called his son to read to him.

"Where shall I read, father?" said Tom.

"Anywhere, my son." The father was ignorant of the names of the books, and knew not how to direct the boy.

Tom opened and read Psalm 103--"Bless the Lord, O my soul; and all that is within me, bless his holy name." When he had finished, Tom asked--

"Who was David, father? he writes pretty, don't he?"

The father had never heard of David before, and he blushed to acknowledge his ignorance to his own child.

"He was a man of God, my son," he evasively answered.

"I suppose so," said Tom, "but I want to know more about him. Where did he live? what did he do?"

The father grew excited with shame, and at last acknowledged that he did not know.

"Why, father," said he, "can't you read?"

His shame was over, and his pride gone; this question humbled him to the dust, for it brought him to a conviction that he was unfit in this state of ignorance for the ministration of the Gospel. Full of solemn thought he did not preach that day, but went to the woods, and there spent the day in secret prayer and meditation. The same night he began to take lessons of Tom as they sat together in their shanty, and lighted the holy page with a blazing pine-knot, and in the course of that winter the black man learnt to read.

About three years after this, the condition of the family was again improved by a new engagement under Mr. Risley, who was a man of higher character and attainments than Mr. Hibbard. He now began to reflect on the condition of the blacks, who were getting numerous in Canada, in consequence of escapes from the States; and these, too much joyed at having effected their deliverance, were forgetting that industry and sobriety were necessary to make freedom acceptable. Most of the colored persons were working for hire on the lands of others, and had not yet dreamed of becoming independent proprietors. Meetings were called, and at last it was determined that a number of blacks should associate, and settle on a suitable plot of land, where they might hope to be rewarded with independence and comfort, and attain a permanent standing in the world. Henson was dispatched to explore the country, and at last it was determined to settle on an estate which the government granted them temporarily, determining, however, to purchase the land by contract, before competition was invited.

After seeing his people thus far provided for, he set about the labor of liberating slaves, and undertook most arduous journeys, and no end of perils, to relieve his brethren in bondage. So nobly did he work in this cause, that although crippled in body and uneducated in mind, he has succeeded in delivering 118 human beings out of the cruel and merciless grasp of the slave-owner. In one of these expeditions he travelled on foot 400 miles, through the States of New York, Pennsylvania, and Ohio, into Kentucky, to assist the friends of one James Lightfoot, who had himself escaped out of bondage. Reaching these people, he found them unprepared to go, and promised to return for them in a year; then he pushed on fifty miles into the interior of Kentucky, and there released a large party, whom he landed safely on the Canadian shore. Then he made a second journey for the Lightfoots, and encountered innumerable perils in their behalf; and these too, he succeeded in releasing, and landed safe upon the freeman's shore.

He now set about improving the condition of his people at home, and in order to stimulate them to habits of good husbandry, commenced lecturing upon crops, wages, and profits, and soon effected such salutary reforms as to lay the basis of a true independence amongst the negros, who now bless his name, and teach their children to lisp "Josiah Henson."

He now formed an alliance with Hiram Wilson, a congregational missionary, who took an interest in the blacks; and by the aid of this gentleman and Mr. Fuller, (who brought back from England fifteen hundred dollars for the benefit of the negros) a fund was raised for the establishment of a manual labor school; which was finally settled at Dawn, on the River Sydenham, and two hundred acres of rich land, purchased at four dollars the acre. Henson bought a patch of land here at the same time; and in 1842 removed his family to the lot, and commenced the operations for founding a permanent settlement. From that time to the present, his exertions have been devoted without stint to the advancement of the welfare of his own people--a Wilberforce to those in bondage--a Robert Owen to those that are free.

A short time since, Henson, accompanied by his son, came to this country; and, like the others whom we have spoken of, he has been engaged since he arrived here in speaking on slavery. He has spoken with much effect before large audiences, sat at the tables of some of our principal preachers and philanthropists, and has become a general favorite.

A short time after, Earl Grey sent to him, and requested an interview, which Henson granted. The object of the interview was to know if Henson would undertake a mission to India, to ascertain the capabilities to produce cotton, and other slave-grown products. We regard this as a remarkable indication of the progress of the Anti-Slavery cause. For some time past, a great deal has been said in this country and America, about checking slavery by discontinuing the use of slave-produce. It has been agitated by philanthropists and merchants, until it has reached the feelings and thoughts of statesmen. The very circumstance of the Secretary of our Colonies soliciting an interview with an American fugitive slave, must gall the slaveholders of "the model Republic" keenly; but that he was conferred with on such a subject must wound them to the quick. We regard this interview as one of the most remarkable of the kind which has taken place in this country during this remarkable year. It indicates a tendency. England takes from the slave-states of America every year more than one-half their produce; in fact, we are the great patron and substantial sustainer of American slavery. And, if we cultivate in our colonies the articles we are now taking from America, the slave system in that country is doomed. May its death-day soon come! Henson told the Earl that he had a mission to perform in this country, which he could not, on any consideration, relinquish; but, after its termination, he should be in a position to make an arrangement with the English Government.

We need not pursue this narrative further. Scanty as it is, it yet affords an illustration of the capabilities of the negro; not only to profit by favorable circumstances, but amidst the crushing influences of an unjust, heartless, despotic, and blasphemous slavery, to create those circumstances for himself. How it shames the pride of the pale Saxon to note the career of such a man as this; to see him cast off his chains, and fly to a land of liberty, over hundreds of miles of country, with a wife and two children at his side, and two younger ones at his back. He must face hunger, cold, ravenous beasts of prey, and all the dangers of a midnight journey unarmed, through desolate forests and marshes, or risk the safety of life, limb, and the liberty for which he is ready to sacrifice all else, in the open ways of the market and the thoroughfare, where bloodhounds lie in wait to scent him, and men with bloodier purposes than the hounds themselves, are ready to entrap him in their snares. How many of our well-fed, well-educated citizens, would dare such trials, even for a higher boon--if such there be--than personal liberty? How many of your slave-owning, chapel-going hypocrites, who talk of "mild treatment," and "fit for nothing else," can pass through such a fire as this, unscathed, preserving honor all the while, and bating no one jot of so righteous a purpose; but fulfilling it in the sternest integrity, and with not the slightest moral stain? The master lies and cheats, and sells his slave twice to himself (or intends it); he plots against his life; he strikes him, taunts him, and looks down upon him, imagining in his own slave-owning imbecility, that a black skin marks an inferior order of creation--a legitimate beast of burden; but the slave nurses his head on his knee when sickness comes, follows him faithfully when perils are near, and spares his life when no help is at hand, even though the tyrant has turned the whole current of the negro's blood by repeated cruelties and wrongs. So far the capabilities and moral virtues of the negro as exemplified in Josiah Henson. There are thousands such in the west, groaning in chains, perishing body and soul, the victims of this hellish "institution." Let the hand of benevolence be extended from these shores; the loud voice of British opinion be sounded so loud as to penetrate every labyrinth of that huge spider's web of man-catchers, and every effort which noble hearts, guided by wise heads, can make, be used for the enfranchisement of the slave.

CHAPTER IV
WILLIAM WELLS BROWN.

No doubt, many of our readers are in the habit of walking through Fleet-street or the Strand. If so, perhaps they have occasionally met an intelligent, fine looking colored man, neither black nor white, but combining a mixture of the both; in fact, a mulatto. Such an one is William Wells Brown, who may frequently be seen at meetings in the principal thoroughfares of London. He is a fugitive slave, and is legally the property of another man, and cannot return to his native country for fear of being taken back to slavery.

Mr. Brown was born in Lexington, Kentucky. His mother was the slave of Dr. John Young. His father was a white man, a slave-holder, and a relation of his master. This Dr. John Young was the owner of forty to fifty slaves. He had a large farm, on which was principally grown tobacco and hemp.

Like slaves on most all other plantations, those on Dr. Young's were worked hard. They were summoned every morning at four o'clock, by the ringing of a large bell, to the field. They were allowed half an hour to get their breakfast; at half-past four a horn was blown, and the slave who was not at his post in time received ten lashes.

One morning, Brown's mother was ten or fifteen minutes too late; and when she got to the fields, the overseer commenced whipping her. She could only say, "Oh, pray! oh, pray! oh, pray!" these are the words which slaves generally utter when imploring mercy at the hands of their oppressors. The son heard it, though he was some way off. He heard the crack of the whip, and every groan and cry of his poor mother. The cold chill ran over him, and he wept aloud; but he was a slave like his mother, and could render her no assistance. He learnt from bitter experience that nothing could be more heart-rending than to see a dear and beloved mother or sister tortured, and to hear her cries, and not be able to render the slightest assistance.

Among the slaves on Dr. Young's farm, was one called Randall. He was a large well-built man, possessing great physical power. He was considered the most able-bodied and valuable slave on the plantation, but that did not screen him from the lash. The overseer, whose name was Cook, entertained a strong malicious feeling against Randall, and though he was told by the master not to attempt to whip Randall, he was determined to try. One day he gave Randall a very hard task, much more than he could possibly do, and at night, the task not being performed, performed, he told the slave that he would be remembered next morning.

On the following morning Cook told Randall he was to be whipped, and forthwith ordered him to cross his hands and be tied. Randall asked why he was to be whipped, and was told, because he did not finish his task the preceding night. Randall said the task was too great, or he should have done it. Cook said it made no difference, he should whip him. Randall stood silent for a short time, and said--.

"Mr. Cook, I have always tried to please you. Since you have been on this plantation, I have worked as hard as I possibly could; morning, noon, and night, I have always obeyed orders, and done my utmost to please you and I find you are determined not to be satisfied, let me do what I may. No one has laid hands on me, to whip me, for the last ten years, and I have now come to the conclusion not to be whipped by any living man."

Cook saw from Randall's determined look and gesture, that he was in earnest, and fearing to tackle him alone, called three of the hands from their work, and commanded them to hold Randall. Knowing the immense strength of the man, and not liking to be brought into too close contact with him, they refused, and the overseer, with all his commands and entreaties, could not induce them to commence operations. For some days the matter appeared to rest there, but the overseer, whose dignity was so-sadly compromised, only bottled up his rage, so that he might vent it all the more powerfully on a future occasion; pretense, or no pretense, what was that to him, He was a white man, and Randall was a black, and he would let the nigger know whether he would obey his commands or not. So one morning when the hands were at work in the field, Cook, with three of his white companions, made their appearance. Randall was commanded to leave his work, and proceed to the barn. This he refused to do, as he anticipated what they intended doing. The overseer and his companions immediately fell on him, and commenced pummeling him with all their might. Randall put forth all his strength, and laid the ruffians prostrate one after another. Whereupon one of them fired at him, and brought him to the ground by a pistol ball. The poor fellow was no sooner down, than the whole four rushed upon him, wounded as he was, and commenced beating him over his head and face, until they succeeded in tying him. He was then taken to the barn, and tied, in a bleeding state to a beam. And in this condition Cook gave him one hundred lashes with a cowhide, and then washed him with salt and water, and left him tied during the dry. The following day he was untied, and taken to a blacksmith's shop, where he had a ball and a chain attached to his leg. And in this weak, exhausted, and humiliated state, he was compelled to labor.

What think you of this, men of civilized nations? Are you not ashamed of the human form and name? Do you not wish to be transformed into some other shape out of shame, that things calling themselves men, should act so demon-like? and especially when you know that these things are done in the meridian blaze of the civilization of the nineteenth century, by professedly advanced republicans, and even under the consecrated banner of the Christian faith?

When William Wells Brown (how he came by this name we shall see further on) had answered the purpose of his master, he was hired out by a Major Freeland, who was a public-house keeper, also a horse-racer, cock-fighter, gambler, and to crown the whole, an inveterate drunkard. Little charity or benevolence could be expected from such a character. In fact he was a blood-thirsty tyrant. He had ten or twelve servants whom he would knock and kick about as if they were as many barrels of swipes. He would tie up his slaves in the smoke-house, whip them, then smoke them, by burning around them tobacco stems, and call it all "Virginia play."

Brown not very well liking the tender treatment of so kind a master, after living with him five or six months, took it into his head to run away, and went into the woods, where he stayed for some days scarcely knowing whether he should make towards the land of freedom or return. One day while in the woods, he heard the barking and howling of dogs, and in a short time they came so near, that he knew them to be bloodhounds, kept for the purpose of hunting runaway slaves.

Seeing there was no chance of escape, he took refuge on the top of a tree, and the hounds were soon at its trunk. He remained there about half-an-hour until the hunters came up. They immediately commanded him to descend, and finding there were no means of escape he came down, was tied and taken to St. Louis' jail.

He was not there long before Major Freeland made his appearance, and took him out of jail, and ordered him to follow him home. Immediately on his arrival there, he was, as he expected, tied up in the smoke-house, and whipped to his heart's content. After the Major had flogged him to his own satisfaction, he put the cowhide into the hands of his son Robert, who being a chip of the old block, gave him more lashes. Freeland, the younger, then made a fire of tobacco stems around him, smoked him well, and after being well whipped and smoked, he was untied and sent to work.

Major Freeland soon after failed in business, and Brown was put on board a steam-boat, which plied between St. Louis and Galena. He remained in this situation during the sailing season, which was the most pleasant time he had ever experienced. It was one of the sunny spots of his life, and was forever after treasured among his brightest recollections.

It was, however, too good to last, as, at the close of the voyage, he was hired to a Mr. John Colburn, keeper of the Missouri Hotel. His situation there was as painful as his preceding one was pleasant. This Colburn, though from the Free States, was a most inveterate hater of the negro race. He was as abusive to his wife as to his slaves; but Mrs. Colburn was as kind as her husband was cruel. She never said a harsh word to any of her servants. Her husband never uttered a kind one.

Among the slaves employed at the Hotel was one by the name of Aaron, who belonged to a Mr. Darby, a lawyer. Poor Aaron was the knife-cleaner. One day one of the knives was put on the table, not as clean as it might have been. For this trivial offence, Mr. Colburn tied Aaron up in the wood-house, and gave him a hundred lashes on his bare back. Brown was then commanded to wash the poor fellow down with rum. This put him into greater agony than the whipping. When untied, Aaron went to his master, and complained of the treatment he had received. But Mr. Darby took no notice of what he said, and immediately sent him back. Colburn having learnt that the man had been complaining to his master, tied him up again, and gave him a more severe whipping than before. The poor slave's back was literally out to pieces, so much so, that he was not able to work for a fortnight.

The next change in Brown's life took place by his being hired by a Mr. Lovejoy; and while with him, Brown was very fortunate. Mr. Lovejoy was the Editor of the "St. Louis Times," and also a very good man and master. Brown was taken into the printing-office, and while there, managed to gain some instruction. Though Mr. Lovejoy was kind and considerate, many of his neighbors were infinitely cruel. One of them, a Colonel Harvey, whipped a slave woman to death. In the same town of St. Louis, Francis Macintosh, a free colored man from Pittsburgh, was taken from the steam-boat "Flora," and burned at the stake. These things took place previous to Brown residing there; but during a residence of eight years in the city, numerous cases of extreme cruelty came under his observation. We will give one as an illustration.

A Captain Brant, who resided near Brown's master, had a slave named John, who, on one occasion, while driving his master from the city, the streets being very muddy, and the horses going at a rapid rate, some mud was spattered upon a gentleman by the name of Moore. This of course insulted the dignity of the white man, and three or four months after the occurrence he purchased John, for the express purpose, as he said, "To tame the infernal nigger." Poor John was whipped regularly three times a week for the first three months, besides having a ball and chain fastened to his leg, and kept at hard labor until the iron had so worn into the flesh of the leg, that it was thought mortification would ensue, and all this was done to "tame" him. John, when he first went to St. Louis, before he fell into the hands of Moore, was a noble-minded man; but he soon became a degraded and crushed being. His physical courage and noble bearing were tamed out of him; and the last time Brown saw him, he had almost lost the use of his limbs. Who in England would treat a horse in such a manner?

While living with Mr. Lovejoy, Brown was sometimes sent on errands to the office of the "Missouri Republican." On one occasion, when returning from that office with type, he was pelted well with snow-balls, by several large boys, sons of slave-holders. Having the heavy type in his hands, he could not well escape with his heels, so he laid down his load, and gave ball for ball; but they were too many guns for him. Not only using snow, but stones and sticks until they overpowered him, and would have captured him for his refractory impudence for having thrown snow-balls at while boys. So he was obliged to run, and leave his type behind, which was immediately taken possession of by the boys.

Poor Brown was now in a pretty pickle, and what to do he knew not. But knowing Mr. Lovejoy to be a very humane man, he went and explained the matter to him. Mr. Lovejoy took one of his apprentices with him, and went after the type, and soon returned with it. During the snow-ball skirmish, Brown hit one of the boys pretty heavily, the white boy showed the white feather, and went home blubbering to his father. Soon after, the father made his way to Mr. Lovejoy's office, for the purpose of executing "Lynch law" on Brown. But Brown seeing him approach made his escape through the back door. When the enraged father found the bird had flown, he swore that when he got him in his power, he would whip him to death. A few days after, as Brown was walking in the street, McKinnie, the boy's father overtook him, seized him by the collar, and commenced beating him with a large cane, over the head in the most terrible manner, which caused the blood to gush from his ears and nose in such a manner, that his clothes were completely saturated. After being so beaten, he was let go, and he returned to the office so weak from the loss of blood, that Mr. Lovejoy was obliged to send him home to his master. Here he was obliged to remain five weeks before he could again walk, during which time it was necessary to have someone to supply his place at the office, and he lost his situation.

After his recovery he was hired to Captain Reynolds, as a waiter on board the steam-boat "Enterprise." This boat was then running on the Upper Mississippi. Brown's employment on board was to wait on gentlemen, and the captain being a kind man, the situation was a pleasant one. But, whilst passing from place to place, and seeing new faces day by day, and knowing that the people who wore them could go where they pleased, he wished to go where he liked also. Though his employment was not irksome, he soon became very unhappy. He wanted to be free. Why should he not? The mighty Mississippi rolled beneath him, the breezes flaunted freely above him, the song of the birds, and the sound of human voices awoke within him the desire to be free also. He, consequently, several times thought of leaving the boat at some landing-place, and making his escape to Canada.

But, whenever such desires and thoughts arose in his soul, he remembered that his dear mother was a slave in St. Louis, and he could not think of leaving her in that condition. It was beautiful to be free, but much more beautiful if his mother could be free also. She was a kind mother, she had often told him how tenderly she had loved him when he was young, and how she carried him upon her back when he was an infant; how often she had been whipped for leaving her work to nurse him, and how happy he would appear, when kindly attended to. When reminiscences like these passed through Brown's mind, his resolution to escape would get shaken, so he resolved never to leave the land of slavery without his mother. Besides this material tie, he had three brothers and a sister there, two of his brothers having died, but even their dust was sacred; and the recollections that hung around their graves and their memories attracted him to St. Louis. But, of all his relatives, his mother was the nearest and dearest, and his sister next.

One evening, while visiting them, he made some allusion to a proposed journey to Canada: his sister took her seat by his side, and, taking his hand in hers, said, with tears in her eyes--

"Brother, you are not going to leave mother and your dear sister here without a friend, are you?"

He looked into her face, as the tears coursed swiftly down her cheeks, and bursting into tears himself, said--

"No, I will never desert you and mother!"

She clasped his hands in hers, and said--"Brother, you have often declared you would not end your days in slavery. I see no possible way in which you can escape with us; and now you are on a steam-boat, where there is some chance for you to escape to a land of liberty, I beseech you not to let us hinder you. If we cannot get our liberty, we do not wish to be the means of keeping you from a land of freedom."

He could restrain his feelings no longer, and an outburst of his own feelings caused her to cease speaking upon that subject. In opposition to their wishes, he pledged himself not to leave them in the hands of the oppressor. He took leave of them and returned to the boat, and laid down in his bunk, but "sleep departed from his eyes, and slumber from his eyelids."

A few weeks after, when Brown was on the river, they took in at Hannibal a drove of slaves bound for the New Orleans market, they numbered from fifty to sixty, consisting of men and women from eighteen to forty years of age. A drove of slaves on a southern steam-boat, bound for the sugar or cotton regions, is an occurrence so common, that no one, not even the passengers, appear to notice it, though the poor slaves clank their chains with every motion.

There was, however, one in this gang, that very much attracted the notice of the passengers and crew. If was a beautiful girl, apparently about twenty years of age, almost white, with straight hair and blue eyes. But it was not the whiteness of her skin that created such a sensation among those who gazed upon her. It was her dazzling, unparalleled beauty. The common topic of conversation was the beautiful slave girl. She was not like those by her side--in chains. The man who claimed this article of human merchandise was a Mr. Walker, a well-known slave-trader residing in St. Louis. There was a general anxiety among the passengers and crew, to learn the history of the girl, but her master kept close by her side, and would not permit any one to have any conversation with her. When they reached St. Louis, the slaves were removed to a boat bound for New Orleans, and the history of the beautiful slave girl remained a mystery. Who she was, or who was her father, perhaps she herself did not know. It might have been some rich slave-holder, who was obliged to sell her to propitiate the favor of his wife; or perhaps that beautiful girl was the daughter of the President, or of one who had been, or who would be, the President of the United States. But because she had a dash of African blood in her veins, inherited from her grandmother, she could not call him--father, or enjoy his paternal love. No! she was a slave, the property of another man; and, because she was beautiful, her person was highly prized in the slave market, and hence, she must go where she would be sold at a high price, not for the purpose of working in the field, bad as that might be, but to become the unwilling instrument of a master's base passion, which, to the sensitive woman's nature, is worse than death. But she was a slave, born to submit to a cruel destiny.

Towards the latter part of the summer, Captain Reynolds gave up the boat, and Brown was sent home to his master. He was then placed on the farm, under Mr. Haskill the overseer. Being unaccustomed to work in the open fields under a burning sun, he found it very hard, and did not savor the change, but it was useless to complain; for every complaint he received a stripe. He was compelled to keep up with the best of the hands; but he did not remain there long, as he was soon removed from the farm, and sent to the house to serve as waiter. Whilst he was away with Captain Reynolds, his master "got religion." New regulations were made on the plantation. One was, that of family worship at night and morning. At night-times the slaves were called in to attend, but in the mornings they had to be at their work whilst their master did the praying.

Brown's master and mistress were great lovers of mint julep, and every morning a pitcher full was made, of which they all partook. After drinking freely all round, they would have family worship and then breakfast. Brown loved julep as well as any of them, and not being able to have such a luxury openly, he saw no harm in taking a little on the sly. During prayer-time, he had "an eye to business." He always took good care to seat himself close to the table where the julep stood.

Whilst they were busy at their devotions, he being devotedly fond of the julep, helped himself. By the time prayer was over, he was about as happy as any of them.

One morning, whilst slyly partaking of the favorite liquid, and at the same time keeping an eye on his old mistress, he accidentally overturned the pitcher on the floor, breaking it into pieces, and spilling the contents. This sadly interrupted the family devotion. The old lady, instead of clenching the sonorous supplications of his master with a hearty "Amen," gave a hearty shriek and clenched poor Brown. It turned out to be a sorry affair for him, for as soon as prayer was over he was taken and severely whipped. So his carelessness got him the cowhide, and lost him the julep.

One of Brown's duties was to take care of the horses, and to drive the coach. It consequently fell to his lot to drive the family to church. But he did not very well like the approach of the Sabbath, for during service he was obliged to stand by the horses in the hot broiling sun, or in the rain; just as it happened. One Sabbath, as they were driving past the house of a Mr. Page, a person who owned a large baking establishment, Brown, who was sitting upon the box of the carriage, saw the master baker pursuing his slave around the yard with a long whip, cutting him at every jump. The man soon cut over the yard-wall and was followed by Mr. Page. They came running past the coach, and the slave, perceiving he would be overtaken, suddenly stopped, and Page tumbled over him, and falling on the stone pavement fractured one of his legs, which crippled him for life. This richly served him right. Page was a cruel master, as it was but a short time previous he had tied up a slave woman of his, by the name of Delphia, and so whipped her that her life was for some time despaired of.

Brown was afterwards hired by a Mr. Walker, a negro speculator. Walker knowing him to be a rather clever nigger put him to superintend a gang of negros who were to be sent to New Orleans. In a few days they were on their way thither, and Brown, knowing the duplicity of the white man, was afraid he was sold also, and his hopes of gaining his freedom began to decay in his breast, but he was agreeably disappointed. There was in the boat a large room on the lower deck in which the slaves were kept, men and women promiscuously, all chained two and two together, not even leaving the poor slaves the privilege of choosing their partners. A strict watch was kept over them, so that they had no chance of escape. Cases had occurred in which slaves had got off their chains and made their escape at the landing-places, while the boat stopped to take in wood. But with all their care they lost one woman who had been taken from her husband and children, and having no desire to live without them, in the agony of her soul jumped overboard and drowned herself. Her sorrows were greater than she could hear; slavery and its cruel inflictions had broken her heart. She, like Brown, sighed for freedom, but not the freedom which even British soil confers and inspires, but freedom from torturing pangs and overwhelming grief.*

> * Tom drew near, and tried to say something; but she only groaned. Honestly, and with tears running down his own cheeks, he spoke of a heart of love in the skies, of a pitying Jesus, and an eternal home; but the ear was deaf with anguish, and the palsied heart could not feel.
>
> Night came on--night, calm, unmoved, and glorious, shining down with her innumerable and solemn angel eyes, twinkling, beautiful, but silent. There was no speech nor language, no pitying voice or helping hand from that distant sky. One after another, the voices of business or pleasure died away; all on the boat were sleeping, and the ripples at the prow were plainly heard. Tom stretched himself out on a box, and there, as he lay, he heard, ever and anon, a smothered sob or cry from the prostrate creature--"Oh, what shall I do? O Lord! O good Lord, do help me!" and so, ever and anon, until the murmur died away in silence.
>
> At midnight Tom waked with a sudden start. Something black passed quickly by him to the side of the boat, and he heard a splash in the water. No one else saw or heard anything. He raised his head--the woman's place was vacant! He got up, and sought about him in vain. The poor bleeding heart was still at last, and the river rippled and dimpled just as brightly as if it had not closed above it.
>
> Patience! patience! ye whose hearts swell indignant at wrongs like these. Not one throb of anguish, not one tear of the oppressed, is forgotten by the Man of Sorrows, the Lord of Glory. In his patient, generous bosom he bears the anguish of a world. Bear thou, like him, in patience, and labor in love; for, sure as he is God, "the year of his redeemed shall come." Uncle Tom's Cabin

At the end of the week they arrived at New Orleans, the place of their destination. Here the slaves were placed in a negro pen, where those who wished to purchase could call and examine them. The negro pen is a small yard surrounded by buildings, from fifteen to twenty feet wide, with the exception of a large gate with iron bars. The slaves are kept in the buildings during the night, and turned into the pen during the day. After the best of the gang was sold off the balance was taken to the Exchange coffee-house auction rooms, and sold at public auction. After the sale of the last slave, Brown and Mr. Walker left New Orleans for St. Louis.

After they had been at St. Louis a few weeks another cargo of human flesh was made up. There was amongst the lot several old men and women, some of whom had grey locks. On their way down to New Orleans Brown had to prepare the old slaves for market. He was ordered to shave off the old man's whiskers, and to pluck out the grey hairs when they were not too numerous; when they were, he colored them with a preparation of blacking with a blacking brush. After having gone through the blacking process they looked ten or fifteen years younger. Brown, though not well skilled in the use of scissors and razor, performed the office of the barber tolerably.

When they had got to a place called Natchez, Brown saw a slave, whose name was Lewis, very cruelly whipped. Having to go on shore, and knowing that Lewis was there, he inquired for him of another slave. "They have got him," said the slave, "hanging between the heavens and the earth." Brown asked what that meant, and was told to go into the warehouse and see. He went and saw poor Lewis tied up to a beam with his toes just touching the floor, having been kept there a long time. Brown asked him the reason, and ascertained that Mr. Broadwell, the slave's master, had sold his wife to a planter six miles from the city, and that he had been to visit her; that he went in the night without his master's permission, expecting to return before daylight, but the patrol took him before he reached his wife. He was then put in gaol, and afterwards taken out and whipped.

Just as Lewis had finished his story, Mr. Broadwell came into the warehouse, and seeing Brown, inquired what he was doing there? He knew not what answer to make, and in a moment Broadwell hit him over the head with a cowhide, the end of which struck him over his right eye, leaving a scar, which he carries to this day. Just before Brown visited Lewis, the latter had received fifty lashes, and immediately on his leaving him, Broadwell gave him fifty more, as Lewis himself afterwards told Brown.

When they got to St. Louis, the slaves, as usual, were dressed and driven into the yard, and there exhibited for sale. Some were set to dancing, some to singing, some to jumping, and others to playing cards. This was done to show them off well, and make them appear cheerful and happy. Brown's business was to see that they were placed in those situations, before the arrival of the purchasers. He often set them to dancing, when their cheeks were wet with tears, and made them appear smiling, when only sighs were breaking from their hearts.

The next time they carried a cargo of human merchandise from St. Louis to New Orleans, a beautiful quadroon girl was among the number. She combined in her person all those attractions which make mulattos surpassingly lovely. She was a native of St. Louis, and the virtues of her soul were as beautiful as the graces of her body. She was bought for the New Orleans market; but before Mr. Walker sold her, he wished to subordinate her to his own guilty purposes. On the first night they were on board the steam-boat, Brown was directed to put her into a state-room Walker had provided for her, apart from the other slaves. He saw in a moment what this meant, and accordingly watched the designing man into the room, and listened to the conversation between him and the beautiful slave. He heard Walker make his base offers, and she indignantly reject them. Walker used all kinds of seductive flatteries, and told her that, if she would accept his proposals, he would take her back to St. Louis, and establish her as house-keeper on his farm, but if she persisted in rejecting them, he would sell her as a field-hand to the most cruel master, on the worst plantation on the river. Neither threats nor bribes prevailed, Cynthia maintained her integrity, and the iniquitous slave-dealer retired, disappointed of his prey.

The next morning poor Cynthia told Brown what had passed, and bewailed her sad fate with floods of tears. He endeavored to comfort her, but foresaw too well her doom. She was not, however, sold, but taken back, and established as the housekeeper at Walker's farm, and soon, alas! became involuntarily, no doubt, his mistress. Before Brown left St. Louis, she had two children. Would you not think, reader, that this man was inspired by love, and that he would forever affectionately cherish the beautiful Cynthia. Yes, you would think so, but slavery withers the purest affections of the human heart. Two years afterwards Walker married; but as a previous measure, sold the poor slave-girl into hopeless bondage. Lovely Cynthia, how similar is thy sad doom to that of the equally beautiful Cassy, as portrayed by Mrs. Stowe, in Uncle Tom's Cabin.*

* "You see me now," she said, speaking to Tom very rapidly, "see what I am! Well, I was brought up in luxury. The first I remember is playing about, when I was a child, in splendid parlors--when I was kept dressed up like a doll, and company and visitors used to praise me. There was a garden opening from the saloon windows; and there I used to play hide-and-go-seek, under the orange-trees, with my brothers and sisters. I went to a convent, and there I learned music, French, embroidery, and what not; and when I was fourteen I came out to my father's funeral. He died very suddenly, and when the property came to be settled, they found that there was scarcely enough to cover the debts; and when the creditors took an inventory of the property I was set down in it. My mother was a slave woman, and my father had always meant to set me free; but he had not done it, and so I was set down in the list. I'd always known who I was, but never thought much about it. Nobody ever expects that a strong healthy man is agoing to die. My father was a well man only four hours before he died--it was one of the first cholera cases in New Orleans. The day after the funeral my father's wife took her children, and went up to her father's plantation. I thought they treated me strangely, but didn't know. There was a young lawyer whom they left to settle the business; and he came every day, and was about the house, and spoke very politely to me. He brought with him one day a young man, whom I thought the handsomest I had ever seen. I shall never forget that evening; I walked with him in the garden. I was lonesome and full of sorrow, and he was so kind and gentle to me; and he told me that he had seen me before I went to the convent, and that he had loved me a great while, and that he would be my friend and protector. In short, though he didn't tell me, he had paid two thousand dollars for me, and I was his property. I became his willingly, for I loved him. Loved!" said the woman stopping, "Oh, how I did love that man! How I love him now, and always shall while I breathe! He was so beautiful, so high, so noble! He put me into a beautiful house, with servants, horses, and carriages, and furniture, and dresses. Everything that money could buy he gave me; but I didn't set any value on all that, I only cared for him. I loved him better than my God and my own soul; and, if I tried, I couldn't do any other way than he wanted me to.

"I wanted only one thing--I did want him to marry me. I thought if he loved me as he said he did, and if I was what he seemed to think I was, he would be willing to marry me and set me free. But he convinced me that it would be impossible; and he told me that if we were only faithful to each other, it was marriage before God. If that is true, wasn't I that man's wife? Wasn't I faithful? For seven years didn't I study every look and motion, and only live and breathe to please him. He had the yellow fever, and for twenty days and nights I watched with him--I alone; and gave him all his medicine, and did everything for him; and then he called me his good angel, and said I'd saved his life. We had two beautiful children. The first was a boy, and we called him Henry; he was the image of his father--he had such beautiful eyes, such a forehead, and his hair hung in curls around it--and he had all his father's spirit, and his talent too. Little Elise, he said, looked like me. He used to tell me I was the most beautiful woman in Louisiana, he was so proud of me and the children. He used to love to have me dress them up, and take them and me about in an open carriage, and hear the remarks that people would make on us; and he used to fill my ears constantly with the fine things that were said in praise of me and the children. Oh, those were happy days! I thought I was as happy as anyone could be; but then there came evil times. He had a cousin come to New Orleans who was his particular friend--he thought all the world of him; but, from the first time I saw him, I couldn't tell why, I dreaded him, for I felt sure he was going to bring misery on us. He got Henry to going out with him, and often he would not come home nights till two or three o'clock. I did not dare say a word, for Henry was so high-spirited, I was afraid to. He got him to the gaming-houses; and he was one of the sort that when he once got agoing there, there was no holding back. And then he introduced him to another lady, and I soon saw that his heart was gone from me. He never told me, but I saw it--I know it, day after day. I felt my heart breaking, but could not say a word. At this the wretch offered to buy me and the children of Henry, to clear off his gambling debts, which stood in the way of his marrying as he wished--and he sold us. He told me one day that he had business in the country, and should be gone two or three weeks. He spoke kinder than usual, and said he should come back; but it didn't deceive me, I knew that the time had come; I was just like one turned into stone; I couldn't speak nor shed a tear. He kissed me and kissed the children a good many times, and went out. I saw him get on his horse, and watched him till he was quite out of sight, and then I fell down and fainted.

"Then he came, the cursed wretch! he came to take possession. He told me he had bought me and my children, and showed me the papers. I cursed him before God, and told him I'd die sooner than live with him.

"'Just as you please,' said he; 'but if you don't behave reasonably I'll sell both the children, where you shall never see them again.' He told me that he always had meant to have me, from the first time he saw me; and that he had drawn Henry on, and got him in debt, on purpose to make him willing to sell me. That he got him in love with another woman; and that I might know, after all that, that he should not give up for a few airs and tears, and things of that sort."

Walker soon commenced purchasing, to make up another gang. On their way down he purchased additional numbers, and when they arrived at St. Charles, a village on the banks of the Missouri, a slave-woman, with a child in her arms appearing to be about four or five weeks old, was sold to him. They travelled by land for some days, and were in hopes, when they got to St. Charles, to get a boat from that place to St. Louis; they could not, and, consequently, were obliged to walk. The slaves were chained together. Walker taking the lead and Brown bringing up the rear, both of whom were on horses. On their way the young child grew very cross, and kept making a noise, during the greater part of the first day. Mr. Walker complained of its crying several times, and told the mother to "stop in noise, or he would." The woman tried to keep the child from crying, but could not.

The following morning, just as they were about to start, the child again commenced crying. Walker stepped up to her and told her to give the child to him.

The mother tremblingly obeyed. He took the child by one arm, as anyone would a cat by the leg, and walked into the horse where they had been staying, and said to the lady, "Madam, I will make you a present of this little nigger, it keeps making such a noise, that I can't bear it." "Thank you, sir," said the lady. The mother, as soon as she saw that her child was to be left, ran up to Mr. Walker, and falling on her knees, begged of him, in an agony of despair, to let her have her child. She clung round his legs so closely, that for some time he could not kick her off; and she cried, "O my child, my child. Master, do let me have my dear, dear child. Oh! do, do. I will stop its crying, and love you forever, if you will only let me have my child again." But her prayers were not heeded, they passed on, and the mother was separated from her child forever.

After, the woman's child had been given away, Mr. Walker rudely commanded her to retire into the ranks with the other slaves. Women who had children were not chained, but those who had none were. As soon as her child was taken she was chained to the gang.

All the slaves having been disposed of, they returned to St. Louis, got another gang, and proceeded as usual towards New Orleans. This time they stopped at Vicksburg about a week. One day while there, several gentlemen called to see Walker, for the purpose of purchasing some slaves, and as was the custom, wine was presented to them, and Brown acted as butler, but having accidentally filled some of the glasses too full, one of the gentlemen spilled the wine upon his clothes Mr. Walker apologized to him for his slave's carelessness and sent a knowing look at Brown, which seemed to say that he would hear from him again on that subject.

As soon as the gentlemen left the room, Brown was told that he would rue for his carelessness, and be taught better manners for the future. The next morning Walker gave him a note to the gaoler, and a dollar in money to give him. Brown suspecting that all was not right and seeing a sailor on his way, walked up to him, and asked if he would be so kind as to read the note. He read it over, and then looked on Brown. Brown asked him what the note contained, and the sailor said--

They are going to give you hell. This is a note to have you whipped, and says you have a dollar to pay for it."

Brown took the note and started off, not knowing exactly what to do, but was determined if he could help it, not to be whipped. While he was meditating, a colored man, about his own size, walked up, when the thought immediately struck him to send the man to the gaoler, instead of going himself. Brown ascertained from him that he was a freeman, and had been in the city but a short time, and wanted a job. Brown said he was very busy, and wanted to get a trunk from the gaol to carry to one of the steamboats, and asked the man if he would do it for him. The man having consented, Brown handed him the note and the dollar, and off he started for the gaol.

Brown rejoicing in the skillfulness of his maneuver, and congratulating his back on the whipping it had escaped, walked round the corner, and there took his station to see how his friend looked when he came out. He had been there only a short time when the young man made his appearance, looking woefully chop-fallen.

Brown came up to him and asked him where the trunk was, when the poor fellow complained bitterly that a trick had been played on him. He said, "They whipped me, and took my dollar, and gave me this note, and told me to give it to my master."

Brown offered him fifty cents for the note, that being all the money he had. The bargain was struck, and he took the note home to his master. Thus Brown exercised his wits and saved his back.

It is not difficult to imagine that one who would try to save his back, would ultimately try to save himself, and that he did so, the sequel will show.

A few days afterwards they reached New Orleans, and arriving there at night-time, they remained on board till morning. While there, Brown saw a slave murdered. The circumstances were as follows:--In the evening, between seven and eight o'clock, a slave came running down the levee, followed by several men and boys. The whites were crying out, "Stop that nigger! stop that nigger!" while the poor panting slave, in almost breathless accents was repeating, "I did not steal the meat--I did not steal the meat." The poor man at last took refuge in the river. The whites who were in pursuit of him, run on board of one of the boats to see if they could discover him. They finally espied him under the bow of the steamboat "Trenton." They got a pike-pole and tried to drive him from his hiding-place. When they would strike at him he would dive under the water. The water was so cold, that it soon became evident that he must come out or be drowned.

While they were trying to drive him from under the boat or drown him, he in broken and imploring accents said, "I did not steal the meat; I did not steal the meat. My master lives up the river. I want to see my master. I did not steal the meat. Do let me go home to master." After punching and striking him over the head for some time, he at last sunk in the water, to rise no more alive.

On the end of the pike-pole, with which they had been striking him was a hook, which caught in his clothing, and they hauled him up on the bow of the boat. Some said he was dead; others said he was "playing possum;" while others kicked him to make him get up; but it was of no use--he was dead.

As soon as they became, satisfied of this they commenced leaving one after another. One of the hands on the boat informed the captain that they had killed the man, and that the dead body was lying on the deck. The captain, whose name was Hart, came on deck, and said to those who were remaining, "You have killed this nigger; now take him off of my boat." The dead body was dragged on shore and left there. Brown went on board of the boat where the gang of slaves were, and during the whole night his mind was occupied with what he had seen. Early in the morning he went on shore to see if the dead body remained there. He found it in the same position that it was left the night before. He watched to see what they would do with it. It was left there until between eight and nine o'clock, when a cart, which took up the trash from the streets, came along, and the body was thrown in, and in a few minutes more was covered over with dirt, which they were removing from the streets. During the whole time Brown did not see more than six or seven persons round the corpse, who from their manner evidently regarded it as no uncommon occurrence.

After the expiration of the twelve months, Brown was sent home to Dr. Young, and glad enough he was to go, for he had seen too much of tearing the husband from the wife, the child from the mother, and the sister from the brother. But he was soon called on to see and feel more, for a most heart-rending trial awaited him. His dear sister had just been sold to a man who was going to Natchez, and was lying in gaol awaiting the hour of her departure. She had expressed her determination to die rather than she would go to the southern plantations, and she was put in goal to prevent her committing suicide. Brown immediately went to the goal, but the goaler not being there, he could not see her.

Crushed with grief, he went to his master, who spoke to him very politely. Brown knew from his kind demeanor that something was the matter. Dr. Young, after making several inquiries about his journeys to New Orleans, told Brown he was hard pressed for money, and as he had sold his mother and all her children to different masters, he thought it would be better to sell him also, as no doubt he would prefer a city to a country life. After a short pause, Brown said--

"Master, mother has often told me that you are a near relative of mine; in fact, that you are my father's brother and I have often heard you admit the fact; and after having hired me out, and receiving, as I once heard you say, nine hundred dollars for my services; after having received this large sum, will you sell me to be carried to New Orleans or some other place?"

"No," said he, "I do not intend to sell you to a negro trader. If I had wished to have done that, I might have sold you to Mr. Walker for a large sum, but I would not sell you to a negro trader. You may go to the city, and find yourself a good master."

"But," said I, "I cannot find a good master in the whole city of St. Louis."

"Why?" said he.

"Because there are no good masters in the state."

"Do you not call me a good master?"

"If you were, you would not sell me."

"Now I will give you one week to find a master, and surely you can do it in that time."

The price set by the Doctor on poor Brown, was the trifling sum of five hundred dollars, and although he endeavored to make some arrangement by which he might purchase his own freedom, his master would not agree to his proposals. He accordingly set out for the city in search of a new master. When he arrived there, he proceeded to the gaol with the hope of seeing his sister, but was again disappointed. On the following morning he made another attempt, and was allowed to see her once, for the last time. When he entered the room where she was seated in one corner, alone and disconsolate, there were four other women in the room, belonging to the same man, who were bought, the goaler said, for the master's own use.

Brown's sister was seated with her face towards the door when he entered, but her gaze was transfixed on nothingness, and she did not look up when he walked up to her; but as soon as she observed him she sprang up, threw her arms around his neck, leaned her head upon his breast, and without uttering a word, in silent, indescribable sorrow, burst into tears. She remained so for some minutes, but when she recovered herself sufficient to speak, she urged hint to take his mother immediately, and try to get to the land of freedom. She said there was no hope for herself, she must live and die a slave. After giving her some advice, and taking a ring from his finger, he bade her farewell forever. Reader, did ever a fair sister of thine go down to the grave prematurely, if so, perchance, thou hast drank deeply from the cup of sorrow? But how infinitely better is it, for a sister to "go into the silent land," with her honor untarnished, but with bright hopes, than for her to be sold to sensual slaveholders.

Brown had been in the city now two days, and as he was to be absent for only a week, it was well that he should make the best use of his time if he intended to escape. In conversing with his mother, he found her unwilling to make the attempt to reach the land of liberty, but she advised him by all means to get there himself if he possibly could. She said, as all her children were in slavery, she did not wish to leave them; but he loved his mother so intensely, that he could not think of leaving without her. He consequently used all his simple eloquence to induce her to fly with him, and at last he prevailed. They consequently fixed upon the next night as the time for their departure. The time at length arrived, and they left the city just as the clock struck nine. Having found a boat, they crossed the river in it. Whose boat it was he did not know, neither did he care; when it had served his purpose, he turned it adrift, and when he saw it last, it was going at a good speed down the river. After walking in the main road as fast as they could all night, when the morning came they made for the woods. They remained there during the day, but when night came again, they proceeded on their journey with nothing but the North Star to guide them, and the star of hope within to sustain them. They continued to travel by night, and to bury themselves in the silent solitudes of the woods by day. They did not walk during the day, for fear they should be seen; not that they feared the light, because their deeds were evil, but because they fled from those whose hearts were shrouded in moral darkness and spiritual death.

The North Star was the harbinger of mercy to the poor slave; for when flying from bondage immured in gloomy forests, it would be impossible for them to find their way without such a faithful guide. No doubt slaveholders would blot it from the geography of the heavens if they could, with just the same impunity as they annihilate the rights of man. But they cannot. That star will shine on, and beckon poor slaves to follow its cheerful light, and so sure as it was made to shine, and men, whether white or black, were made to be free, the time will come when slavery in America will be no more. Well might Pierpont, the American poet, say--

"Star of the North! while blazing day
Pours round me its full tide of light,
And hides thy pale but faithful ray,
I, too, lie hid, and long for night.
I or night--I dare not walk at noon:
Nor dare I trust the faithless moon,
Nor faithless man, whose burning just
For gold hath riveted my chain;
No other leader can I trust
But thee, of even the starry train;
For, all the host around thee burning,
Like faithless man, keep turning, turning.

"In the dark top of Southern pines
I nestled, when the driver's horn
Called to the field, in lengthening lines;
My fellows, at the break of morn.
And there I lay, till thy sweet face
Looked in upon my "hiding place.'
Star of the North!
Thy light, that no poor soul deceiveth,
Shall set me free."

As Brown and his mother proceeded on their way, joy bubbled up from the fountains of their being, at the thought of their approaching freedom. They walked until they were overwhelmed with fatigue.

When they thought they were leaving slavery with its democratic whips, its republican chains, and evangelical bloodhounds, and that the prospect of freedom was before them, they were re-inspired, and went on in spite of their weariness, Tired and hungry they had now been on their way ten days and ten nights. Sometimes they felt as if they must die, and nothing but the hope of realizing that priceless boon--freedom--could possibly have borne them up. Though then they were depressed; they were leaving behind them dear relatives in chains. Being now nearly two hundred miles from St. Louis, they summoned up courage to walk by day.

On one occasion Brown felt very cheerful, and did all he could to keep up the spirits of his poor mother. He was telling her that they would soon be free, and when they were he would work, and get a little farm, and sit down quietly in his free home, and then, after accumulating money, he would purchase his dear sister and brothers, and that they should once more all be happy together.

All at once he heard the click of a horse's hoof, and looking back saw three men on horseback galloping towards them. They soon came up, and demanded them to stop. The three men dismounted, arrested them on a warrant, and showed them a handbill offering two hundred dollars for their apprehension, and delivery of them to Dr. Young and Isaac Mansfield in St. Louis.

While they were reading the handbill, Brown's mother looked him in the face, and burst into tears. "A cold chill ran over me," says he, "and such a sensation I never experienced before, and I trust I never shall again." They took out a rope and tied him, and they were taken back to the house of the individual who appeared to be the leader. They then had something given them to eat, and were separated. Each of them was watched over by two men during the night. The religious characteristic of the American slaveholder soon manifested itself, as before the family retired to rest they were all called together to attend prayers; and the very man who, but a few hours before, had arrested poor panting, fugitive slaves, now read a chapter from the Bible and offered a prayer to God; as if that benignant and Omnipotent One consecrated the infernal act he had just committed.

The next morning they were chained and handcuffed, and carried back in a wagon to St. Louis. So all their bright hopes were at an end; and all their fervent yearnings for a life of independence were extinguished. Their chains were bound closer than ever, and the prospect of freedom darker than before they started.

When brought to St. Louis they were chained and lodged in gaol. Brown had only been in goal a short time when intelligence reached him that his master was sick. Heart-cheering intelligence this. Brown saw through the gloom a glimmer of hope, and he fell on his knees and prayed fervently for him--not for his recovery, but for his death.

After being in gaol about a week his master, who recovered, sent a man to take him out and, convey him home. He was taken into the room where his master was, who told him that if he had not made a promise not to sell him to a negro trader he would do so at once; and Brown was sent to the field--much to his disappointment and delight without a whipping.

He was afterwards sold to a Mr. Willie, a merchant tailor. Mr. Willie soon hired him out on board a steamboat, but he would not have gone if Dr. Young had told his new master he had run away. He had to wait a little while before the boat commenced sailing, and during the interval he had to undergo a trial for which he was completely unprepared. His mother, who had not been taken out of the gaol since her return, was now about to be carried to New Orleans, to die on a cotton, sugar, or rice plantation. This intelligence penetrated him with unutterable anguish. She who loved him so much, who so tenderly watched him while he was young, and in whose heart anticipations of freedom equal to his own were awoke, and who so very recently struggled so bravely to get beyond the reach of man-stealers, was about to be separated from him forever. He had not seen her since she had been thrown into prison, but had several times solicited entrance to the gaol but was not permitted.

At last the fatal day, when he was to see her for the last time, arrived, and about ten o'clock in the morning he went with an anxiously beating heart on board. He found her in company with fifty or sixty other slaves; she was chained to another woman. Here was a spectacle that might make devils laugh, and angels weep. An affectionate son, whose equally affectionate mother was about to be torn away from him, and carried helpless, hopeless, and friendless into slavery. Sad, humiliating spectacle! On seeing Brown she immediately dropped her head upon her heaving bosom. She moved not, neither did she weep; her emotions were too deep for tears. Brown approached her, threw his arms around her neck, kissed her, fell upon his knees begging her forgiveness, for he thought he was to blame for her sad condition, and if he had not persuaded her to accompany him she might not have been in chains then.

She remained for some time apparently unimpressionable, tearless, sighless, but in the innermost depths of her heart moved mighty passions. Brown says, "She finally raised her head, looked me in the face, and such a look none but an angel can give, and said, 'My dear son, you are not to blame for my being here. You have done nothing more nor less than your duty. Do not, I pray you, weep for me, I cannot last long upon a cotton plantation. I feel that my heavenly Master will soon call me home, and then I shall be out of the hands of the slaveholders.' I could hear no more--my heart struggled to free itself from the human form. In a moment she saw Mr. Mansfield, her master, coming toward that part of the boat, and she whispered in my ear, 'My child, we must soon part to meet no more on this side the grave. You have ever said that you would not die a slave; that you would be a freeman, Now try to get your liberty! You will soon have no one to look after but yourself!' and just as she whispered, the last sentence into my ear, Mansfield came up to me, and with an oath, said, 'Leave here this instant; you have been the means of my losing one hundred dollars to get this wench back'--at the same time kicking me with a heavy pair of boots. As I left her, she gave one shriek, saying, 'God be with you!' It was the last time that I saw her, and the last word I heard her utter.

"I walked on shore. The bell was tolling. The boat was about to start. I stood with a heavy heart, waiting to see her leave the wharf. As I thought of my mother, I could but feel that I had lost

> 'The glory of my life,
> My blossing and my pride!
> I half forgot the name of slave,
> When she was by my side.'

"The love of liberty that had been burning in my bosom had well-nigh gone out. I felt as though I was ready to die. The boat moved gently from the wharf, and while she glided down the river, I realized that my mother was indeed--

> Gone--gone--sold and gone,
> To the vice swamp, dark and lone!'

"After the boat was out of sight I returned home; but my thoughts were so absorbed in what I had witnessed, that I knew not what I was about half of the time. Night came, but it brought no sleep to my eyes."

Before the paroxysm of grief had subsided, Brown was called on board to commence his avocation. The boat carried down, whilst he remained on it, four or five gangs of slaves. After the performance of several voyages he returned to Mr. Willie's family, where he again began to lay plans for making his escape. When once the love of freedom is born in the slave's mind it always increases and brightens, and Brown having heard so much about Canada, where so many of his acquaintances had found a refuge, he heartily desired to join them. He would build castles in the air in the daytime, and when night came he would dream of Canada, of freedom, progress and glorified manhood, and on waking in the morning weep to find it was but a dream.

> "He would dream of Victoria's domain,
> And in a moment he seemed to be there;
> But the fear of being taken again,
> Soon hurried him back to despair."

Though Mr. Willie treated him much more kindly than Dr. Young, that did not, nor could not, reconcile him to his servile condition, for Brown, like Frederick Douglass, became more miserable when circumstances improved around him.

He was afterwards sold to a Captain Price at a very high price--for seven hundred dollars. He was wanted as a carriage driver, and Mrs. Price was very much pleased with the Captain's purchase. She was very proud of her servants, and always kept them well dressed, and Brown being a fine looking fellow was duly installed as the driver of the new carriage which Mrs. Price had just purchased.

Mrs. Price, like most of the fair sex, had an itch for match-making, and consequently soon determined on forming a union between Brown and one of her female servants: named Maria. She often talked to him on the necessity of his marrying, and said it would be so pleasant for him to choose a wife from the family, and one day she called Brown into her room to have a little quiet conversation with him, on the all-important subject of love, courtship, and marriage. This was an unusual thing for a master or mistress to so treat a slave. One would have thought that Mrs. Price, if she were not so intent on marrying Brown to another, wanted to love him herself. She, however, soon ascertained that though he was not insensible to the tender passion, he did not love Maria. If capable of loving, and not loving Maria, he no doubt loved someone else, and Mrs. Price was anxious to know who it was. This was pushing the inquiry rather too far, as Brown like other people, did not like to divulge his love secrets, and after blushing a while, he said, he was not in want of a wife. This did not satisfy his mistress. She said that if Brown loved Eliza, another slave, as she, the mistress, was apprehensive he did, why to make matters go smooth, she would buy Eliza.

It was true that Brown loved Eliza, but as he loved liberty better, he determined never to marry any one, until he obtained his freedom. But this he was compelled to keep a secret, and as he wanted to get the unbounded confidence of Mr. and Mrs. Price, he promised the latter he would marry Eliza. Both Eliza and Mrs. Price were much pleased at the decision he had come to.

Two or three months after Captain Price had purchased Brown the family made a voyage to New Orleans, and Brown accompanied them. After this they took a trip to Ohio. But much as Brown was liked, they were rather apprehensive that when he got to a free state he might like to be free himself. He was therefore questioned about it. He soon satisfied the Captain that he did not like the State at all, and also his wife, by promising her that when they returned from Ohio, he would marry Eliza. Brown all this time was meditating the best means of flight.

Soon after the boat left New Orleans, and proceeded up the river. Brown's trials of the past were soon lost in hopes for the future. The love of liberty, which had been burning in his bosom for years, and which at times had been well-nigh extinguished, was now resuscitated. Hopes nurtured in childhood and strengthened as manhood dawned, now spread their sails to the gales of his imagination.

At night, when all around was peaceful, and in the mystic presence of the everlasting star-light, he would walk the decks, meditating on his happy prospects, and summoning up gloomy reminiscences of the dear hearts he was leaving behind him. When not thinking of the future his mind would dwell on the past. The love of a dear mother, a dear sister, and three dear brothers yet living, caused him to shed many tears. If he could only be assured of their being dead he would have been comparatively happy, but he saw in imagination his dear mother in the cotton-field, followed by a monster task-master, and no one to speak a consoling word to her. He beheld his sister in the hands of the slave-driver, compelled to submit to his cruelty, or what was unutterably worse, his lust; but still he was far away from them, could not do anything for them if he remained in slavery, consequently he resolved, and consecrated the resolve with a prayer, that he would start on the first opportunity.

That opportunity soon presented itself. When the boat got to the wharf where it had to stay for some time, at the first convenient moment Brown made towards the woods, where he remained until night-time. He dared not walk during the day, even in the State of Ohio; he had seen so much of the perfidy of white men, and resolved, if possible, not to get into their hands. After darkness covered the world, he emerged from his hiding place--but he did not know east from west, or north from south; clouds hid the North Star from his view. In this desolate condition he remained for some hours, when the clouds-rolled away, and his friend, with its shining face--the North Star--welcomed his sight. True as the needle to the pole he obeyed its attractive beauty, and walked on till daylight dawned.

It was winter-time--the day on which he started was the 1st of January, and as it might be expected, it was intensely cold; he had no overcoat, no food, no friend--save the North Star, and the God which made it. How ardently must the love of freedom burn in the poor slave's bosom, when he will pass through so many difficulties, and even look death in the face, in winning his birth-right, freedom. But what crushed the poor slave's heart in his flight most, was not the want of food or clothing, but the thought that every white man was his deadly enemy. Even in free states the prejudice against color is so strong, that there appears to exist a deadly antagonism between the white and colored races.

Brown, in his flight, carried a tinder-box with him, and when he got very cold, he would gather together dry leaves and stubble and make a fire, or certainly he would have perished. He was determined to enter into no house, fearing that he might meet a betrayer.

It must have been a picture which would have inspired an artist, to see the fugitive roasting the ears of corn that he found or took from barns during the night, at solitary fires in the deep solitudes of woods.

When Brown was young, he was called William. Though Dr. Young, his former master, had no children of his own, he had living with him a nephew called William Young. When he came to reside with the doctor, Brown's mother was told to change her boy's name, which she did. Brown, though young at the time, thought this a very cruel act. He could not see the right or the use of altering his name because another boy was called William. After the orders were given, his mother called him "Sandford," and this name he was known by, but he never liked it.

As Brown pursued his journey alone, the question of what he should be called when he got free, was, the name by which he should be known. He detested the idea of being called by the name of either of his masters, and as for his father, he would rather have adopted the name of "Friday," and been known as the companion of some Robinson Crusoe, than to have taken his name.

So, while he was hunting for his liberty, he was also hunting for a name, and as he travelled, on, he would repeat a variety of names to himself, to hear how they would sound, and by way of getting used to it before he got among civilized beings. He could not choose one to his satisfaction, but he determined to stick to William come what might, and leave it to the chapter of accidents whatever might be added to it.

On the sixth day it rained very fast, and froze almost as fast as it fell, so that his clothes became one glaze of ice, but he travelled on chilled and benumbed until he could go no farther. He accordingly took shelter in a barn, but was afraid to lie down, or he might sleep the sleep of death. He walked about to keep his blood from freezing. The thought of death presented nothing frightful to him compared with being caught and sent back into slavery Nothing but the fire of hope burning within his breast, could have sustained him under such overwhelming trials.

> Behind he left the whip and chains,
> Before him were sweet freedom's plains."

He resolved, when day came, to seek the protection of someone in whom he thought he might place confidence. He thought he might see some colored person, or one who was not a slaveholder, who might render him some assistance. He had an idea he should know a slaveholder as far as he could see him. Accordingly, he perched himself behind some logs and brushwood, intending to wait until someone should pass.

The first person who passed looked too genteel to be addressed. The second, Brown attempted to speak to, but fear deprived him of his voice. A third soon made his appearance. He wore a broad-brimmed hat and a long coat, and was evidently walking only for exercise. Brown scanned him well, and though not much skilled in physiognomy, he concluded he was the man. Brown approached him, and asked him if he knew anyone who would help him, as he was sick? The gentleman asked whether he was not a slave? Brown hesitated; but, on being told that he had nothing to fear, he answered, "yes," The gentleman told him he was in a pro-slaving neighborhood, but, if he would wait a little, he would go and get a covered wagon, and convey him to his house. After he had gone, Brown meditated whether he should stay or not, being apprehensive that the broad-brimmed gentleman had gone for someone to assist him; he however concluded to remain.

After waiting about an hour--an hour big with fate to him--he saw the covered wagon making its appearance, and no one on it but the person he before accosted. Trembling with hope and fear, he entered the wagon, and was carried to the person's house. When he got there, he still halted between two opinions, whether he should enter or take to his heels; but he soon decided after seeing the glowing face of the wife. He saw something in her that bid him welcome, something that told him he would not be betrayed.

He soon found that he was under the shed of a Quaker, and a Quaker of the George Fox stamp. He had heard of Quakers and their kindness; but was not prepared to meet with such hospitality as now greeted him. He saw nothing but kind looks, and heard nothing but tender words. He began to feel the pulsations of a new existence. White men always scorned him, but now a white benevolent woman felt glad to wait on him; it was a revolution in his experience. The table was loaded with good things, but he could not eat. If he were allowed the privilege of sitting in the kitchen, he thought he could do justice to the viands. The surprise being over his appetite soon returned.

"I have frequently been asked," says Brown, "how I felt upon finding myself regarded as a man, by a white family; especially just having run away from one. I cannot say that I have ever answered the question yet. The fact that I was, in all probability, a freeman, sounded in my ears like a charm. I am satisfied that none but a slave could place such an appreciation upon liberty as I did at that time. I wanted to see mother and sister, that I might tell them that "I was free!" I wanted to see my fellow-slaves in St. Louis, and let them know that the chains were no longer upon my limbs. I wanted to see Captain Price, and let him learn from my own lips that I was no more a chattel, but a MAN. I was anxious, too, thus to inform Mrs. Price that she must get another coachman, and I wanted to see Eliza more than I did Mr. Price or Mrs. Price. The fact that I was a freeman--could walk, talk, eat, and sleep as a man, and no one to stand over me with the blood-clotted cow-hide--all this made me feel that I was not myself."

The kind Quaker, who so hospitably entertained Brown, was called Wells Brown. He remained with him about a fortnight, during which time he was well fed and clothed. Before leaving, the Quaker asked Brown what was his name besides William? Brown told him he had no other. "Well," said he, "thee must have another name. Since thee has got out of slavery, thee has become a man, and men always have two names."

Brown told him that as he was the first man to extend the hand of friendship to him, he would give him the privilege of naming him.

"If I name thee," said he, "I shall call thee Wells Brown, like myself."

"But," said Brown, "I am not willing to lose my name of William. It was taken from me once against my will, and I am not willing to part with it on any terms."

"Then," said the benevolent man, "I will call thee William Wells Brown."

"So be it," said William Wells Brown, and he has been known by this name ever since.

After giving the newly-christened freeman "a name," the Quaker gave him something to aid him to get "a local habitation." So, after giving him some money, Brown again started for Canada. In four days he reached a public-house, and went in to warm himself. He soon found that he was not out of the reach of his enemies. While warming himself, he heard some men in an adjoining bar-room talking about some runaway slaves. He thought it was time to be off, and, suiting the action to the thought, he was soon in the woods out of sight. When night came, he returned to the road and walked on; and so, for two days and two nights, till he was faint and ready to perish of hunger. He, consequently, concluded to go to a farm house, and asked for something to eat. A man soon presented himself. Brown cold him what he wanted; the man hesitated, and said that if he would work he would give him something to eat for it. Brown was not in a condition to work first and eat afterwards; but just as he was leaving the door, with a light stomach, but a heavy heart, a woman, who proved to be the man's wife, presented herself and asked what the black man wanted. Brown said, he wanted something to eat. She told him to come in, and she would give him something. The husband still stood in the doorway, as if unwilling to let Brown pass. The wife asked him two or three times to move; but not being inclined to obey her commands, he stood still. She then gave him a push so as to make room for Brown to pass. Ever since that act, Brown says he has been in favor of woman's rights, for the good lady not only satisfied his appetite, but gave him ten cents, all the money she had.

Thanking this angel of mercy, with a satisfied appetite and an overflowing heart, the fugitive, in three days, arrived at Cleveland, Ohio; when, believing himself to be out of danger, he secured an engagement at the Mansion House, as a table-waiter, in payment for his board. The proprietor afterwards hired him for twelve dollars a month. He remained there till Spring.

Here he purchased some books, and during his leisure moments perused them with considerable advantage to himself. While at Cleveland, he saw for the first time an Anti-Slavery paper--"The Genius of Universal Emancipation"--to which he became a subscriber, and read with great avidity. Being out of slavery himself, he felt a desire to do what he could for the emancipation of his brethren; and while on Lake Erie, he found many opportunities of helping many of them. It is well known that a great number of fugitives make their escape to Canada by way of Cleveland. And while on the lakes, Brown made arrangements to carry them as they came there, on a boat, to Buffalo, and thus assist to effect their escape to "the promised land." The friends of the slave knowing that he would take them without charge, brought him into requisition frequently. He sometimes carried four or five at a time. In the year 1842, he conveyed from the first of May to the first of December, sixty-nine fugitives over Lake Erie to Canada. In 1843, he visited Malden, in Upper Canada, and counted seventeen in that village, whom he had assisted to gain their freedom.

Very soon after his escape, Brown became a subscriber to the "Liberator." This paper he also read with heart-stirring delight. He heard nothing of the anti-slavery movement while in slavery; and when he found that there were friends of the slave who were laboring for their emancipation in the North, he joined them with heart and soul. Having tasted the glory of freedom himself, his great desire was to extend the blessing to his race. Consequently, in the autumn of 1843, he commenced lecturing as an agent of the Western New York Anti-slavery Society, and has ever since devoted his time and talent to the cause of his enslaved countrymen.

In 1849 he left America for England, when W. Lloyd Garrison said, in a letter to him, on the 18th of July--"Today you leave the land of your nativity--in which you have been reared and treated as a slave, a chattel personal, a marketable commodity; though it claims to be a Republican and Christian land, the freest of the free, the most pious of the pious--for the shores of Europe, on touching which your shackles will immediately fall your limbs expand, your spirit exult in absolute freedom, as a man, and nothing less than a man. . . . . You have secured the respect, the confidence, and esteem of thousands of the best portion of the American people; and may you continue faithful to the end, neither corrupted by praise nor cast down by opposition, nor intimidated by any earthly power." These are just the words we should imagine the heroic, but much calumniated, Lloyd Garrison to write.

In 1849, Mr. Brown attended as a delegate the Paris Peace Congress, at which he spoke with much effect. Since coming to this country he has delivered four hundred and twenty lectures on Slavery, twenty-three on Temperance, and has addressed eighty-eight public meetings. He has travelled about ten thousand miles through Great Britain. He intended returning to America last year, but the passage of the infamous Fugitive Slave Law prevented it.

He is an eloquent and impressive speaker. He mingles with great facility rich humor with startling facts, and so wins the attention of his audience. He is a contributor to Frederick Douglass' North Star, and to Lloyd Garrison's Liberator.

In a recent number of the North Star, Frederick Douglass says--"We have the pleasure to lay before our readers another interesting letter from W. Wells Brown. We rejoice to find our friend still persevering in the pursuit of knowledge, and still more do we rejoice to find such marked evidence of his rapid progress as his several letters afford. But a few years ago, he was a despised, degraded, whip-scarred slave, knowing nothing of letters; and now we find him writing accounts of his travels in a distant land, of which a man reared under the most favorable educational advantages might be proud. Would to God that the noble example of William Wells Brown were more widely copied among those who escape from slavery! His noble aim, his untiring industry, his unquenchable zeal, and his manly fortitude under afflicting trials, are worthy of all imitation. We have many private assurances from England of the value of Mr. Brown's labors in the cause of freedom and humanity, and are most happy to find that the weapons which have been used here for his destruction have not prevailed there.'

CHAPTER V.
HENRY BIBB.

HENRY BIBB was born in the month of May, 1815, in Shelby County, Kentucky. His mother was a slave, the property of David White, Esq., who reckoned the infant as he would a sheep added to his flock, or an acre to his farm. He "flogged him up," and with the earliest taste of life, this son of the bondwoman, the eldest of seven brothers, felt that gall which breeds bitterness in the heart of a whole race against the teachers of Christianity. Who his father was, he knows not, for the ties of life are not binding to the slave; and if he had known, there would have been no better lot for him. Even from the one parent he knew he was, as a young child, dragged away to labor; and for eight or ten years the wages of his drudgery, first under one master, then under another, went to pay for the education of his owner's daughter! She, in the polished society of the Southern States, sang, no doubt, and tinkled a guitar, and breathed out beautiful sentiments and utterances of affection; not a shade the less charmingly because every note was learned. every grace acquired, from the gains of a wretched boy, toiling under the lash: for, the experience of misery began with him early. Barely allowed a rag of clothes, he worked all day hungry and tearful, lying down at night on a floor of hard earth, or a bench, sometimes treading with bare feet the frozen ground in December, and staining it with footprints of blood.

Aspirations he had indeed to burst these sordid chains, but the vault of Chillon was not more dark than the world in which this fettered child was compelled to move. Reading and writing were forbidden to the slave, and all that was left to his mind, was liberty to plot in secret, an escape, as Henry did, though with many their very souls corroded in the absence of all hope. But he soon began to meditate flight. At ten years of age he was living with a Mr. Vines, in Newcastle town, and the wife of this man was an example of the corrupting influence of the slave system upon human nature. The little boy whom an English woman would rather have fondled in her bosom, was to her, a victim whose miseries might absorb some of her savage feelings. She struck him, flogged him, reproached him for every act, and when he ran away, lacerated his flesh with a cruelty almost more than human. Several times was this repeated, until in despair of taming this negro child's spirit, his master sent him back to Mr. White, whose property he was. That person had married a second wife, and this new tyranny was worse than the former. Half the time that Henry Bibb lived here, he was away in the woods seeking to escape that blood-dripping thong which surely awaited him on his return. His mistress was not only a task-master, but a torturer by predilection. She forced him all day to rub the furniture, to wash clothes, to scrub the floor, rock her chair, tickle her feet, and scratch or comb her hair, and then to reward him, scourged his limbs till they quivered under her hands. Several times he tried to escape, and once or twice by taking a bridle with him, and pretending he was on the look-out for a runaway horse, strangers suffered him to pass, but in the end he was always captured, and condemned to a whipping.

From that time burned in his heart an unquenchable longing--and more than a longing, an unchangeable resolve--to be free. When he was eighteen years old, the twilight of religion dawned over his mind, for in spite of every hostile law, knowledge sometimes came, like manna in the desert, to the slave. A young white girl tried to set up a school for teaching the negros, but police were sent to break up its second meeting, and the attempt was declared an incendiary crime. Far pleasanter was it to the proprietors to see their bond-people degraded by debauch, and sinking into an oblivious apathy, which threatened no revolt against a despotism the most monstrous ever conceived by human nature. In consequence of this, every Sunday was an occasion of riot, fighting, gambling, and profanity, encouraged by the masters, and thus the black population was scientifically debased, in order that every human thought might be deadened, and every yearning for liberty buried in obscenity and vice. The slaves with whom Henry Bibb associated, were like the savages of their original country--superstitious to the last degree, and he himself relates how several times he went to quacks for amulets and charms, in whose efficacy he was taught to believe, in order to save himself from hard work and flogging.

Still there was a star above these clouds. Liberty was more than a name to him; it had penetrated to his heart. He heard that Canada lay somewhere in the north--a country of freedom, whither the slave might fly. Beyond Egypt there was even for him a promised land, but the hosts of Pharaoh were less inevitable than hunters of men, who invariably seized him before he could cross the broad bright Ohio. Often, from the cliff-like banks of that noble river, he stood alone, looking, he tells us, at the blue northern sky, thinking of the happy people there, asking his hope when he might be among them, and wistfully gazing on the thousand splendid steamboats, arriving and departing with men and women, and children, who, made like him, feeling as he did, born in the same nature, and nurtured in the same desires, yet belonged, it seemed, to another creation, for they were all free, and he was a miserable slave. There were birds flying over those waves, that perpetually ran by to the ocean, but they and the brutes enjoyed what he was robbed of by those of his own kind, in a State proclaiming itself the moral glory of the world.

From these reflections he was for some time divested by the society of many young women, in associating with whom he found no little delight. He relates some curious incidents to illustrate the sordid ignorance and superstition in which the negros are bred. Desiring to secure the affections of one, he asked some quack conjuror for a charm. The fellow told him to get the bone of a bull-frog, and if he could rasp with it the naked skin of the girl he liked, she would reciprocate his affection. He selected one whom he knew to be already as affianced as slaves are ever allowed to be, and as he humorously relates--"I happened to meet her in the company of her lover one Sunday evening, walking about; so when I got a chance, I fetched her a tremendous rasp across her neck with this bone, which made her jump. But in place of making her love me, it only made her angry with me." The poor fellow did not then know that he himself possessed the mightiest amulet with which man can subdue women to his heart--a faithful and loving disposition, that could express itself in the genuine language, that needs no interpretation. He soon afterwards met a mulatto slave-girl, named Malinda, who lived in Oldham county, Kentucky, about four miles from the residence of his owner. She possessed a beautiful form; her skin was soft and smooth; her cheeks had a dark bloom upon them, and her eyes were as bright as those of the New Orleans quadroon. She associated with slaves of the first rank, for there are castes and grades even among these wretched people, and for the sweetness of her voice, was admired by many of the free population.

Henry Bibb visited Malinda two or three times, without thinking of more than an acquaintance. But even the code of those Southern States cannot change the nature of man. There was soon an union of feeling between them; every visit deepened the impression, and it was speedily apparent that the girl loved him too-- for her eyes sparkled when he came, her hand lingered in his, and she asked him to come, when her mother wished he would stay away. She allowed him to pass through every phase and sentiment, until he became attached to her by all that can bind the heart. Solemnly, however, does he declare that had he then fully known to what miseries and humiliations the child of the slave is born, he would not have taken a wife, and propagated inheritors to such a curse. One Saturday evening, however, which he remembers to have been lit by a bright moon, he met Malinda at her mother's door. As he approached, she flew to him, and took his hand; he told her then what was the chief emotion of his mind; that he desired her as his wife, and would forever love her as such, but only on certain conditions would ask her to make the pledge. He was religious, he said, and she also yearned through an untaught faith to heaven. He was determined to be free, and if she would consent to be his partner in the troubles and dangers he saw in view, then the nuptials of their hearts were complete. She required a week to choose her decision, and when he met her again, it was agreed, that if they still remembered this promise at the end of a year, they should be married, that they should lead a pious life, and never forget that the promised land they desired was beyond the Niagara Falls, under the sacred flag of England. Legal wedlock they could not enter into. What is immorality to the white, is forced upon the American slave. They are forbidden to seal their union before the altar, and they may be torn asunder whenever their remorseless owners may require. But there was not for these, less faith in the mutual pledge, now sworn between these young lovers. They clasped each other by the hand; they pledged their sacred honor they would be true; they called on heaven to witness and bless these night-nuptials, and in this manner they stood bound by the only ties by which they could ratify their promises of love.

Many difficulties arose in the way of this marriage. Henry's mother opposed it, because she thought he was too young; Malinda's mother because she desired to match her daughter to the favorite slave of a wealthy man. His own master objected, because he thought he would steal for his wife's sake, but her's consented willingly, and at last a festival took place to celebrate the occasion.

For some time Henry could only visit his wife on Saturday night, returning punctually to his master's estate on Monday, under pain of a flogging. The oppression he suffered was so great, that his owner feared his running away, and sold him to William Gatewood, the proprietor of his wife. Then the unmitigated bitterness of slavery plunged the iron deeper into his heart. He was forced to stand by while Malinda was tortured, insulted, and abused; to see her staggering at her toil, to see her stripped naked, and whipped by coarse and cruel men, whom he, without power to interpose, saw handling her with licentious brutality, and then giving her over to him, humiliated, bleeding, and blushing with unutterable shame.

A few months after this, a daughter was born to these affectionate but unhappy slaves. Scarcely had she grown to be able to walk, when her mother saw her the victim of the same inhumanity that was practiced on herself. She saw Miss Gatewood whipping her, bruising her face with her heavy hand, and reiterating her savage blows at every heavy sob extorted by pain from the feeble creature. She was named Frances, and was a quiet, playful, vivacious and interesting little girl, with a keen black eye, and in her face a reflection of her mother's beauty. But with such a wife, and such a child to love, Henry Bibb was wretched, for separation stripping, tying up, flogging, insults, hard tasks, and a denial of every soothing influence of life, rankled every day more deeply in his soul.

In the fall of the winter of 1837, the climax of this, tyranny had come. There was, perhaps, little worse to endure, but there was more already than the most abject could bear. Henry Bibb resolved to attempt to escape. It was a perilous trial. Two dollars and fifty cents, with a suit of clothes he had never worn before, were all he possessed. Had he told his wife this intention, it is improbable that he could have succeeded; but he desired work, not liberty, for her as well as for himself. Gaining permission from his master to work for himself on Christmas, he went on the 25th of December, down to the Ohio, pretending to seek for employment. Instead of this, however, he managed to cross in a ferry-boat, and found himself in a free State, though not in one whither he could not be pursued. Steam-boats were landing passengers here every night, so Henry concealed himself until the sound of one coming up the stream came like the welcome of freedom to his ears. In a few moments he was on her deck, bound for Cincinnati, but bewildered by fear and excitement, for he was liable at any moment to be seized, fettered hand and foot, and sent back to his master. The advantage he had--in his complexion, which was not black, but somewhat fair, since there was some slave-holding blood in his veins. Every time, nevertheless, that the mate came with a lantern to the steamer, he trembled in anticipation of a discovery, but contrived at last to hire a hammock, in which he lay, muffling the clothes about his face till morning. No questions were asked, and about nine o'clock next day, the vessel moored off the quay of Cincinnati. The fugitive stepped on shore, walked as calmly and gracefully as he could, up the main street, and escaped observation. But Canada was his destination. how should he find the way? An inquiry might cause suspicion. In this exigency he had faith in the honesty of his race. He would ask someone kindred to him by blood, and sure he was that none of that color would betray him. Nor was he disappointed. A poor wood-chopper gave him directions, told him of the Abolitionists, feasted him hospitably, and gave him God's speed on his way. Then striking-out at the high road, the escaped slave walked rapidly along, and as the night approached his eyes sought in the depths of heaven for that North Star, which hung like a lamp of hope over the unreached haven of his desire. For forty-eight hours he struggled on without food or rest, and then, half frozen with cold, barefooted and hungry, he knocked at a door, and asked leave to warm himself at the fire. They were latter-day Christians indeed, who were within, for they refused him this little dole of charity, and at the next house the same inhospitable answer met him. In the morning, however, he saw a low-roofed cottage, and through a window the breakfast-table spread with all its bounties. A woman sat near it, and stepping up to her with his hat off, Henry asked for sixpence worth of bread and meat. She gave it, and when he offered payment, burst into tears, bade him take it as a gift, and go in peace on his journey. Mungo Park fed with milk under a tree, by the poor African woman, was not more gladdened by her cheer, than the fugitive who now, it might be said, was receiving similar kindness at the hands of one of that traveller's race. In this way Henry Bibb got through the State of Ohio, faring at public-houses on the road, and at length earning a meal by assisting the cook at an hotel. She wanted to hire him for the winter; but he went in fear of being pursued, though at Perrysburg he was persuaded to remain, gaining a livelihood as a wood-chopper, until the next Spring.

On the first of May 1838, he hasted on his return to Kentucky, though a dangerous expedition. He could not live without his wife, and having saved fifteen dollars, resisted the advice of his friends, and determined to risk the perils of the enterprise. He laid out his cash in pedlar's ware, bought a pair of false whiskers for disguise, and set off in search of his little family. The journey was comparatively easy. When he reached Cincinnati, he had sold all his goods at a profit; he then took passage in a steamer, and in due time landed about six miles from Bedford where his mother resided, near the estate of his former master. It was glowing moonlight, and he walked rapidly through the plantation until he reached her house. He knew she slept in the kitchen, and that her bed lay near the window. He tapped on the glass. A woman put her head out, and inquired who was there. With his false whiskers she did not know even her son; but when he took off this disguise, and claimed her as his mother, her affection recognized its own at once, and she bounded out through the door to embrace him. Happily Malinda and little Francis happened to be staying a night with her, so that the meetings all took place at once. There was weeping and laughing for joy, delight and fear, hope flickering through the gloom of doubt and dread, so fearful, that they were only not despair. Henry Bibb, however, was not easily depressed. He gave his wife money to pay her passage to Cincinnati, and arranged to meet her there on the next Sunday. He would not long remain in the neighborhood. On the Wednesday following, therefore, he once more said farewell, promising himself however that this was only a prelude to her welcome in the sweet land of liberty. Ferrying himself across the Ohio, he again made his way to Cincinnati; but there all his resources were exhausted, and some friends were obliged to subscribe for his support. Among others two white men knew his secret, and each gave him fifty cents. They wormed the story from him, cajoled him into telling his master's name, and left the room bidding him a treacherous God speed. These sneaking spies, who in public would probably act if they could as the General Monks of America, took passage on board the steam boat down the river, found the owners of Henry Bibb, got a promise of three hundred dollars for betraying him, and returning to Cincinnati engaged a pack of ruffians to aid them in capturing the poor slave, who had committed the crime of breaking from unnatural chains.

Henry Bibb had engaged to excavate a cellar for the good woman with whom he was stopping. While he was digging under the house, he heard a man enter above; another came to the door; he attempted to pass out, but this fellow drew a pistol, and declared he would shoot him if he moved. Then all the hopes he had cherished melted like serial delusions before his eyes; his dear wife's coming would be to a desolate place; his child's escape would be into a land where no father awaited her, and he whose wife and whose child were looked for there, was going back in fetters to the toil of a galley-slave.

He was dragged to a "justice. office," claimed by Mr. Gatewood, delivered over to him, and locked up in a gaol. The gaoler's wife with another woman pointed out a way of escape, but for their sake he would not attempt it; and waited until all was ready for his embarkation a third time on the rolling Ohio. On his way, an offer was made to him by some professional slave-catchers, that if he would enter into their employment they would set him free, and soon pay him money enough to purchase his wife and child out of their bonds. But with manly indignation he refused these wages of a bloodhound, and they immediately took him to Louisville, where he was offered for sale. Three of them remained in his room all night to prevent the possibility of escape, and next morning one stayed with bowie-knife and pistols to guard him, while the others went in search of a purchaser.

The man that remained was Dan Lane--a Jonathan Wild of America--a sort of human mastiff hired to rob a slave mother of her children, to kidnap the young girl by her parent's side, to drag the wife from her husband--to do all the vilest and basest work of the vilest and basest trade. Drunkard, gambler, scoundrel, as he was, no fitter agent could be found for the nefarious slave system of America. Dan, while the others were away, was compelled to go to the stables, situated in one of the most public streets in Louisbergh. Henry Bibb of course accompanied him, marshaled by the arm. When arrived, he was ordered to stand by until his guardian was ready to come out, but the door was open; a glimpse of liberty beckoned him away; he made two or three cautious steps in that direction, and then with a sudden impulse of courage rushed through and shot like an arrow along the street. Dan was not ready to follow. He was only half dressed, and a moment or two must elapse before he could come out of the stall. With this advantage therefore, Bibb turned a corner before he was perceived, and by doubling at every point, jumping a number of fences, and diving through archways, succeeded in deluding his pursuer. At last he sprang over a high wooden paling and came down on a hencoop, with such a clatter of dogs barking about him, that he almost gave himself up for lost. There was, however, close by, a huge pile of boards and scantling, where he found a hiding-place, and remained ten or twelve hours enduring the worst agonies of fear.

There was a workshop on either side, and men were at work within eight or ten feet of him. Night came on however without his being discovered, and about nine o'clock, groping about, he found his way through a low brick tunnel out into the street. There, as once before, he trusted his secret to a man of his own race's color and was not betrayed. It was an old man who gave him something to eat, and told him that he was about forty miles from the residence of William Gatewood, where his wife, whom he still hoped to rescue, was living. There was a good road, but he preferred making his way over the rocky hills, woods, and plantations, back to Bedford. So he started off, cheered that night by the stars, and in the morning by the larks that sang merrily in the fields all around him. A slave, working in a meadow, gave him a piece of bread, in return for which Bibb taught him the idea of escape, which he pledged himself to do within six months from that day. Soon after, he met an old friend, who managed to procure him an interview with Malinda. They met with tears, and despondent looks, for the avenues of hope seemed closing, and life was passing away, while Canada was yet a vision of the soul, a laud half fable, too happy for the slave. The fugitive remained several days in concealment, attended by his wife who brought or sent him food; but not daring to move, for Dan Lane actually went to the house in which he was hidden--near enough to have been reached by his hands, and he heard that there was a large reward offered for his capture.

Evidently no safety was there. He must once again go his way alone, and in the middle of the night he bade a sorrowful adieu to Malinda and his child, and started off in the darkness. "O," he says, "that was almost like tearing the limbs off my body." Should he ever see them again? It was not sure. They both cried bitterly at parting; and might they not have been forgiven if a silent curse went out from their hearts upon those sordid tyrants, who thus made the life which Heaven had given them for happiness, a life of affliction and despair. Henry Bibb then left, and through his knowledge of the way succeeded early in reaching Perrysburgh in Ohio. There he waited eight or nine months without hearing of his family. It was clear that Malinda could not escape. Of what use therefore was liberty to him? He could make a new effort for her rescue, and if need be, he would sacrifice himself in the attempt, for this unhappy toil-worn man had not forgotten the sweet hours of his youth when he pledged himself to that young girl by moonlight, near her mother's door.

Again was Henry Bibb on the scene of his early life's suffering--the place where he had been tortured while a child by stripes, when a man by the humiliation of his wife, and where ever since his fancy had been with those who were dear to it, and who now seemed drifting into oblivion. As one risen from the dead he appeared before his mother. No one was in her room when he entered, except a little female slave, fast asleep. The woman shrieked with joy at beholding her son, and that cry of rapture woke the slumbering girl. This creature, nurtured in chains had been abased by them, for the teachings of servitude had rotted her heart, and corrupted it with the darkest vices of human nature. She kept perfectly still, she gave no sign of being awake, she plotted--the pigmy spy--to overhear all and report it to her mistress. She continued skulking with closed lids while the fugitive spoke of his wife, of his child, of his plans, of all he hoped and desired to do. He then went away, promising to come back next night about seven o'clock. At that hour he was punctually approaching the house when he was alarmed by seeing several men, with dogs, moving to and fro. He hid among the bushes until midnight was past, and then tapping at his mother's window, heard from her that the little girl had betrayed him, though she said, if he kept quiet for a few days, people would believe that the young informer had lied.

Bibb accordingly went to a friendly slave who concealed him, and generously located him. Happy we are to say, that that man is now enjoying the liberty he helped to secure for another. He carried messages between the husband and wife, and confiding in him alone Henry might have succeeded, but he trusted his secret to another professed friend, who betrayed him for twenty shillings. All was arranged for the start to Canada. It was to take place on the next Saturday night. The heroic adventurer lay waiting the hour under a heap of flax in a barn. Suddenly a tumult awoke him. Loud and savage but familiar voices grated like curses on his ear. "Shoot him down! Shoot him down!" "If he offers to run or resist, kill him!" Such were the greetings of the dawn to him, and a mob of slave-holders, their faces glaring with diabolical self-gratulation, stood around him, brandishing cutlasses and guns, and threatening death upon the slightest attempt at flight. Farewell then to the long-cherished hope of liberty for Malinda and her child; farewell to his own free breathing of the air of heaven; all his labor was in vain. He once more found himself bound with a cord, robbed of his watch and money, with other things which he prized far more, and led away a helpless and all but hopeless slave. To a Blacksmith's shop they go, that he may be heavily manacled with fetters, that the ox never wears, and then to a moist cold dungeon in Bedford gaol. There he was visited by numerous "gentlemen" of the neighboring plantations, who came to taunt him, to tell him he ought to be hung, and to chill in his mind a lingering hope of some future success. They brought Malinda too, and made her look at her husband from without the door; and as he sat there, his bosom swelling for an embrace, he could only see her weep, and hear her broken sobs, for they would not allow her to approach.

In the dead of the next night, when he was alone, two of his fellow-slaves came to the grating, and asked him to tell them about Canada. He gave them directions, and afterwards learned that within a week they were on the road, and successfully reached that country. For himself, however, there was a longer tribulation to come. On the third day he was brought out of prison heavily ironed, fastened with cords on a horse's back, and guarded by two armed men to be marched to Louisville for sale. Following him, and bound on a nag, was his wife and child. Many who had known them, shed tears as they went away; but the mother most bitterly wept--for she was now growing old, and her own and her adopted daughter were going from her forever. In a miserable posture, and subject to the jeers of every wretch who passed in possession of liberty, these captives entered Louisville, and were carried to the common jail. There Henry Bibb was visited by a physician who prescribed for him; not for his own sake, but to increase his value in the market. Nevertheless the den he was confined in, stunk and swarmed with vermin. Thrice he was transferred to the workhouse, where a ponderous log-chain was riveted about his leg, and he was set to labor at sawing stone. The fare of this hell on earth was coarse corn bread, beef full of worms, and nauseous pot liquor; and even of this a very scanty allowance. At night the prisoners were confined; two together, in a damp stone cell, with scarcely a rag of bedding, and bugs and mosquitos infesting every corner.

Murderers and swindlers were here placed on a level with this man, whose crime was claiming liberty, while Malinda was thrust amid crowds of female pickpockets, forgers, and the most shameless and abandoned of her sex. Yet, though their ribaldry and ferocity were shocking, they sympathized with the recaptured slave, and endeavored to aid him in escape; but the plan failed, and despair began to blacken over his mind, when one morning the door of his cell opened, and Garrison, the slave-dealer, with brutal oaths and abuse, thrust in Malinda. She fell upon her husband's neck, moaning and sobbing, and bursting forth into a piteous wail, "Oh, my child, my child; my child is gone. What shall I do? my child is gone." He could not then learn how, but that evening she told him the story. Garrison had taken her to an infamous house, inhabited by female slaves. He had, with loathsome obscenity, told her she was there for the vile purposes of vice. He had, like a miscreant, assailed her modesty, and when she repelled him, flogged her naked body till it bled under the lash. Her clothes were blotted with deep red stains that showed how the scourge had cut into her flesh. Then he attempted, through her motherly love, to betray her virtue, and declared if she did not submit he would sell the child. The child had disappeared, and now she was allowed only two days of companionship with him who was her only friend in that place of desolation.

Little Frances, however, had not been sold. At the expiration of three months, the slaves, handcuffed, and guarded by a savage dog, were marched to a boat at the Ohio, and floated down to New Orleans. The horrors of the voyage were like those of the middle passage--chains, crowding, cramping, and scarcely any air to breathe. At Vicksburg they were examined by a city officer, to ascertain their bodily and mental capacities, and at New Orleans were taken at once to a trader's yard prison, at the corner of St. Joseph Street. There, men and women, young and old, were exposed, trimly combed and washed, for sale. They were compelled to stand in rows, to be questioned by the spectators; and if they failed to answer promptly, suffered the indecent punishment by the paddle.

The paddle, says Henry Bibb, is made of a piece of hickory timber, about an inch thick, three in width, and eighteen in length. The part which is applied to the flesh is full of holes, through which the blood gushes at every blow. The persons who are thus flogged are always stripped naked; and one of the bitterest aggravations of this abject people's lot is, that men are compelled to see their wives, their unwedded brides, their sisters, or their daughters, unclothed, and quivering under the hands of some low, moneyed roué, delighting in the inhuman occupation. At length Henry Bibb was relieved from the Orleans' prison. He was purchased with his Malinda and her child, by Deacon Whitfield, of the Baptist Church, who lived on his plantation, at Clartom, almost fifty miles up the Red River. With a saintly tone of voice, an affectation of humanity, and professions of kindly feeling, he was among the most cruel of a cruel race--the slave-holders of America. His negros were a dull, feeble, half-starved, and overlabored herd. The first impressions that Bibb received, were by no means encouraging. First, he saw a man compelled to strip his own wife and flog her; then he saw the Deacon give a young girl two hundred stripes on her bare flesh, and was himself compelled to wash her back with strong brine, under which the tears fell like burning drops from her eyes. Appointed to the office of overseer, he was forced daily to witness and participate in horrors which few hearts can conceive, or the pen of man describe. Every morning, long before sunrise, each slave was ordered to light a pine-torch, and go into the fields,--so that a number of brilliant stars seemed to be glimmering, low down among the cotton trees. But at the same time, the pitiable overworked poor wretches, under the lash, converted that which might have seemed a paradise, with all its flowers, into the semblance of a hell. Labor, the most tedious, was apportioned among the females as well as males;

cotton planting and picking, grinding corn, and tillage. If a slave was sick, the Deacon, a Christian minister, swore it was hypocrisy, and dosed him with a powerful and dangerous medicine. There was no care for the ailing. Malinda was afflicted, and she might have perished, for all that her mistress would have done to aid her; her second child did die, and the father was compelled to bury it, coffinless, in a hole.

Shortly after, for attending a prayer-meeting, Henry Bibb was condemned to five hundred lashes, on his naked back. Under fear of this, he attempted to escape, with his wife and remaining child. They took their way through the green wilderness on the borders of the Red River, wandering for eight or ten days, and eating parched corn, grapes, and wild fruits, that hung bountifully on the wild trees. By means of a crooked tree they crossed the stream, and entered on the swamps of Louisiana, where snakes, and alligators abounded and where bloodhounds would probably be employed to hunt them down. Still, all this was preferred to the Deacon's chains. They were attacked by a troop of wolves, though by yelling and striking at them with a bowie-knife, Henry contrived to keep them at bay. Wolves, however, were not so ferocious as men: for escaping them, these fugitives saw themselves pursued one day, by horsemen and dogs, so that again bound with cords, cursed and maltreated, Bibb, with Malinda and little Frances, were taken back to their melancholy bondage.

His clothing was stripped off; he was compelled to lie with his face on the ground; his hands and feet were tied to stakes, and he was scored from head to foot with the whip. When the regular number had been given, the Deacon took the bloody thong into his own hands, and saying there was a spot left where the flesh was not ripped open, laid on a few heavier strokes than any. Eight or ten blows with the paddle were next applied, and after this, salt water was poured into the wounds. A weighty iron collar was riveted round his neck, with prongs reaching above the head, to which a small bell was attached, which he could not reach with his hand. But by the man determined not to be a slave, the bonds of slavery may be broken. Henry Bibb had been captured and tortured, but his soul was not subdued, and he was once more in the woods with an old negro named Jack, who consented to be the companion of his flight. They started for the city of Little Rock, in Arkansas, travelling only by night, under the guidance of the North Star, and concealed themselves all day. At length their provisions were exhausted, and coming in sight of a large plantation, where people of color were at work, Jack said, that after dark he would ask them for some food. They both hid until sunset, but when a female cook was asked, for charity's sake, to give bread to the poor wayfarers she, to curry favor with her master gave the alarm, and they had to fly for life. Nevertheless, they managed to get some little sucking pigs, and a turkey, which when in the depth of a forest, they cooked, and satisfied their hunger. That night, however, about ten o'clock, when emerging through the skirts of the woody country, five men sprang upon them with fire-arms, threatening them with instant death, if they stirred. There had been a reward offered of fifty dollars for Henry Bibb, whether dead or alive. We, therefore, for a third time, find him on the Deacon's farm, manacled, flogged, tortured with unendurable toil, and offered for sale to any slave-owner who would buy him.

In December 1840, he was sold to a party of sportsmen, who treated him with humanity, and from sympathy with his misfortunes, endeavored to buy his wife and child; but the Deacon would not consent, and swore he would punish her if she attempted to cling to her husband. She did cling to him, and the scoundrel, with a brutality that made even slave-dealers, who were standing by, cry, "Shame!" laid on the bloody lash, to her back, and answered every appeal for mercy, by an oath and a blow. Henry, consequently, was parted from Malinda, but the humane men, with whom he was now in company, promised to sell him to some person travelling, and give him a part of the money, to aid him in escaping to Canada. They advised him to feign stupidity, but to be alert on every opportunity, and they employed him to drive their wagon, black their boots, and curry their horses. They passed from State to State, giving him more indulgence than ever he had enjoyed as a servitor before, and led a curious life, racing and gambling at every populous place they reached. At last they entered the territory of the Cherokees, where a wealthy half Indian saw Bibb, and took a fancy to him, as a sort of body servant, for his personal attendance. He offered nine hundred dollars to the sporting dealers, and they struck a bargain; but they gave Henry full directions as to the Canadian route, by which he determined to profit on the first occasion. His new master, however, prevented him, not by cruelty, but by confidence, for he allowed him to ride a beautiful horse, and to carry a large money-bag, full of gold and silver. The temptation was strong, and the opportunity good, but there was a feeling of honor to check such a desire, and Henry settled for a while on his master's plantation.

The Indian was a humane and reasonable man, employing many negros in cultivating grain on a considerable plantation. He gave them good food to eat, and decent clothes to wear, employed no overseers to flog them, and only occasionally chastised them himself, which is generally done by all Indian masters. They sometimes make a rule never to scourge their negros, but only attack them, when they are free to defend themselves, and occasionally put the aggressor to flight! With these people the slave led a comparatively happy life mingling in their dances and festivals; but this did not last long, the old chief was in a declining state, and shortly died, tended with every care, by the man whom he had won by kindness. Henry Bibb watched over him night and day, until the last breath exhaled his soul into eternity, and even prepared his body for the tomb; though then, still longing to reach Canada that Eden of hope--he plunged into the woods, and commenced anew the adventures of a fugitive. Wet weary, hungry, he trod on his way, never daring to enter the Indian huts, for a long while, when, desperate with want, he feigned drunkenness, and staggered to a cottage door. The inmates gave him a blanket, and fed him, refusing the payment he offered; for, among those half-savage natives of that continent, where slavery brands the beautiful face of liberty with a deforming scar,--among those heathen dwellers in the forest, with their tomahawks, their bows, and arrows, and guns, and hunting knives; with their faces painted red, and grotesque ornaments, disfiguring the natural dignity of their faces, Henry Bibb, the outcast slave, wandering and persecuted, was more safe from treachery and wrong, than among the polished and peaceful citizens, who crowded the churches, and prayed to the God of all Christians in the stateliest cities of the land.

He felt this; he felt his danger multiplied a hundred fold when he left the Indian country, and struck out on a prairie, where men of the imperial white race might be seen again, but finding a number of horses running loose in a plantation, he manufactured a bridle from a pliant grape wine, mounted one of them, fled like Mazeppa over the Tartar plains, and found himself, next morning, far away, and out of reach of that community. Then he let the animal go, and blessing it for the service it had rendered him, wished it a safe journey back. For himself, he never paused until he crossed the frontiers of Ohio, and entered that State. There he put up at the best hotels, talked of buying land and stock, passed as an admiring traveller, and made a pleasant companion on the road, who lent him a spare horse. Thus, as in a kind of solitary triumph. he rode on, borne up by the exulting joy of his heart, until he reached Jefferson city. There he heard that a steamboat was that day expected down the river, for St. Louis. He knew that the captain would not take a colored person on board, without ascertaining that he was legally free; but he adopted an ingenious stratagem to overcome, this obstacle. He bought a large trunk, placed it on his shoulders, as though it were full packed, and followed a party of white people, as though he had been their slave. Thus he got safely between decks. There he met a number of Irish persons, whom he treated to whiskey, and when deep in their good graces, asked one of them to get his ticket for him. In this way escaping observation, he came to Portsmouth, on the Ohio. His money was now exhausted; he had to hire himself to an hotel-keeper, for twelve dollars a month, and this, with the little gratuities he received, enabled him to save. Here he encountered one of the sportsmen who had formerly sold him, but no discovery took place.

Indeed, the end of his wanderings had come. In Detroit he went to school, and learned the rudiments of reading and writing--one of the first available exercises of which, was the perusal of a letter from his old master William Gatewood. There was no chance now of recovering him, so that individual thought proper to be polite. The emancipated slave condescended to reply to his former master; he told him that should he ever travel that way, "I will use you better than you did me, while I was your slave." He forgave him, he said; he begged to be lovingly remembered to his mother, and he advised him, in future, to treat his negros more humanely. For, he added, many a fugitive slave would never have thought of escaping from a kind master; but to see his wife stripped and scourged, and his child bruised, until its skin was purple, was more than even the most abject of humanity could suffer.

From that day, Henry Bibb devoted himself to the cause of the slave. He travelled from State to State, manumitted by law, and preached against the iniquities of that traffic, abhorred by the nature of man. Sometimes he was still insulted by the white-skinned puppies, on board a steamboat, or at an hotel; but the gall of slavery was gone, he was free, and but one wish remained unfulfilled.

That wish was the recovery of his wife--the restoration of his child. In 1845 he went to his native county,--at some peril to himself, and inquired for Malinda. Then he tasted the last bitter ingredients of the curse of slavery. Malinda was not with Deacon Whitfield. With her child she was living on another estate--a life of shame,--a life of hopeless infamy, with her master. For a time he could not believe this miserable truth,--but a truth it was, and henceforward, dead to him Malinda remained, a victim to that nefarious system, which, in the Southern states of America, has ruptured every holy and sacred relation, between man and man. We will not record a curse against that woman. Her husband, indeed, bitterly spurns the thought that she could be faithful to him, and yet yield to another; but he may think of her kindly, when the memory returns to him that she suffered the deepest humiliation, which a woman could endure; that she mingled her tears with her blood, for the sake of his love; that she writhed in long agony under the dripping lash, because she would not wrong his honor by sacrificing her own, and who can tell what agony--worse than the rack, worse than the stake, worse than crucifixion,--the torturing of her child, perhaps, or even its threatened murder, extorted from her, what was wrong from her own bleeding flesh, and cheeks blushing with indignant shame.

However this may be, Henry Bibb cast her image out from his heart, and married another wife at Boston, in June 1848. She was a kind, good person, full of affection for him, and of enthusiasm for his cause. May he long enjoy his remnant of happiness, and see some fruits of his pious labors in behalf of the poor slave population of America.

And what is the knowledge gained from this narrative, incontestably true, of slave life in the United States? It is that the deepest colored pictures that imagination can employ, the warmest tints of fiction, the amplification of the most fertile and rhetorical pen, cannot exaggerate the infamy and cruelty of the slave system there. We may decry the agitators of liberty, as the fanners of a dangerous flame; we may reject the delineations of romance, and the declamation of earnest oratory; but the story of Henry Bibb, the authenticated history of his sufferings, and the damning evidence he has given against the oppressors of his race, place beyond contradiction the facts now circulating through the world. If there be in the heart of universal humanity, that conscience which knows good from evil; if there be in our common nature that warmth and charity, elevating while they soften; if our hearts are not dead to the eloquent appeal of the wronged--the basely and bitterly wronged negros of America,--then all the service our pity and sympathy can bestow, will be given to them; our voice will be raised for their deliverance from chains, which we could not, would not wear an hour, and if the echo of that voice does not come back to us over the Atlantic in blessing for the bestow, sure we may be that in the deep and silent joy, that will beat in the pulse of those dusky millions, will be found a grateful all the prayers that liberty can raise for their the happiest country of the world.

HENRY HYLAND GARNET.

ANOTHER noble specimen of the negro race now in this country, who dares not return to the United States for fear of the passers of the Fugitive Slave Law. No doubt, most of our readers have seen and heard him, as, since he has been in this country, he has addressed a great number of public meetings.

He was born in Maryland, in 1815. His great-grandfather was the son of an African chief, stolen from his native country in his youth, and sold into slavery on the shores of Maryland. The branch of his family thus transplanted into America were all held in slavery till 1822, when they escaped to the non-slaving states. Henry, the subject of this notice, was then about eight years of age, and with his father, mother, and sister, and eight fugitive slaves, found an asylum in New York. They were the property of Colonel Spinar, on whose death they passed into the hands of his nephew, who was the very personification of tyranny. His mother, who was a woman of great energy of character, seeing what sort of life they might expect from the hands of such a wretch, resolved to make her escape. Having on one occasion obtained permission to be absent two days, to attend the funeral of a relative, ten miles off, they started at sunset, travelling all night towards the land of freedom, hiding themselves in the wood by day, till they found themselves safe in New Hague, a village in Pennsylvania. At last they reached New York city, where they remained about seven years, when it was their misfortune to be again hunted by man-stealers, who came upon them at their residence. The father and mother escaped as by a miracle, the former by leaping from the top of the house into a yard, and the latter by hiding herself till the hunters were gone. The day following the daughter was seized and thrown into prison to await her trial. The best legal assistance was obtained by the friends of the girl, and, by great exertions, they obtained her discharge from custody, and she was borne out of court in the arms of her friends.

While those things were transpiring, Henry was at Washington, in the capacity of cabin-boy, on board a schooner. After completing the voyage, he returned to New York, and received the terrible intelligence concerning the persecution of his family. He at first intended to revenge himself by some desperate acts, but the prudence of his friends prevailed on him to return to New York, when he entered the African free school, and soon reached the highest class. In 1833 he was admitted into the Canal-street Collegiate School, with several other colored youths, and commenced the study of the Latin language. But little time or pains were bestowed on his instruction, as the colored boys were not permitted to mingle with the white boys; and, consequently, to him the opportunities which the school afforded were limited.

In 1835 he travelled to New Hampshire, a distance of five hundred miles, and became a member of Canaan Academy. He had not been there but three months when the inhabitants assembled, and, with a mob, removed and burned the house. They next attacked the house in which the colored pupils boarded, but were met with stern resistance, and driven back. The day on which the academy was destroyed, a young and lovely colored girl, called Julia Williams, entered the village, hoping to drink from the same fountain of learning. She had been a member of Miss Crandall's school, at Canterbury, until that noble lady was imprisoned in a dungeon, for the crime of instructing colored females in learning and religion. When Mr. Garnet beheld her, he admired her modest and gentle demeanor, as well as her heroic spirit, and formed an ardent attachment for her, which was reciprocated, and resulted in their marriage in 1841.

In 1835, he experienced a religious change of mind, and turned his attention to the Gospel ministry, and repaired to the Oneida Institute in 1836, where he was received with great kindness by the president, and was treated with equality by the professors and his fellow students. There he gained the reputation of a courteous and accomplished man, an able and eloquent debater, and a good writer. He graduated at the school at Whilestoun in 1840, and received his diploma. He then repaired to the city of Troy, State of New York, where he was ordained a minister of the Presbyterian Church in 1833. He is a very acceptable preacher, his discourses being both evangelical and poetical. Having complete command of his voice, he uses it with skill, never failing to fill the largest houses with perfect case. He is a most strenuous advocate of freedom, temperance, and education. He had a hearing in relation to the restoration of the elective franchise to his oppressed brethren, before the legislatures of New York and Connecticut. One of his most remarkable speeches was an address to the negros at a National Convention at Buffalo, in 1843, when, for two hours, the mighty assembly was swayed as he pleased. Sometimes they wept, and at other times they cried for revenge, and frequently they shouted aloud for joy or for sorrow. He made another remarkable speech at Boston; and has also published a discourse on the past and present condition and destiny of the colored race. He was for some time connected with the National Watchman.

In 1847 he retired from the Presbyterian Church in consequence of its connection with slavery, and left Troy and repaired to Geneva, and became the pastor of an Independent orthodox congregation, which relation he now holds. Last year he came to this country by invitation of the friends of the Free Labor Movement; and also attended the Peace Congress at Frankfort, as a Delegate from his own country. He has been laboring during ten months successfully in the Anti-slavery cause, especially in the North of England and in Ireland. He has been received with great kindness by Christians and philanthropists in this country. He is soon to be joined by his wife and children, intending to remain here until he has finished his Anti-slavery mission, and then proposes to go to the island of Jamaica as a missionary, as it would not be safe for him to return to Republican America while the Fugitive Slave Law is in existence.

Mr. Garnet is a tall, fine-looking black man, about thirty-five years of age. He is very gentlemanly in his manner, and a most decidedly agreeable companion. A vein of quaint humor runs through his conversation. He is very well informed on the great leading movements of the age; and though he is stern and unbending when a principle is involved, he is more moderate in his language towards those who disagree with him, and is disposed to use less harsh means in altering their opinions than many who are similarly situated to himself.

MOSES ROPER.

THE subject of this sketch, whose vicissitudes and sufferings, like those already given, have been published to the world by himself, was a native of North Carolina, in Caswell County, but, as in almost all other cases, the time of his birth is unknown. His father was a slaveholder and his mother a slave. For the particulars of his infancy, we are indebted, through himself, to the narrations of his mother, which show that almost as soon as he came into the world, the miseries of slavery began to crowd upon him, while his mother's sufferings were such that one cannot mention them without blushing for that corrupted humanity by which they were inflicted.

A few months before Roper was born, his father married his mother's young mistress. As soon as she heard of his birth, she sent one of his mother's sisters to see whether he was black or white. On returning, she told her mistress that the child was white, and that he was the image of Mr. Roper, her husband. No sooner had she received this intelligence, than the savage propensities of her nature were aroused. She procured a large club stick and knife, and hastened to the place in which the mother was confined, with the full determination to do Herod's bidding, and murder the young child. But, just as she raised the knife to do the bloody deed, his grandmother entered the cabin, caught hold of the murderer's arm, and saved the child's life. But the murder being prevented, something else must be done to appease the wrath of the green-eyed monster--jealousy. Both the mother and child were, therefore, sold or sent to some slave master soon after the confinement.

Till young Roper was about seven years of age, we have no further knowledge of his condition, but, at that period, his mother's old master, who was his father's wife's father, died; and, in conformity with a slavery usage, all the slaves were divided among the children. That every-day horror of slavery now befell him; his mother, whom he tenderly loved, was drawn with the other slaves, and was sent he knew not whither. In consequence of being so very white,--for he was the child of a white father, and a half-white mother--he was sold to a "negro trader" who took him to the Southern States. This trader in men and women, after travelling several hundred miles, and selling a good portion of his livestock, found that young Roper was not at all a marketable article; his skin was too white and called up too many unpleasant reminiscences in the minds of the slave mongers. He, therefore, left him with a Mr. Sneed who kept a large boarding-house, and who was commissioned to do two things--learn him to wait table, and sell him--if he could. Mr. Sneed used a year's-worth of energy in trying to sell young Roper, but without success; no one would give his gold for a nigger with so white a skin. He was therefore removed by his son-in-law to meet Mr. Mitchell, at Lancaster, who was then on his way from the north to the south with another drove of slaves. In this town he was sold to a Doctor Jones, who, in addition to his profession as a son of Æsculapius, was also a cotton planter. Here Roper, for a brief season, had a nice easy time of it; his employment being to beat up and mix medicines, but even the mystery-man didn't like his white skin, so he sent him to the plantation to have it burnt darker by the sun. Poor Roper's white skin was a sad drawback to him. From the plantation he was removed to a tailor, but, even among the knights of the thimble, his skin was the sore place in his character. Either the journeymen objected, or he was wanted for domestic purposes, for, during the whole time he was in the employment of Mr. Bryant, the tailor, he was only once in the workshop, and then only for two or three hours. Whatever, were the reasons, as a juvenile tailor he made no progress, so his owner re-called him home--no, not to home, slaves have no home--and he was sent along with a load of cotton to be sold with it; and was sold to a Mr. Allen, who soon, to suit the caprice of his wife, exchanged him for a female slave. Messrs. Cooper and Lindsey, however, the 'respectable' traders who bought him, had the mortification to find that they also had got a bad bargain in the whiteness of his skin, and so they made the best of it by changing him to a Mr. Smith of Fazettnill, North Carolina, for a nigger of more sable complexion. With this gentleman he remained about a year, when he was again sold to a Mr. Hodge, a negro trader, from contact with whom the beginning of more severe hardships dated.

Few slaves have had a more checkered history than Moses Roper. We have seen already how frequently he changed masters. After having been sold to Mr. Hodge, and travelling several hundred miles, he was again sold to a Mr. Gooch, a cotton planter of South Carolina; and this anti-liberty transaction took place at a town called Liberty Hill. As soon as he got to the plantation--we will not call it home--he was put under the surveillance of overseers, and subjected to every other indignity which slaves usually suffer. Here he had plenty of stripes, labor, and grief, with just enough of food to keep him in remembrance of the delights of hunger. But changes were still in store for him. Mr. Gooch had bought him, not for himself, but for his son-in-law, Mr. Hanmans, to whose tender mercies in due time he was consigned. This son-in-law had only two other slaves. For a time he was treated with tolerable kindness, but his new master's severity seemed to have a kind of affinity with the growth of cotton, for when it was ready to hoe, he gave him task-work which, failing to do, a plentiful application of the lash was superadded. So plentiful, indeed, was the punishment, and so limited the pleasure--there was so much of shade and so little of sunshine, that Roper, for the first time in his life, resolved to be a hero--to do an act of nobility by running away. This feat he at once performed, escaping into the woods half naked, but was soon caught by a slaveholder, who put him into Lancaster gaol. In almost every part of England when an animal strays, it is secured and put into what is called the "pinfold," and, if not claimed within a certain time, after a process of advertising, it is sold to pay fold dues. A similar custom exists in America with reference to slaves; the only difference being that the gaol is the slaves pinfold. Moreover, when a slave runs away, the owner always adopts a more rigorous system of punishment, and Master Roper had the benefit of this wholesome regulation. He made several attempts to gain his freedom, but either he went about his object clumsily, or the circumstances were unfavorable to his making a clean job of it, for in every attempt he failed. In one thing he was successful; he secured one hundred lashes, heartily applied, for each attempt to escape. His present owner had quite a relish for the lash; he used it often and with peculiar facility, and even Mrs. Hanmans, his mistress, was also accomplished in the same department. She, however, didn't like the extra trouble of making him smart through his clothes, and therefore did her part of the bloody business when he was naked.

Roper made so many attempts to run away, that Mr. Hanmans resolved to part with him. He wanted a slave who had no aspirations for freedom, who was content with his condition, and less anxious to hide in the woods. So he handed him back again to Mr. Gooch for an equivalent in land. Roper was averse to returning, and Gooch knew it, so, to secure him, he was chained by the neck to his chaise, and in this dignified manner taken to Mac Daniel's Ferry, in the county of Chester, a distance of fifteen miles. He was now sixteen years of age and but a small boy, but his lack of muscular development and manly strength went for nothing in the estimation of Mr. Gooch. Though a boy only he must do a man's work. He had, as on another occasion already mentioned, a very short allowance of food, which, of course, was a rather equivocal kind of advantage to a youth who had to do the labors of a full grown man. Even if he had been physically qualified to perform the task which was set him, starvation was not very likely to stimulate him to exertion: but because he did not do that which was impossible, he was severely flogged and put into irons. He was, however, soon delivered from this kind of bondage. Mr. Gooch took his irons off, "in the full anticipation," says Roper, "that I could never get across the Catarba River even when at liberty. On this I procured a small Indian canoe which was tied to a tree, and ultimately got across the river in it. I then wandered through the wilderness for several days without any food, and but a drop of water to allay my thirst, till I became so starved, that I was obliged to go to a house to beg for something to eat, when I was captured and again imprisoned. Mr. Gooch having heard of me through an advertisement sent his son after me, who tied me up and took me back to his father. He then obtained the assistance of another slaveholder, and tied me up in his blacksmith's shop, and gave me fifty with a cowhide. He then put a log chain, weighing twenty-five pounds, round my neck, and sent me into a field into which he followed me with the cowhide, intending to set his slaves to flog me again. Knowing this, and dreading to suffer in this way, I gave him the slip and got out of his sight . . . I got to a canal on the Catarba River, on the banks of which I forced the ring of my chain and got it off, and then crossed the river."

Roper was now again on the high-road of an attempt to free himself from the bondage and cruelty of slavery, and might perhaps this time have been successful had he not met with a Mr. Ballad, a slaveholder, who knew him. He also knew the slaveholder to have the reputation of being one of the best planters in the neighborhood, and he therefore begged that he would buy him. Mr. Ballad, however, had neither the means nor the inclination, but with the fear of the law before him,--for heavy fines attach to all who harbor runaway slaves,--secured Roper, and immediately proceeded to take him back to his owner. At this Roper's soul sunk within him. He says--"As we came in sight of Mr. Gooch's, all the treatment I had met with there, came forcibly upon my mind, the powerful influence of which is beyond description. On my knees, with tears in my eyes, with terror in my countenance, and fervency in all my features, I implored Mr. Ballad to buy me, but he again refused, and I was taken back to my dreaded cruel master. Having reached Mr. Gooch's, at the hands of this man monster, Roper received a severe lashing. "This he did by first tying my wrists together and placing them over the knee, he then put a stick through, under my knees and over my arms, and having thus secured my arms, he proceeded to flog me, and gave me five hundred lashes on my bare back. This may appear incredible, but the marks which they left, at present remain on my body a standing testimony to the truth of this statement of his severity. He then chained me down in a log-pen with a forty pound chain, and made me lie on the damp earth all night. In the morning after his breakfast he came to me, and without giving me any thing to eat or drink, tied me to a large heavy harrow, which is usually drawn by a horse, and made me drag it to the cotton-field for the horse to use in the field. . . . . He then flogged me again, and set me to work in the corn-field the whole of that day, and, at night, chained me down to the log-pen as before. The next morning he set me to work in the cotton-field, and gave me a third flogging. At this time I was dreadfully sore and weak with the repeated floggings and harsh treatment I had endured. He put me under a black man, with orders that if I did not keep up my row in hoeing with this man, he was to flog me."

This is the kind of treatment to which Roper was now exposed, and for which there was no redress. Flogging and otherwise punishing slaves seems to have been a kind of amusement to Mr. Gooch. Roper was not the only subject upon whom he wreaked his hellish rage. He had no feelings of compassion even for women, much less for men. He had a female slave about eighteen years of age, upon whom he inflicted the most degrading punishment with apparently as little remorse as if she were even a stick or a stone. She also had attempted her freedom, and had also failed to obtain it--had attempted it because she had been called upon to perform duties for which she was unequal; and, for not doing which, though impossible, she was most unmercifully and brutally punished. Roper was chained round the neck to this female slave, with a chain weighing forty pound, and although restrained from free movement by this enormous weight--they were compelled to work with the other slaves for a whole week, and do an equal amount of labor. One can easily conceive how painful it must have been to his feelings to witness such humiliating conduct heaped upon one for whom he appears to have had an earnest attachment, for he says--"I would rather have suffered a hundred lashes myself than that she should have been thus treated." And again--"Words are insufficient to describe the misery which possessed both body and mind while this punishment was being inflicted, and which was dreadfully increased by the sympathy which I felt for my poor degraded fellow-sufferer." So intense was the agony which he endured, both on his own account and that of his fellow-sufferer, that he besought his master, most imploringly, to set them free from their chains, promising to do the task which had been him and more if possible. But the slave-master was not to be moved by any appeal to his compassion. Firm to his purpose, they were to drag their chains, and did so until life seemed to be fast ebbing out, when his selfishness suggested what the most earnest importunity on the part of Roper had failed to obtain.

These inhuman proceedings created in Roper's mind a renewed determination to deliver himself from the fangs of such a monster. He, however, remained for several months, during which time he was repeatedly reminded of the luxury of the lash:--reminded that the tender mercies of the wicked are cruel, and sometimes most cruel when better things were to be expected. Mr. Gooch called himself a Christian. He was a member of the Baptist Church known as "Black Jack Meeting House." Surely, the very stones of the building will be witnesses against him at the day of judgment. Religion, however, with him was simply a profession. We will not libel so sacred a thing by supposing that the veriest iota of its Divine spirit ever found a resting-place in his bosom. He was truly a black sheep, a lump of cruelty, and had no more affinity with the religion of Jesus than hell with heaven. He, however, went to church, and had the reputation of being a member of a Christian society. Roper says he attended Mr. Gooch's church for many years but was never inside. This anomaly is accounted for by the fact, that the colored population is never allowed to mix with the white. This is true of many Protestant churches, but the Roman Catholics make no such distinction. Whether otherwise pure or impure, they are at least free from the taint of this horrible and devilish prejudice. These white-skinned and refined disciples of the doctrine of the distinction of class and of color have, no doubt, sufficient reason to object to sit on the same seat in the same sanctuary with their slaves--the dark presence of a negro may well make them unhappy by reminding them of their own dark deeds; but will they object to sit with them in the same paradise, or grudge to hear the benediction of the same Saviour, or refuse to join in singing the same eternal song? But of this we may be very certain, that none can enter that pure place who do object.

We are anxious to believe that Roper's present master was a rather foul specimen of the slave-holding class, though the best of them are bad enough, but he was decidedly worse than bad. Not only were the young and robust the victims of his cruelty, but even old age did not escape him. He had a slave, named Phil, who was between seventy and eighty years of age, and so feeble that he was wholly unfit for labor. This old man Gooch used to chain round the neck and run him down a steep hill, apparently as a matter of amusement, for he never relinquished it to the time of his death. Another slave, named Peter, he almost flogged to death, and after having done that, pulled out his pistol to shoot him, and would have done it had not his daughter--who, despite having so brutal a father, and being exposed to such in-humanizing circumstances, had still something of woman's nature--snatched the pistol out of his hand.

The favorite mode of punishment was that of using horns, with bells attached to the back of the slave's neck; this method was adopted to prevent the slaves from running away. The instrument was several feet high, and the cross pieces two, four, and six feet in length. Mr. Gooch, however, was not alone in his adoption of this mode of punishment; it is the one usually observed by the slaveholders of South Carolina and other States. As specimens of the way in which the slave holding gentry of America treat their human chattels, Roper gives the following instances, all of which he had himself seen when going over other slave states with his owner.

A large farmer, Colonel M'Quiller, in Cushan country, South-Carolina, was in the habit of driving nails into a hogshead so as to leave the point of the nail just protruding in the inside of the cask; into which he used to put his slaves for punishment, and roll them down a very long and steep hill. Roper said, that in this way he killed six or seven of his slaves. This plan was first adopted by Mr. Perry, who lived on the Catarba River, and being rather effective was soon seized upon by others; for slaveholders are in no way nice as to the means, provided the end--subjection--be accomplished.

Another instance of slave-holding barbarity, was that of a young lad, who had been hired by a Mr. Bell, a member of a Methodist Church, to hoe three-quarters of an acre of cotton per day. Having been brought up as a domestic slave, he was not able to do it. On Saturday night, he left three or four rows unfinished and did them on the Sunday morning. As it rained on Saturday night, his master discovered that a part of the work had been done on Sunday; on the Monday he tied him up to a tree in the field, and kept him there the whole of that day, flogging him at intervals. At night, when he was taken down, having a mile to go, he was so weak that he could not get home. Two white men, who were employed by Mr. Bell, put him on a horse, took him home and threw him down on the floor, just as a sportsman would throw down a stag or a load of game, and then proceeded to supper. In a little time they heard some deep groans come up from the kitchen, when they, indifferently, or as a matter of sport, went to see him die; but he had breathed his last. Even for this crime, horrible as it may seem, and as it really is, American slave law provides no means of redress. But if a man kill a slave belonging to another master, he is compelled to pay the worth of the slave. In this case a jury met, returned a verdict of "willful murder," against Bell, and sentenced him to--pay the value. The life of a negro in the slave States of America is therefore worth so many dollars--the market price, neither more nor less. Mr. Bell, however, was unable to pay the market price, but found a friend, in a Mr. Cunningham, who it seems regarded him with a rather favorable eye, and as a reward for his successful flogging operations made him his overseer. An additional noticeable element in the character of Mr. Bell was the fact that he was a Methodist--an American Methodist--very different we believe from the character known by the same name in this country. Whether he considered it a less offence, or not, we cannot positively affirm, but this may be stated without fear of contradiction that Mr. Bell killed a man, because he broke the Sabbath; the man breaking the Sabbath, moreover, not as a matter of free will or choice, but from necessity to save a flogging. Many similar instances of cruelty might here be given, affecting women as well as men, but we will proceed with Mr. Roper's narrative.

Mr. Gooch, the amiable gentleman in whose possession we left Mr. Roper, continued to hold his property for several months, that is to say, he continued to hold him because Roper didn't attempt to run away. In the life of a slave, incidents ever new and ever distressing are continually arising, and the history of Roper is rather a notable illustration of this fact. In August, 1831,--this was his first acquaintance with any date, which he accidentally happened to learn by hearing it mentioned, and inquiring what it meant; was told that it was the number of the year from the birth of Christ. Sometime in this month some cows broke into a crib where the corn was kept, and ate a great deal. For this offence against that decorum which slaves are required to maintain amongst cattle, their brother chattels, they all, except Roper and another, were tied up and received several floggings. Roper and his fellow slave, frightened by the groans of the others, remained in the field, and for that day escaped the lash. Not "catching it then," Roper was comforting himself in the prospect of escaping altogether. But, on Monday morning, although he could not see Gooch, on account of the great height of the Indian corn, he heard him flogging the other man. Roper being afraid that he also would now drop in for his share of the whip, and evidently dreading a good whipping a great deal more than a good breakfast, he determined to run for it--this was always his favorite expedient when he wanted to get out of the way of anything unpleasant--and he did so, arriving, after a forty miles journey, at the estate of Mr. Crawford, North Carolina, in Mecklinburg County. Having heard people talk a great deal about the Free States, he determined upon going there. In making this effort he had also a strong desire to meet with his mother, who was in slavery, several hundred miles away from Chester. He had, however, but a very faint hope of ever seeing her.

On his journey, the first night he slept in a barn, upon Mr. Crawford's estate, but oversleeping himself was awoke by the overseer, who in rather alarming tones demanded to know what he was doing there. Poor Roper, who appears to have been a most unlucky wight in his runaway excursions, was dumb-foundered, and made no reply. The overseer at once jumped to the conclusion that he had taken a prize--that the victim of Morpheus was also a subject of slavery, and he therefore secured

Master Roper, and made no further present inquiry. On their way to the house, however, Roper made up the following story, which he told to the overseer in the presence of his wife. He said, that he had been bound to a very cruel master when he was a little boy, and having been treated very badly he wanted to get home to see his mother. "This statement," says Roper, "may appear to some to be untrue; but as I understood the world bound, I considered it to apply to my case, having been sold to him, and thereby bound to serve him; though still I did rather hope that he would understand it--that I was bound when a boy till I was twenty-one years of age." This "story" did not have any manifest effect upon the mind of the overseer, who overlooking the fact that Roper was white, fixed tenaciously on his woolly hair as supplying the most conclusive evidence that he possessed enslaved blood. The overseer's wife, however, was rather taken with his appearance, and urged that she did not think that he was of African origin--that she had seen white men darker than he was; and so changed the mind of her husband that after he had given Roper as much buttermilk as he could drink, and something to eat, which was very acceptable, as he had had nothing for two days, he let him go. Roper set off for Charlotte, in North Carolina, the largest town in the county. The country all around and on each side of the road was thickly studded with wood, and very thinly inhabited, the houses being, in most cases, two or three miles apart, so that he had every chance of secreting himself if pursued. When he got a glimpse of any one coming along the road he immediately rushed into the thickest part of the wood, and thus eluded their search. In this way he proceeded all day, until at night he came up with two wagons. The regular road wagons do not generally put up at inns, but encamp in the roads and fields. He told the wagon men the same story as that he had told Mr. Crawford's overseer, and met with a more unequivocal success. He was admitted into their circle, fed at their homely, but plentifully supplied table, which was one of the things Roper was fond of, and put up with them for the night. With these wagon men he made very good friends, they consenting to his going with them on their journey, on condition of his helping them. This of course he consented to do; but in the morning he was frightened by one of the men putting several questions to him. And when within a mile of the town his fears were again aroused, by observing the men whispering together while watering their horses at the brook; and fancying he overheard them say they would put him in Charlotte gaol when they got there, he made his escape into the woods, pretending to be looking after something till he got out of their sight. He then ran on as fast as he could, but without going into the town of Charlotte lest that should lead to his detection. And here he was at a loss how to get on, as houses were not very distant from each other for nearly two hundred miles. What also increased his perplexity, and at the same time, paradoxical as it may seem, facilitated his progress, was his observing at a short distance some other waggons. He was afraid to approach them lest the wagon men should seize him but when he met any one on the road he asked them how far the waggons were off, with the hope of inducing them to believe that he belonged to them and was wanting to overtake them. At nights he slept on the ground in the woods, just far enough from the wagons to know that they were a little in the distance, but still not so near as to allow himself to be observed by the drivers. All this time be had but little food, and that little was principally fruit, which he found on the road. Being afraid that his master was in pursuit of him, he left the usual line of road; and took another direction, principally through fields and woods; making his way to Creswell courthouse, a distance by the route he went of nearly two hundred miles from Salisbury. On his way, he was stopped by a white man to whom he told his old story, and again succeeded in disarming suspicion and smoothing the way for his escape. He also met with a poor man who had been roving into some of the western territories and was going back to Virginia, for more luggage. The road lay in the exact direction in which Roper was going, so he made friends with him, and they travelled on together to a place called Red House, only two miles from Hilton, where Mrs. Mitchell took him from when he was six years old to go to the Southern States. Here he hoped to find his mother. For that purpose he left the poor man with the cart at Red House, wandering about for a long time, not knowing which way to go. After a while he determined to take the road leading over Ikeo Creek. He had not passed this far before he came up with a little girl about nine years old, and asking her where she was going, and she said to her mother's, pointing at the same time to a house on a hill about half a mile off. The thought immediately flashed across his mind that he was really going to find the object of his anxious search. In his breast then sprang up an indescribably joyous emotion, such as he had never before experienced. There was something in the appearance of the girl which seemed to remind him of a form dear to him as his own life, but which slavery had torn from him while he was incapable of estimating the value of a mother. As a pretext for getting a glimpse of the dear object of his search, he told the girl that he was very thirsty, and would go with her to get something to drink. On their way he asked the little girl several questions, such as her name and that of her mother. She renewed his anxiety by informing him that her's was Maria, and her mother's Mary. He then asked her if her mother had any more children, to which she replied, that there were five besides herself, and that she had been told that one had been sold when a little boy, and that his name was Moses. These answers deepened his anxiety to see his mother, while in the little girl he was now sure he saw his own sister.

    They were not long before they reached the house, but the mother had no knowledge of her son. She took him for one of the men employed in digging a well on the estate of her master. "I told her," says Roper, "that I knew her very well, and thought that if she looked at me a little, she would know me; but this had no effect. I then asked her if she had any sons. She said, yes; but none so large as me. I then waited a few minutes, and narrated some circumstances to her attending my being sold into slavery, and how she grieved at my loss. Here the mother's feelings on that mournful occasion--feelings which a mother only can know--rushed through her soul. She saw her own son before her, for whom she had so often wept and in an instant we were clasped in each other's arms, amidst the ardent interchange of fervent caresses and tears of joy."

After the first gush of joy had subsided, he had then an opportunity of reviewing his position, when his mother and he talked over the trials they had passed through, and the sorrows they had endured. At night, his mother's husband, a blacksmith, belonging to Mr. Jefferson at the Red House, came, and of course was rather surprised to find a strange man in the family, not knowing at all who he was: The blacksmith had been married to Roper's mother when he was a babe. And when it was made known to him who the stranger was, as he had been excessively fond of him in his infancy, he was equally affected with joyous surprise at his return.

The next morning Roper wanted to go on his journey, in order to make sure of his escape to the Free States. But as might be expected in such circumstances his mother, father, brothers, and sisters, could ill part with their long-lost one; and in order to evade the evil chances of pursuit, persuaded him to go into the woods in the daytime, and return to their cabin at night to sleep. This he did for about a week. But on the following Sunday evening, after retiring to rest on a pallet, which his mother had prepared for him and on which he slept between his two brothers, he was suddenly awoke by a posse of slaveholders whom he found standing around his bed armed with pistols, and who immediately seized him, and without giving him opportunity to bid his friends farewell, conveyed him to the Red House, where he was confined in a room the remainder of the night, and in the morning was lodged in the gaol of Creswell courthouse.

Unutterable anguish now wrung the hearts of his relations. Even before the first ebb and flow of their rejoicing on the arrival of the lost one had well passed, he was again in the hands of the selfish and cold-blooded abettors of slavery, and never saw his friends more.

In the gaol of Cresswell courthouse, he was confined in a dungeon underground, the grating of which looked to the door of the gaoler's house. While in prison his grandmother, went to him every day, taking him, besides the regular gaol allowance, something to eat, which extra supply of food enabled him better to sustain the hardships to which he was now exposed. But the gaoler's wife had a desperate antipathy to him, and whenever her husband went out, would go to Roper's dungeon and shut the door which was over the grating, and which increased the unhealthiness of the place so much that he was almost suffocated.

In this damp and noisome place he was confined thirty-one days before his owner heard of him; but on hearing that he was there he immediately sent his son and son-in-law, Mr. Anderson, after him. They arrived in a horse and chaise--of course slaveholders are all gentlemen and keep such things--and took Roper from gaol to a blacksmith's shop, tied his hands, got an iron collar fitted to his neck with a heavy chain attached, the other end of which was fastened to a horse and he placed on its back. Just before starting, his grandmother came to bid him farewell. Roper gave her his hand as well us he could, into which she secretly placed a few presents, and they parted. Through grief and ill-usage he was now in a very weak state, and the sorrow which sat like a load of lead upon his heart was still further increased from having to part with his grandmother--she was the last relative he ever saw.

Amidst the war of the elements they now proceeded on their journey. The thunder was one continued roar, and the lightning flashed with terrific vividness from every quarter. So desperate was the lightning that to the present punishment of Roper was added a new terror, he expected every moment that the iron collar round his neck would attract the fluid, and either strike him dead, or inflict some other physical injury little less to be dreaded.

In this way, the first day they travelled fifty miles; he being so very weak as scarcely to be able to sit on the horse. Having been long in prison, he had now partly lost the southern hue, and as he had his hat on, the people could not see his hair, and therefore took him to be a white man--a criminal--and were solicitous to know what crime he had perpetrated. Late at night they arrived at the house of Mr. Britton. This gentleman, a year or two before had joined the Society of Friends, and as they do not allow slave-holding in their members, he liberated his slaves and sent them into Ohio. Here Roper was treated well for the night. They gave him a hearty supper, which in his weak state was of the greatest service to him. They did not however allow him over much liberty; he had just so much as his chain gave after being locked to the bed-post on which they slept. Next morning they went on to Salisbury. At this place they stopped to water the horses, and while doing so they chained Roper to a tree in the yard by the side of the chaise.

And now occurred an incident which is worth giving in his own words--"On my horse," he says, "they had put the saddle bags which contained the provisions. As I was in the yard, a black man came and asked me what I had been doing. I told him I had run away from my master, after which he told me several tales about the slaves, and among them he mentioned the case of a Quaker, who was then in prison waiting to be hung for giving a free passage to a slave. I had been wondering all the way how I could escape from my horse, and once had an idea of cutting his head off, but thought it too cruel, and at last thought of trying to get a rasp and out the the chain by which I was fastened to the horse's neck. As they often let me get on nearly a quarter of a mile before them, I thought I should have a good opportunity of doing this without being seen. The black man procured me a rasp, and I put it into the saddle bags which contained the provisions. We then went on our journey, and one of the sons asked me if I wanted anything to eat; I answered no, though very hungry at the time, as I was afraid of their going to the bags and discovering the rasp. However they had not had their own meat at the inn as I supposed, and went to the bags to supply themselves, when my intention was discovered. Upon this they fastened my horse to the horse in their chaise, and kept a stricter watch over me. Nothing remarkable occurred till we got within eight miles of Mr. Gooch's, where we stopped a short time, and taking advantage of their absence, I broke a switch from some boughs above my head, lashed my horse, and set off at full speed. I had got about a quarter of a mile before they could get their horse loose from the chaise; one then rode the horse and the other ran as fast as he could after me. When I caught sight of them I turned off the main road into the woods, hoping to escape their sight. Their horse being much swifter than mine, they soon got within a short distance of me. I then came to a rail fence, which I found very difficult to get over, but, breaking several rails away, I effected my object. They then called upon me to stop, more than three times, and I not doing so, they fired after me, but the pistol only snapped. This is according to law, after three calls they may shoot a run-away slave. Soon after the one on the horse came up with me, he caught hold of the bridle of my horse, and pushed his pistol to my side. The other soon came up, and breaking off several stout branches from the trees, they gave me about one hundred blows. They did this near to a planter's house. The gentleman was not at home, but his wife came out, and begged them not to kill me so near the house. They took no notice of this, but kept on beating me. They then fustened me to the axletree of their chaise, and one of them getting in, the other took my horse, and they ran me eight miles as fast as they could; the one on the horse going behind to guard me."

In this way Roper was brought to his old master, Mr. Gooch, who, on their arrival, was the first person who showed himself. At first he seemed disposed to treat him rather kindly, unchaining him from the chaise with rather a gentle hand, and asking, in tons of unusual softness, where he had been. The first thing the sons did was to show the rasp which he had secreted in the provision bag, with the intention of cutting his chain. His owner then gave him a good dinner, the best he ever did give him, but it was with the view, Roper thought, of keeping him from dying, before he gave him something else--the best flogging he ever gave him in his life. After dinner he took him to the log-house, stripped him quito naked, tied his hands to a rail, which he had previously fastened up very high, fastened his feet together, put a rail between his fect, and stood on one end of it to hold it down. The two sons then gave him fifty lashes each, the son-in-law another fifty, and Mr. Gooch himself, by way of desert, fifty more. Mrs. Gooch, on this occasion, and for the first time in her life, so far as Roper had ever observed, manifested a little sympathy, and begged them not to kill him. But they were not so soft as to be influenced by her intreaties, although they did spare his life. When he asked for water, they brought in a pailful, and threw it mercilessly over his lash-ploughed back. After this they took him to the blacksmith's-shop, got two large bars of iron, each weighing twenty pounds, and put a heavy log-chain round his neck. All this was done on the Saturday, and on Monday, Roper had a repetition of an old experiment--he was chained to the same female slave as before. In the evening they were obliged, as a matter of punishment, to walk round the estate, by all the houses of the slaves, in order that they might taunt them. They had also imposed upon them long and severe labor, being obliged to be up and out in the fields before daybreak, while the other slaves were still in their cabins. It was in the morning that Mr. Gooch performed his flogging operations, and on being ordered to be early in the field, Roper and his companion knew what was going to be stirring. They therefore made up their minds to escape to the woods and secrete themselves. They did so, when forty slaves and the sons were sent out to hunt them. However, they were not to be found, and at midnight, believing that the search for them would be abandoned, they came from their hiding-place and went on to the banks of the Catarba. Here Roper got a stone and opened the ring of the chain on the neck of his female partner, and as the chain round his neck was only passed through a ring, it was now easily slipped off his own. "We then," says Roper, "went on by the banks of the river for some distance, and found a little canoe about two feet wide. I managed to get in, although the irons on my feet made it very dangerous, for if I had upset the canoe, I could not swim. The female got in after me, and gave me the paddles, by which we got some distance down the river. The current being very strong, it drove us against a small island, round which we paddled to the other side, and then made towards the opposite bank. Here again we were stopped by the current, and made up to a large rock in the river, between the island and the opposite shore. As the weather was very rough, we landed on the rock and secured the canoe, as it was not possible to get back to the island. It was a very dark night and rained tremendously, and as the water was rising rapidly towards the top of the rock, we gave all up for lost, and sometimes feared to hope, that we should never see the morning. But Providence was moving in our favor; the rain ceased, the water reached the edge of the rock, then receded, and we were out of danger. We remained all night upon the rock, and in the morning reached the opposite shore, and then made our way through the woods till we came to a field of Indian corn, when we plucked some of the green ears and eat them, having had nothing for two days and nights. We came to the estate of ----, where we met with a colored man who knew me, and having run away himself from a bad master, he gave us some food, and told us we might sleep in the barn that night. Being very fatigued, we overslept ourselves, and the proprietor came to the barn, but as I was in one corner under some Indian corn tops, and she in another, he did not perceive us, and we did not leave the barn before night. We then went out, got something to eat, and strayed about the estate four days, till Sunday." Roper now met with a man who had the irons on his feet, and who sympathizing with a brother in distress, proposed to try and relieve him of his load. They both tried to cut the irons with a file, but, in consequence of their thickness, were unsuccessful. He, however, started for Lancaster with the irons on, and when within three miles, purposed to try to obtain some food from some of the slaves belonging to the plantation of Mr. Crocket, but the dogs smelt him, and made such a noise that they brought out the old gentleman, armed with a rifle, instead of the slaves. Mr. Crocket at once took him into custody, put him on horseback, marched him off to Lancaster gaol that night, where he had the rather exceptional consolation of being placed in a dungeon next to a man who was going to be hung, and whose cries and groans, as he prayed to God for mercy, were most distressing. Here he remained for several weeks before Mr. Gooch heard of him, when his son-in-law was again dispatched to bring him back. Mr. Gooch himself went within a mile of Lancaster, in order, no doubt, to assist his son-in-law to keep Roper quiet, provided he should prove at all obstreperous. He had already a chain on one leg, and in addition to this they tied his hands, in order to make a tolerable certainty of death, doubly sure, and taking him home again, flogged him, put extra irons on his neck and feet, and put him under a driver with a greater share of work than he ever had before. After some time, and a fair share of drill, they took his irons off, which had no sooner been done than he again attempted to escape. He got as far as North Carolina, when a reward was offered; Roper was caught, and taken back to Mr. Gooch. That gentleman, always ingenious, in the process of punishment, had already tried a new plan, by tying him up by the wrists to a kind of swing, and then flogging him as it was whirled round in a true gymnastic fashion, by a horse. But he now adopted a different and more terrible device. He had Roper's hands and face covered with pitch, and then, in his own merciful and delicate way, applied a lighted torch, burning nearly the whole of his hair and face, while the pain was most distressing. But neither brutal threatenings, nor still more brutal burning and flogging, were sufficient to quench Roper's impetuous and burning desire for freedom. Before two days were over he was off again, and was again caught. This time Mr. Gooch was concerned to know how he got off his irons. Roper, however, was dumb, he would answer no questions, and Mr. Gooch, supposing that the feat had been performed by his own hands, which by the way, was a slight mistake, as the irons were taken off by another slave, had his hands put into a vice and his nails squeezed off. His feet were made to undergo a similar process, and he was then chained down in a log house, but the chain not having been made sufficiently secure, he again effected his escape, but was almost at once recaptured, when he received from Mr. Gooch the most severe, and also the last, flogging that gentleman had the gratification of inflicting.

Mr. Gooch seemed now to be tired of trying to break in Roper, and he, therefore, passed him over to a Mr. Britton, a slave dealer. And being once more fairly in the market, he seems to have been regarded as a rather more suitable article than when we last saw him in the same condition, for in a very short time he was the property of several new masters, whom he served in the capacity of a domestic slave, evidently with much more satisfaction to himself than when he was under the control of Mr. Gooch.

After passing severally through the hands of Messrs. Wilson, Rowland, Goodley, and Louis, he became the property of a Scotchman of the name of Beveridge, who had lived in America eighteen years without being contaminated by the polluting contact of slavery, and who, even after his soul was touched by its leprosy, and degraded by identification with it, continued to be a man of remarkable kindness, so much so, that he awoke in the bosom of Roper an attachment which was never effaced. With this gentleman he travelled through several of the Southern states, was made steward on board the Versailles, one of his steamboats, which, ceasing to run, in consequence of the lowness of the river, he proceeded with his master to Appulachicola, a town in West Florida, where he became a bankrupt, and all his property was sold.

Roper was now bought by a Mr. Register, a planter of the same state, who was a perfect savage. Previous to the purchase, he frequently taunted him by saying, "You have been a gentleman long enough, and, whatever may be the consequences, I intend to buy you." This change so exasperated him, that he cared not whether he lived or died, and resolved on making himself tipsy, and then plunging into the river, in order to get out of the hands of Mr. Register. This gentleman was a very precious specimen of his class, for, in addition to his being a slave-holder, he was also a slave-stealer, and of other cattle and property as well. Roper had, by some means, become acquainted with his character, and, by way of discharging a portion of the indignation which was pent up in his bosom, at having become the property of so vile a fellow, he said to some of Register's acquaintances, that "he had been accustomed to live with a gentleman, and not with a rogue." This coming to the ears of Mr. Register, Roper's fears were desperately excited, lest a few hundred lashes should be his reward for this trifling freak of wit and gratification of temper. But this passed off without any serious results. Roper was requested to prepare to proceed to Mr. Register's home, and had provided for his use a half-starved old nag, whose backbone was so sharp that it seemed like the edge of a rough saw; and, on this sprightly animal, he was to travel a distance of about eighty miles. This felicitous mode of conveyance, if it secured no other good, gave him, at least, opportunity for reflection, and he immediately began to plan his escape. About twelve at night, they arrived at Marianna, where they were to rest till the morning. Here, Mr. Register, whose suspicion had been somewhat awakened, put the question, "Do you intend to run away." Roper, although he had made some progress in intelligence and morals, was not yet so far advanced as to make a reply, representing the exact fact of the case. In fact, his reply was exactly the reverse of his intentions, but he states, that he had not then a knowledge of the sin of lying. As a kind of security, Mr. Register took Roper's spare clothes into his bedroom with him, and left his own, which were very wet, with his slave to dry. When these were done, he took them into his master's bedroom, and, finding him apparently fast asleep, said that he would take his own to dry too. He took care to make this announcement with a rather sonorous voice, in order to test the reality of his master's slumbers, and knowing, moreover, that he had a dirk and pistol by his side, he was anxious to take every precaution of avoiding their effects upon his own person. This was especially necessary, as Mr. Register was rather a dangerous character, and was known not to be over nice as to the mischief he did with such pitiless weapons. Roper, however, found that the drinking indulgences of the previous day, had induced a profound sleep, and that now was his chance for getting away; and, therefore, without loss of time, he started into the woods, running many miles, until he came to the river Chapoli. This river brought fresh difficulties. as it was deep and beset with alligators. He was, therefore, at a loss how to proceed. But pacing up and down for nearly two days, he at last discovered an Indian canoe, by which he conveyed himself across.

Landing on the opposite bank, he found himself surrounded by planters looking for him, when he hid himself until night. In the morning he proceeded on his journey, guided by the sun, and after passing the Chattahoochee river by a ferry-boat to the Georgian side, he came up to a slave-hut, where he found a man seventy or eighty years old, from whom, after telling the story of his troubles, he obtained some food, a piece of dry Indian bread, which the old man cheerfully gave him. Being refreshed with food and rest, he proceeded on his journey, and met with no further disaster, except a fright from the howling of a pack of wolves, till he came to Flint river, where he saw a man who knew him, and it was only by inventing what he called "a hasty and wicked deception," that he was saved from being committed to the gaol of Bainbridge, a town close by. Leaving Bainbridge, he started for Savannah, winding his way, and intriguing if he met with anyone who was likely to recognize him. On the road he met with some cattle drovers, who were collecting cattle to drive to Savannah, and being desirous of obtaining a passport, he determined on the following plan--He called at a cottage, and after talking some time with the wife, whose interest he excited by telling her his little story; he pretended to feel for his passport, and not being able to find it, went out to look for it, but returned, stating, that he was sorry he did not know where it was. The wife pleaded with her husband to give him a passport, and he consented, employing his son to write it. Roper had to dictate the terms, which he was enabled to do from memory, having heard passports read on several occasions. The lad sat down, and filled a large sheet for the passport, and another with recommendations. These being completed, Roper dined with his friends, and then proceeded on his journey. Going along, he examined the papers, and although he could not read a word, he observed they were much blotted, and was, therefore, afraid they would not answer his purpose, and began to think how he should obtain a more respectable and authentic looking document.

Having again met with the drovers before mentioned, he showed them his passport, calling their attention to the blotted parts, which he had been careful to immerse in water, in order to give it the appearance of a spoiled document, and asked their advice as to how he should obtain another. They recommended him to go to a rich cotton-merchant, who lived in the neighborhood, and engaged to go with him, in order to state that they had seen the passport before it was wet. Influenced by their representations, the cotton-planter readily wrote a free pass and recommendation, to which the cow-drovers affixed their marks. The recommendation was as follows:--"John Roper, a very interesting young lad, whom I have seen and travelled with for eighty or ninety miles, on his road from Florida, is a free man, descended from Indian and white. I trust he will be allowed to pass on without interruption, being convinced, from what I have seen, that he is free, and, though dark, is not an African. I had seen his papers before they were wetted."

With this passport, Roper went to Savannah, one of the greatest slaveholding cities in America, where they are always on the look-out for runaway slaves. When at this city, he had travelled about 500 miles, having had to make an exceedingly circuitous route. Though not over certain of his success, he marched down the main street with a tolerable confidence, and went to the docks and inquired for a berth, as a steward to a vessel bound for New York. Five minutes he arrived, he was engaged, and in an equally short time the schooner "Fox" was away from the docks into the river. His spirits now began to revive, as he anticipated soon reaching a free country, where he would be entirely safe. When they got out into the stream they cast anchor, and were detained there several days, and having business in the city to transact, he was obliged to go there. And as, moreover, it was known that his master was on the look-out for him, Roper felt that his position was not over safe. He therefore made an attempt to get an engagement on another vessel, but was unsuccessful. In about two days, however, the schooner "Fox" sailed from Savannah to New York. Roper now was full of transport. Visions of bliss and freedom flitted before his mind, and he began to feel as if he was something more than a slave--a man. But the sailors treated him badly on the voyage. They observed some indications of African blood in him, and that, in their estimation, was sufficient to justify any and every kind of indignity. They threw a rope round his neck, and nearly chocked him, the blood streaming from his nose profusely. They also took up ropes with large knots, and knocked him on the head, taunting him at the same time with being a negro, and telling him that they despised him.

On arriving at New York he thought he was free, but to his sad disappointment he soon ascertained he had been deceived. It was necessary that he should cast about in order to take care of himself, and he therefore determined to go into the country and try to get employment. This he obtained about eighty miles up the Hudson River, but his bliss was blighted by being seized with the cholera. The landlord of the house where he had put up, told him that he must leave there, as he could not keep any one in his house who had so alarming a complaint. No one would enter his room, except a pious and amiable young lady, who procured him medicine at her own expense, and administered it herself. With the good nursing, and genial smiles of this young lady, he soon recovered his health, and went on to the city of Albany in a steam-boat, a distance of about eighty miles. Not being able to get work here, he proceeded to Vermont, one of the New England States, where he found the people so opposed to slavery, that he frankly told them that he was a fugitive, and from where and for what reasons he had run away. He now hired himself to a firm in Sudbury, but because the people persuaded him that his wages were too little, and from fear also that his master might betray him, he was induced to leave, whence he travelled to Ludlow, where he formed some agreeable acquaintances, and then on to Boston. Here he had an engagement in a shop, but he was still haunted with the fear of being discovered, and therefore had his head shaved, bought a wig, and engaged himself to a Mr. Perkins of Brooklin, three miles from Boston. But the family soon discovered that he wore a wig, and was a runaway slave, when in order to avoid unpleasantness, he returned to Boston to his former situation. Some weeks after this he discovered, from information which his friends gave him, that a gentleman was in Boston anxiously inquiring for a person, whom, from the description, he knew to be himself, and that a considerable sum was offered for his recovery. He therefore at once got out of the way; went into the Green Mountains for several weeks, and from thence to New York, where he remained in secret several days, till he heard of a ship, the "Napoleon," sailing to England, and on the 11th of November, 1835, he embarked for this country, where freedom exists not in name only but in reality, bringing with him letters of recommendation to the Rev. Drs. Morison, Raffles, and Fletcher; and thus, after a period of sixteen months, sometimes hotly pursued by slaveholders, and at others equally excited by his own fears, he was fairly out of the reach of his enemies, and speeding his way to that country where slaves cannot breathe--

> If their lungs receive our air, that moment they are free,
> They touch our country, and their shackles fall.

On the 20th of November, 1835, he landed at Liverpool. "My feelings," he says, "when I first touched the shores of Britain, were indescribable, and can only be properly understood by those who have escaped from the cruel bondage of slavery." At Liverpool he was surrounded by an atmosphere of kindness and attention. Dr. Raffles, to whom he had a letter of recommendation, introduced him to several of his friends, who paid him every attention, and secured him, many temporal, intellectual, and spiritual advantages, to which he had hitherto been an entire stranger. From Mr. Clare of Liverpool, he was introduced to the Anti-Slavery Society in London, and was received kindly by its secretary, Mr. Scoble. He now lost no time in delivering his letters to Drs. Morison and Fletcher, the former of whom, through the "Patriot" newspaper, invoked the sympathy of the British public in his behalf, and the response was of such a nature, as to awaken undying gratitude in the mind of Roper, especially towards Mr. Christopher, a member of Dr. Morison's church, for whom he felt an attachment which words are inadequate to express. Roper now went to an academy at Hackney, where he remained six months, going through the rudiments of an English education, and regularly attending the ministry of Dr. Cox, which was exceedingly helpful to him in the development of a religious life. The kindness he received while at Hackney, deserves to be recorded in his own words. He says, in the sketch from which we have chiefly drawn the facts of this narrative, "I feel it my duty to present my tribute of thankfulness, however feebly expressed, to the affectionate and devoted attention of the Rev. Dr. Cox, from whom, under God, I received very much indeed of spiritual advice and consolation, as well as a plentiful administration of my temporal necessities. . . . . I would not also forget to mention the kindness of his church generally, by whom I was received with Christian love and charity. Never, I trust, will be effaced from my memory, the parental care of the Rev. Dr. Morison, from whom I can strictly say, I received the greatest kindness I ever met with, and to whom, as long as God gives me lips to utter, or mind to reflect, I desire to attribute the comfort which I have experienced since I set my foot upon the happy shores of England." Moses has long since returned to America, and such a simple but effective tribute comes with peculiar grace from the pen of one, the greatest part of whose life had been spent in the most abject slavery, and whose means of mental and moral culture must therefore necessarily have been exceedingly imperfect. But if under the most unfavorable circumstances, with scarcely any opportunities of developing their mental and spiritual attributes, there are to be found in the ranks of slavery, such brilliant specimens of moral greatness and intellectual strength, as this volume portrays, what may we not expect of the race--the colored and despised race of Africa--when the morning star of their freedom shall arise--when they shall have the same chances of becoming good, and great, and distinguished, as other races of free-born men.

In the career of Moses Roper, it has been seen how cruel are the mercies of the wicked--how dangerous a responsibility is unlimited power--in what an abject condition the African race are placed in the Slave States, of what is called "the land of the free," to what cruel vicissitudes and adverse tides of fortune a man is doomed, who may happen to be born with the slightest tinge of color in his skin, or the finest sprinkling of negro blood in his veins--how desperately the moral nature of men may sink, and still be called respectable--still be beneath the shelter of public opinion, and the protection of the law; but revolting as the picture may appear to those who are seeking either in the limited range of social life, or by the pulpit, or the pen, to secure the rights and the happiness of all in every clime, and of every grade, there is this enduring consolation, this ever abiding and inspiring thought, that even the basest elements of human life and society have a corrective influence, and that therefore it is still possible that the wrongs of the negro race may yet awaken the redeeming energies of the free-born in every land, and also that slaveholders themselves, base, brutal, and degraded as they are, may yet comprehend the wickedness of their position, and be induced to rise to the dignity of a stainless and Christian life.

PETER WHEELER.

THUS spurned, degraded, trampled, and oppressed,
The negro exile languished in the West.
With nothing left of life but hated breath;
And not a hope, except the hope in death,
To fly for ever from the Creole strand,
And dwell a freeman in his father's land.

MONTGOMERY.

IN 1839 was published at New York a small duodecimo volume, entitled, "Chains and Freedom: or, the Life and Adventures of Peter Wheeler, a Coloured Man yet living. A Slave in Chains, a Sailor on the Deep, and a Sinner at the Cross. Three volumes in one. By the Author of the 'Mountain Wild Flower.' " We are particular to give the title of this book because it is somewhat of a curiosity in a literary sense, and displays some peculiar traits of authorship. It is in substance an autobiography of Peter Wheeler, told in a straight, rough style, which quite please a Saxon ear with its rugged honesty, and sufficiently attests its genuineness as a record of facts. But there is no necessity to be satisfied with the internal evidences of genuineness which the book contains, inasmuch as abundance of external evidence exists of its truth; otherwise it is a book which we should hold in doubt sooner than any of the kind we are acquainted with. The reason why we should have little respect for such a book is the egregious vanity which its literary editor displays, and the very inartistic jumbling of absurdities with which he is content in the introduction. He dedicates his work to "everybody who hates oppression, and don't believe that it is right, under any circumstances, to buy and sell the image of the Great God Almighty," &c. Peter is then advised to put on his "thinking cap," that the author may write while Peter talks; the author finally begging him to "think correctly, and speak accurately," so that we may have "a true story and a good one." Peter winds up the preliminaries by averring that "a man must he pretty bad to tell a lie in a book, for if he has ten thousand books printed, he will print ten thousand lies, and that lying on too big a scale." Now, the reader knows the nature of our chief source for the facts of Peter's history, we may proceed at once to recite that history, first premising that Peter was well known to a vast number of men eminent in the clerical and medical professions, and that the truth of his narration has been certified by sixteen gentlemen of high professional standing in New York.

Peter Wheeler was horn on the 1st of January, 1780, at Little Egg Harbor, a parish of Tuckertown, New Jersey. He was born a slave, and many a time, he says, "like old job, I've cussed the day I was born." "My mother has often told me," he continues, "that my great grandfather was born in Africa, and one day he and little sister was by the sea-side pickin' up shells, and there came a small boat along shore with white sailors, and ketches 'em both, and they cried to go back to see mother, but they didn't let 'em go, and they took 'em off to a big black ship, that was crowded with negros they'd stole; and there they kept 'em in a dark hole, and almost starved and choked for some weeks they should guess, and finally landed 'em in Baltimore, and there they was sold." Such is the African's version of a fact which has become patent as a matter of history. "Grandfather," he says, "used to set and tell these 'ere stories all over to mother, and set and cry just like a child, arter he'd got to be an old man, and tell how he wanted to see mother on board that ship, and how happy he and his sister was, a playing in the sand afore the ship come; and jist so mother used to set and trot me on her knee, and tell me these 'ere stories as soon as I could understand 'em."

The mother of Peter was owned by a professing Quaker who "warnt a full-blooded Quaker," that is, not a Quaker at all, but a mere attendant at the Quakers' meetings. We are particular to note this, because nobody has so strenuously, and with such a holy ardor, labored for the emancipation of the slave as the members of the Society of Friends, and this half Quaker was the first and last of that body, as Peter says, whoever owned a slave.

The mistress of Peter's mother happened to have a child at the same time as Peter himself was born, and the baby of the mistress happening to die, Peter was transferred to the disconsolate mother, to alleviate somewhat the pangs of maternal bereavement. Thus the young negro fell in luck's way, and drew his first nourishment from the breast of a white woman. The bond thus created between the mistress and the foster child, maintained its integrity for many years, and Peter was kept "in master's family almost jist like his own children." Dressed in a suit of "red scarlet," with a "good many buttons, all up and down, before and behind," he strutted about as proudly as any of his young masters, and though black, yet fat and happy.

Peter's mother was owned by an old man named Mather, and by his will, she or her son were entitled to freedom at Mr. Mather's death. When that happened the mother was set free, and Peter was retained in the service of Mr. Mather's son, and enjoyed every external privilege of a freedom from slavery. He had a sister Hagar, who lived with her free mother, and with her Peter enjoyed many childish sports. One Sunday when the master and mistress had gone to meeting, the two minute Wheelers set off on a fishing expedition. She stood on the bridge, and he waded out and got a fine basket full. But just then a tremendous flouncing in the water took place, and something seized Peter's hook, and "yauked it arter him, pole, line, nigger and all," so that the young Sabbath-breaking piscators were so terrified as to run home and hide their heads under the bed-clothes, "trembling like a leaf," and afraid to stir one inch. By-and-bye the master came home and heart the story, and says he, "why, sure enough 'twas the devil, and all cause you went a fishin' on a Sunday, and if you go down there a fishin' again on Sunday, he'll catch you both, and that'll be the end of you two.

The "big thing in the creek" was a shark, which the boy of nine years old had hooked, and for hooking which, without permission, he did not get a whipping.

Peter's life at this time was a sort of fulfilment of the nigger notion of happiness. He lived in the house, and "had the handlin' of the victuals," and so had his fill of that class of comforts. He knew "jist like a gal," when washing-day was near, and tackled the pounding barrel and the big kettle, as heartily as any Sussex damsel. He did the heavy cooking too, and carried the dinner out to the field hands, besides ringing the changes on the mop, the broom, and the scrubbing-brush. Your negro is a first-rate hand in the kitchen; he cooks as well as Soyer, and his dishes are wholesomer; and in all those miscellaneous duties which we (male) Londoners never acknowledge to doing, but stigmatize as "molly coddling."

This was the rough commercial comfort prevalent as at the present day amongst the thriving portion of the trading class. The London life of our minor men of business, active shopkeepers, and tradesmen of moderate means, is just of this sort. The motto is, "plenty to eat, plenty of work, and enough sleep;" artistic amusements, literary studies, and the cultivation of the moral and devotional sentiments, give them little concern, and hence the mind is active in the schemes which trade suggests; but otherwise the head remains ignorant, and the heart unrefined, and the slow accumulation of worldly wealth is balanced against the waste of life. Just so in this family, where it was said to be wicked to catch fish on Sunday, but was not thought wicked to train the young in spiritual and temporal darkness, and where, though it was admitted the nigger had a body which must be fed, it was never supposed he had a soul to be saved. Peter went to school once in his infancy, when his young master was absent through illness; and moral and religious teaching he knew nothing about. During this time of good feeding and warm covering, Peter enjoyed a few boyish adventures, such as could only be enjoyed by a very privileged youngster. One day he mounted a spirited young horse with his legs tied under the horse's belly, and got flung off, and his ten-year old skull cracked in two or three places. At another time his young master got into a pen with some fierce hogs, which attacked him, and Peter flying to the rescue, got a slice bitten out of his hand. Escorting his mistress through a wood, he was attacked by an old cat-owl, which jumped on his head, and planted his claws in Peter's wool, and began to peck, while he "hollered like a loon." The mistress came to his relief with a club, and pounded the owl till he was dead, giving Peter a few poundings also by accident; but the claws of the assailant were fixed so tight in the nigger's wool, that the mistress had to cut them out with a jack knife. Once, when permitted to go to meeting, he took a fit of laughing at the peculiar ways of an old dame, who rose and spake as follows--"Oh, all young gentlemen beware of them 'ere young ladies--ahem!--Oh, all you young ladies beware of them 'ere young gentlemen--Ahem!--Pennyroyal is good for a cold." Peter thought, that if the Lord had prompted her to rise, he had forsaken her the moment she had risen; and so "snorted out straight," and was condemned to go no more. Soon after this he received "a tuning with a bunch of sprouts," for driving a calf up to a fence, and then sticking pins in its nose; though for stealing eggs to play at egg pelting, he appears never to have been whipped.

Such was Peter's boyhood, full of jollity and abandon, with abundance of creature comforts and an indulgent master and mistress, who if they had added to these bounties an education, such as would form a foundation for an intellectual and moral manhood, would have left the foster child as well fitted for time and eternity as any children of their own. After such trifles we may profitably turn to something more serious.

The end of Peter's fun came at last. His mistress died, and his troubles began, the tale of which is painful in the extreme. He was eleven years of age, a sleek, active, and clever lad, and "free by law." His master, however, had less moral regard for Peter than the mistress whom death had snatched away; and, although Peter was free by law, and free by right--even the right of a slave owning community--this man's sense of justice had been ruined by the small taste of slave labor which the possession of the lad afforded him. The plantation was advertised for sale; the announcement including "a plantation well stocked with oxen, horses, sheep, hogs, fowls, &c., and one young, smart nigger, sound every way." He was on the stock-list, and being black, could give no certification of his freedom, and would only have been laughed at if he had. Besides, what is a poor ignorant black boy, of eleven years of age, to do against a man who can bring half a nation of scoundrels to second his villainy, and who scruples at no violation of personal rights, and will use force if he finds it necessary. But the sale took place, and the "young nigger" was made to mount a table, while the auctioneer cried out--"Here's a smart article, sound, well-trained, young nigger, he's a first-rate body servant, good cook and all that; now give us a bid." His little sister, stung with anguish, leaped upon the table and stood wringing her hands and sobbing, and as the two infants clung together, in tears, their little hearts half broken at the pain of parting, and a dread of cruelty which the boy would have to undergo, the bidding steadily proceeded. At last he was "knocked down" to Gideon Morehouse, for one hundred and ten dollars, the purchaser making an agreement with the seller to give the boy three quarters' schooling. Now in the slave States, owners are not merely unwilling to educate their slaves, but they have a good plea for studiously keeping them in ignorance, inasmuch as it might happen, that among the items of a negro's knowledge, that of his right to liberty would occur. Peter Wheeler, therefore, got no schooling as promised, a slaveholder's word being worth as little as a slaveholder's sense of justice. "Now how could that man get any right to me," says Wheeler, in his simple way, "when he bought me as stolen property; or how could anybody have even a legal right to me? And yit that's the way that every slaveholder gits his right to every slave, for a body must know that a feller owns himself." But the sister, who yet enjoyed her freedom, had, during the time that this iniquitous bargain was pending, been busily engaged in borrowing small sums of her friends, and adding these to the savings of her free labor, came back to the auction room with one hundred and ten dollars, and offered them to the purchaser of her brother as the price of his liberty, "No," said he, "I'll take nothing short of one hundred and fifty silver dollars." She had raised the highest sum in her power, and for want of forty dollars more the boy was torn from his sister and mother, while none put forth a hand to help them, nor offered a word of solace to stay their tears. They were both black women, and, in America, the blacks are not reckoned susceptible of human feelings.

Reaching his master's house, he was put to the cabinet-making, and worked at this assiduously. One day he blunted a chisel by accident, and received kindly intimation that he should have "his head split open with the broad axe." Few accidents occurred further until he was taken by his master to New York State, a Mr. Abers, his master's brother-in-law, being of the party. On the road an offer was made for the purchase of the boy, and he begging his master to sell him, received a score of kicks for his pains. Then the team taking fright, and getting beyond his controul, he received a heavy whipping and a fresh kicking in the back which rendered him a cripple for several days. When the wagon came to a deep rut the master made the boy lift as hard as he could to assist in raising the wheels on the level again, standing over him at the same time with a whip, crying "lift, you black * * *, lift," and thus they trudged on, one lifting and the other whipping.

At last they got into thick woods, and the master halted and began farming. The first work was to build a log hut. The master made a mistake in cutting a log, and when he found it would not fit, he pounced upon the boy and knocked him down with his fist, flinging the log at the same time on his foot. The boy's foot swelled and gave him great agony, but the wretched white man kept him to his labor, and kicked him till he stood up on his crushed foot, and made him hold the logs breast high, while he himself refrained from lifting a pound, but employed himself in crying-- "Lift, lift, you black cuss." Presently down went the boy exhausted, and the logs fell on him again. "Get up you wretch," cried the master; "or I'll split open your brains with a hatchet." He rose again, and stood trembling at his labor, and was presently knocked down again for failing in his strength. Then he had to thatch the barn in the coldest weather, while clad in thin ragged clothes, the master relieving him from a sense of cold by incessant floggings, varied now and then by threats against his life. The brutality of his master now became so great, and so disgusting to the labourers on the farm, that they all advised Peter to run. "Why," said they, "do you stand there to be beat, and whipped, and starved, and banged to death? Why don't you run?" Squire Whittlesey, too, who lived hard by, had heard of Peter's treatment, and, says he, "You're free by law, why don't you run, Peter?" His answer was, "Wait till I git a leetle older, and I clear the coop for a ruest." But the master was not only cruel but mean, and robbed Peter of many perquisites which fell to his share in accordance with the usage of the forest. Peter killed large quantities of fish, but was allowed none himself; and, when entitled to certain bounty money for killing a ravenous beast, the master took it from him and kept it. "But the slave aint a man," says he, in his narrative, "a slave is a thing: he's jist what the Slave Laws call him, a chattel, property: jist like a horse; and, like a horse, he cant own the very straw he sleeps on."

Another instance of the master's meanness occurred when Peter had, by dint of great courage, and peril of life, saved the daughter of a neighbour from drowning. The father of the girl was full of gratitude, and, to reward Peter, made a grand suit of clothes, including a coat of blue cloth, and pantaloons of green, with a handsome vest, a linen shirt, a pair of shoes, and a hat worth seven and a half dollars. Then Peter's pockets were filled with raisins, and his pate beautified with a new French crown; and, leaving his thin rags behind him, he set out to drive the folks to church. When his master saw him in this suit of seventy dollars, "he stared a bit;" but Peter took it coolly, and, hitching up his trowsers, walked along the church straight to the "black pew," and "there warnt any crook in his back that day."

But the master was so astonished to see Peter in this gay garb, that he sat all day viewing him from head to foot, and without hearing "a bit of the sarmint all that day." When they got home, he cries out--"Nigger, where did you get that suit from?" Peter tells the story of the girl's danger, and his own heroism. "Hand me that coat." says the master, taking it and putting it on himself. Then his daughters begun to expostulate, but were silenced by a few oaths, concluding with the assertion that "the * * * nigger" had no right to the clothes; and, "I'll do as I please with my nigger's things. He's my property. It's a * * * pity if my nigger's things don't belong to me." And, with the same propriety, might he say, that his nigger's soul belonged to him; or, if he possessed salvation by Christ, that his title to heaven belonged to him. With such premises, he could logically prove that he could kill his slave, and do no wrong, as he would innocently kill his ox, or other property. Here we see the legitimate and necessary inference of this barbarous, inhuman, and wicked position, that it is right, under certain circumstances, to own property in man. A man is not safe, as long as he acknowledges this right; for if he sbelieves it ever can exist, he will exercise it as soon as circumtances are favorable, and become one of the most barbarous and abandoned of slaveholders in an hour.

CHAPTER VI.
PETER'S LOT GROWS HARDER THAN BEFORE.

WITHOUT repining, Peter labored with diligence, and discharged with integrity all the offices of trust reposed in him by his besotted master. One day they were engaged in digging a cellar: Peter was holding the scraper while the master drove it into the earth. Presently it came in contact with the root of a tree, and Peter was jerked head over heels into the hole. "Come up here," says his master, taking a halter in his hand. He was then made to strip and hug an apple tree. He was then tied to the tree and whipped with an ox good, while he was stark naked, "till he'd cut a good many gashes in my flesh, and the blood run down my heels in streams; and then he unties me, and kicks me down into the cellar to hold scraper agin."

By being so cruelly treated during the winter, when spring came, poor Wheeler was knocked up with the typhus fever, and was laid on a bed of straw, behind the kitchen door, where he lay for six months almost dead. The doctor came one day and told his master--"If you want that boy to get well, you must give him a better place to lay down than he has got, for 'taint fit for a sick dog." After this, Wheeler was removed, by his master's daughter, upstairs. By their kind and assiduous attention he gradually got better, and even sufficiently strong to vindicate his manhood. We will let him speak for himself in his own quaint manner.

"Well, next Sunday a Methodist preacher comes along, and was agoin' to preach at Ingen Fields. And so he and his wife come down to dine with us, and we cooked a leg of mutton we had on hand, for dinner, and got it on the table, and all sets down, and master begins to cut it, and come tu, 'twas distressedly tainted round the bone, and smelled bad.

"Well, master orders it off the table; and I goes and knocks over five chickens, and dresses 'em, and fricazeed them in a hurry, and got 'em on to the table; and I guess we didn't hinder 'em mor'n half an hour.

"Well, nobody could stand the mutton, it stink so; but master tells the folks to give me nothin' else to eat; and I eat, and eat away upon it, day after day, as long as I could; and then I'd tear off bits, and hide 'em in my bosom, and carry 'em out, and fling 'em away, to git rid on it; and one night, when it stunk so bad it fairly knocked me down, I takes the whole frame and leaves for the lot with it, and buries it; and thinks, says I, now the old mutton leg won't trouble me anymore. But it happened, that a few days arter this, that we was ploughin' that lot, and he was holdin' the plough; and up comes the mutton leg, and fust he looks at it, and then at me, and takes it up, and scrapes the dirt off it--and, oh! how he biled! and says he, 'You black rascal, what did you hide that mutton for?' And he took the whip out of my hand, and cut me with it a few times; and says I, 'Master, I won't stand this;' and off I run towards the house, and he arter, as fast as we could clip it; and he into the house and gits the rifle, and I see it, and, oh, how I cleared the coop into the lots; and as I was a goin' over a knoll, he let strip arter me, and I hears the ball whistle over my head. I tell ye, how it come!--and I scart enemost to death.

"Well, I wanders round a while, my heart a pittepattin' all the time, and finally comes back to the house. But I see him a comin' with the rifle agin' as I got into the lot, and I fled for shelter into the shell of an old hemlock-tree left standin' (you've seen such arter a lot is burnt,) and he see me, and he let strip agin', and whiz went the ball through, the old shell, about a foot over my head, for I'd squat down, and if I hadn't he'd a fixed me out as stiff as a maggot. He comes up, and sings out, 'You dead, nigger?' 'Yis, sir.' 'Well, what do ye speak for, then, you black scoundrel?'

"Then he catches hold on me, and drags me out, and beats me with a club, till I was dead for arnest; and then, lookin' at the hole in the tree, he turns to me lyin' on the ground, and says, 'Next time I'll bore a hole through you. Now drive that team, and straight, tu, or you'll catch a junk of lead into you.' Well, I hobbled along, and we ploughed all day; and come night, I boohooed and cried a good deal, and the children gits round me, and asks 'What's the matter, Peter?' I tells 'em, 'master's been a poundin' on me, and then he shot arter me, and I don't know what he will do next.' Julia speaks, and says, 'I declare its a wonder the devil don't come and take father off.'

"He orders the family not to give me any supper, but arter he'd gone to bed, the gals comes along, and one on 'em treads on my toe, and gin me the wink, and I know'd what it meant; and so I goes into the wood-house, and finds a good supper laid on a beam, where I'd got many a good bite; and went off to bed with a heavy heart."

Soon after this Peter encounters a bear, and succeeds in shooting him. His master proceeds to the wood and finds the bear, and then proceeds to Philadelphia with the skin of that and five others that Peter had killed, and sells them for over a hundred dollars "to say nothin' at all 'bout meat," and "he never" says Peter, "giv me a Bungtown copper out of the whole." This is another exemplification of the abominable doctrine of the right of property in man. Concede this right, and you justify the master, and leave Peter no reason to complain.

But now Peter gets an insight into the forms of religion, and takes part in some of the camp meetings, where he learns to pray; and after this he frequently turns aside from his labor to pray behind a tree. His master detects him spending a little time this way, and, as a punishment, he orders him to the woods at dark, and after whipping him severely, ties him up to a tree, saying, "now stay there, you black devil, till morning." A kindly hand cuts Peter away, but he is afraid to venture near the house and spends the night in the woods screaming to keep the wild beasts from attacking him.

Peter gets delivered from his perilous position, and the following day returns to his work.

"One day," says he, "he tells me to get up the team, and go to drawin' wood to the door. I used to have nothin' to eat generally, but buttermilk and soup, except now and then a good bite from some of the gals or neighbors. The buttermilk used to be kept in an old-fashioned Dutch barrel-churn, 'till 'twas sour enough to make a pig squeal. Well, I drawed wood all day, and one of the coldest in winter, and eat nothin' but a basin of buttermilk in the mornin', and so at night I goes to put out the team, and he says, 'Nigger, don't put out that team yit; go and do your chores, and then put up ten bushels of wheat, and go to mill with it, and bring it back to night ground, or I'll whip your blood out.'

"Well, I hadn't had any dinner or supper, and it was a tremendous cold night; but 'Lecta puts into the sleigh one of these old-fashioned cloaks, with a hood on it, and says she, 'Don't you put it on till you git out of sight of the house, and here's two nut-cakes; and if I was in your place, I wouldn't let the horses creep, for its awful cold, and I'm afraid you'll freeze.'

"Well, I come to the mill, which was ten miles off, and told the miller my tale, and what master said, with tears in my eyes; for my spirit had got so kind 'a broken by my hard lot, that I didn't seem to have anything manly about me." Oh! how you can degrade a man, if you'll only make him a slave!

"The miller axed me to go in and eat; but I didn't want to. And so about twelve o'clock at night I got my grist, and starts for home, and gets there, and takes good care of everything; and then I begins to think about my own supper. The folks was all abed and asleep: but I finds a basin of buttermilk and samp down in the chimney corner, and I eats that; and, if anything, it makes me hungrier than I was afore; and I sets down over the fire and begins to think!

"I had had many a time of thinkin' afore, but I had never before felt master's cruelty as I felt it now. Here he was a rich man; and I had slaved myself to death for him, and been a thousand times more faithful in his business than I had ever been in my own; and yit I must starve. I felt the natur' of injustice most keenly, and I bust into tears, for I felt a kind 'a broken-hearted and desolate. But I thought tears wouldn't ever do the work! I axed myself if I warn't a man--a human bein'--one of God's crutters: and I riz up, determned to have justice! 'And now' says I, 'I may as well die for an old sheep as a lamb; and if there is anything in this house that can satisfy my starvation, I'll have it if it cost me my life!'

"So I starts for the cupboard, and finds it locked, and I up with one of my feet and staves one of the panels through in the door, and there was everything good to eat; and so I eat till I got my fill of beef, and pork; and cabbage, and turnips, and 'taters; and then I laid into the nicknacks, such as pies, cakes, cheese, and sich like. Well, arter I'd done and come out, and set down by the fire, master opens his bedroom door and sings out, 'away with you to bed, you black, infernal nigger, you, and I'll settle with you in the mornin,' and he ripped out some oaths that fairly made my wool rise on end, and them shets the door. Well, thinks I, if I am to die, and I expected he'd kill me in the mornin', I'll go the length of my rope, and die on a full stomach. So I goes to an old-fashioned tray of nut-cakes, and stuffs my bosom full on 'em, and carries 'em up stairs, and puts 'em in my old straw bed, and I knew nobody ever touched that but Peter Wheeler, and I crawled in, and I had a plenty of time to think.

"In the mornin' the old man gits up and makes up a fire, a thing he hadn't done afore all winter, and then comes to the head of the stairs, and calls for 'his nigger'; and I hears a crackin' in the fire--and he'd cut a parcel of withes--walnut, of course, and run 'em into the ashes, and wythed the eends of 'em under his feet, and takes 'em along--and a large rope--and hits me a cut, and says, 'out to the barn with me, nigger;' and so I follows him along.

"Well, come to the barn, the first thing he swings the big doors open, and the north wind swept through like a harricane.

" 'Now,' says he, 'nigger, pull off your coat;' I did.

" 'Now pull off your jacket, nigger;' I did.

" 'Now off with your shirt, nigger;' I did.

" 'Now off with your pantaloons, nigger;' I did.

" 'And be d--d quick about it too.'

"Arter I gets 'em off, he crosses my hands, and ties 'em together with one eend of a rope, and throws the other eend up overhead, across a beam, and then draws me up by my hands till I clears the floor two feet. He then crosses my feet jist so, and puts the rope through the bull-ring in the floor, and then pulls on the rope till I was drawn tight--till my bones fairly snapped, and ties it, and then leave me in that doleful situation, and goes off to the house, and wanders round 'bout twenty minutes; and there the north wind sweeps through: oh! how it stung; and there I hung and cried, and the tears fell and froze on my breast, and I wished I was dead. But back he comes, and says he, as he takes up a writhe, 'now, you d--d nigger, I'm agoin' to settle with you for breaking open the cupboard,' and he hits me four or five cuts with one and it broke; and he catches up another, and he cuts all ways, cross and back, and one way and then another, and he whipped me till the blood run down my legs, and froze in long blood icicles on the balls of my heels, as big as your thumb, and I hollored and screamed till I was past hollerin' and twitchin', for when he begun, I hollered and twitched dreadfully; and my hands was swelled till the blood settled under my nails and toes, and one of my fect hain't seen a well day since: and I cried, and the tears froze on my cheeks, and I had got almost blind, and so stiff, I couldn't stir, and near dyin'. How long lie whipped me I can't tell, for I got so, finally, I couldn't tell when he was a whippin' on me; it was a sight to make anybody that has got any feelin' weep; and there I hung, and he goes off to the house, and arter a while, I can't tell how long, he comes back with a tin cup full of brine, heat up, and says he, 'Now nigger, I'm going' to put this on to keep you from mortifyin',' and when it struck me it brought me to my feelin', I tell ye; and then, arter a while, he lets me down and unties me, and goes off to the house.

"Well, I couldn't stand up, and there the barn doors was open yet, and I was so stiff, and lame, and froze, it seemed to me I couldn't move at all. But I sat down, and begins to rub my hands to get em to their feelin', so I could use 'em, and then my legs, and then my other parts, and my back I couldn't move, for 'twas as stiff as a board, and I couldn't turn without turnin' my whole body; and I should think I was in that situation all of an hour, afore I could get my clothes on.

"At last I got my shirt on, and it stuck fast to my back, and then my tother clothes on, and then I gits up and shuts the barn doors, and waddles off to the house; and he sees me a comin', and hollers out, 'Nigger, go and do your chores, and off to the woods.'

"Well, I waddled round and did my chores as well as I could, and then takes my axe and waddles off to the woods, through a deep snow. I gits there, and cuts down a large rock oak tree, and a good while I was 'bout it, tu, and my shirt still stuck fast to my back. I off with one eight foot cut, and then flung my axe down on the ground, and detarmined I'd die afore I cut another chip out of that log that day; and I gets down and clears away the snow on the sunny side of the log, and sets down on the leaves, and a part of the time I cried, and a part of the time I swore, and wished myself dead fifty times.

"Well, settin' there I looked up, and to my surprise I see a woman comin' towards me; and come to, it turned out to be my old friend 'Lecta, and the first thing, she says, when she comes up was, 'ain't you most dead, Peter?' 'Yis, and I wish I was quite, Miss 'Lecta;' and she cries and I cries, and and she sets down on the log, and says, 'Peter, ain't you hungry? here's some victuals for you;' and she had some warm coffee in a coffee-pot, and some fried meat, and some bread, and pie, and cheese, and nut-cakes; and says she to me, 'Peter, eat it all up if you can.'

At last, Peter goes home, and the greeting from his mistress is, "You come home agin, have you, you black scoundrel?" But the master was very mild, and still in bed, slowly recovering from his pounding, and says he, "I'm almost dead, Peter, you must be a good boy and take care of the stock." So away went Peter to the barn dancing and singing, to think what a capital thrashing his master had had.

But as the bully grew stronger, and was no longer at the mercy of his slave, his old brutality comes back, and seizing an opportunity to avenge the beating which Abers had given him, struck at Peter with a dung-fork, and pinned him to the floor. What followed, Peter shall tell himself.

"I run out of the big door, and he arter me, with the fork in his hand; and he run me into the snow where 'twas deep, and got me to the fence, where I was up to my middle in snow, and coldn't move; and he was agoin' to thrust arter me, and I hollers and says, 'Master, don't stick that into me.' 'I will, you black imp.' I see there was no hope for me; and I reaches out, and got hold of a stake, and as I took hold of it, as 'twas so ordered, it come out, and, as he made a plunge arter me, I struck arter him with this stake, and hit him right across the small of his back, and the way I did it warn't slow, and he fell into the snow like a dead man; and he lay there, and didn't stir, only one of his feet quivered; and I began to grow scart, for fear he was dying'; and I was tempted to run into the barn, and dash my head agin' a post, and dash my brains out; and the longer I stood there, the worse I felt, for I knew for murder a body must be hung.

"But bien'bye he begun to gasp, and gasp, and catch his breath; and he did that three or four times; and then the blood poured out of his mouth; and he says, as soon as he could speak, 'Help me, Peter!' and I says, 'I shan't.' And he says agin', in a low voice, 'Oh! help me!' I says, 'I'll see you dead afore I'll help you, you old heathen, you!' and at that he draws a dreadful oath, that fairly made the snow melt; and says agin, 'Do you help me, you infernal cuss.' I uses the same words agin'; and he tells me, 'If you don't, I'll kill you as sure as ever I get into the house.'

"Soon he stood clear up, and walked along by the fence, and drew himself by the rails to the house; and I went to thrashin' again'. Pretty soon 'Lecta come out to the barn, and says, 'Peter, father wants to see you.' I says, 'If he wants to see me mor'n I wants to see him, he must come where I be.' And she speaks as mild as a blue-bird, and says, Now, Peter, 'tend to me. You know I'm always good to you; now, if you don't mind, you'll lose a friend.' That touches my feelin's, and I starts for the house; but I 'spected to be killed as sure as I stepped across the door-sill.

"Well, I entered the old cellar-kitchen, and mistress locks the door, and puts the key in her side pocket, and master set in the chair, and his arm a restin' on another, as I set now and he raises up and takes down the rifle that hung in the hooks over his head, on a beam; and I knew I was a dead man, for I had loaded it a few days before for a bear; and says he as he fetches it up to his face, and cocks it, and pints it right at my heart, 'Now, you d-- nigger. I'll end your existence.'

"Now death stared me right in the face, and I knew I had nothing to lose; and the minute he aimed at me, I jumped at him like a streak; and run my head right atwixt his legs, and catched him, and flung him right over my head a tumblin', and I did it as quick as lightnin', and, as he fell the rifle went off, and bored two doors, and lodged in the wall of the bed-room, and I flew on to him, and clinched hold on his souse, and planted my knees in his belly, and jammed his old head up and down on the floor, and the way I did it warn't to be beat.

"Well, by this time old mistress come, and hit me a slap on the back, with one of these 'ere old-fashioned Dutch fire-slices and it didn't set very asy 'nother; but I still hung on to one ear, and fetched her a sidewinder right across the bridge of her old nose, and she fell backwards, and outcome the key of the door out of her pocket; and 'Lecta got the key, and ran and opened the door for the noise had brought the gals down like fury and I gin his old head one more mortal jam, with both hands, and pummelled his old belly once more, hard, and leaped out of the door, and put out for the barn.

"At night I come back, and there was somethin' better for my supper than I had had since I lived there. I set down to eat, and he come out into the kitchen with his cane, and swore, and ripped, and fore; and I says, 'Master, you may swear as much as you please, but, on the peril of YOUR LIFE, don't lay a finger on me;' and there was a big old-fashioned butcher-knife lay on the table, and I says to him, 'Just as sure as you do, I'll ram that butcher-knife through you, and clinch it!' I had the worst oath I ever took in all my life, and spoke so savage, that I fairly scart him.

I told him to give me a paper to look out a new master: for you see, there was a law, that if a slave in them days, wanted to change masters, on account of cruelty, that his old master must give him a paper, and he could git a new one, if he could find a man that would buy him. At fust he said he would give me a paper in the mornin', but right off, he says, 'No! I swear I won't; I'll have the pleasure of killin' on you myself!'

"So he swore, and finally went into the other room; and the gals says. 'Peter, now is your time; stick to him, and you'll either make it better or worse for you.'

"So I goes off to bed, and takes with me a walnut flail-swingle; and I crawled into my nest of rags, and lay on my elbow all night; and if a rat or a mouse stirred, I trembled, for I expected every minute he'd be a comin' up with a rifle to shoot me, and I didn't sleep a wink all that night; and I promised, in the presence of Almighty God, that the fust time I got a chance I'd clear from his reach; and I prayed to the God of freedom, to help me to get free."

The treatment of Peter had become so desperately cruel, that the neighbors interfered. Mr. Abers, brother-in-law to the master, Morehouse, taxes him with his cruelty, but receives for answer--"I'll do with my nigger as I please, he's my property, and I have a right to use my property as I please." A quarrel follows, Abers knocks Morehouse down, and then kicks him nearly to death, and takes Peter away with him.

So after breakfast, Mrs. Abers takes some warm water, and then she tries to pull Peter's shirt off, but it stuck so fast, says he, that she got some castile soap, and thus got off all the wool that had come off his woollen shirt, the hairs of which clung to his wounds and caused him terrible pain; then bathed with oil and bound up in linen, he goes to bed, feeling like a "new crutter," and spends a fortnight in ease and luxury.

CHAPTER VII.
THE MASTER PUNISHED, AND THE SLAVE SET FREE.

PETER, was resolved to obtain his freedom, but as yet he knew not how. While he was determining on some course to save his life and liberty, Morehouse prosecuted Abers for assaulting him, Abers returned the compliment by prosecuting Morehouse for ill-using his slave. For once, justice held the way, and the master was fined five hundred dollars, and put under bonds of two thousand dollars, to behave respectfully towards his slave in future. The fine was paid and the scoundrel went home muttering, "I wish I'd killed the nigger, then I should not have had this five hundred dollars to pay."

Now Peter fared better, though he was still a slave, and that conviction stung him to the quick. The daughter of his master entered, with heart and soul, into a conspiracy with Peter, to aid in setting him free. They made a suit of clothes for him, and the time soon came for to start. After a variety of difficulties, hair-breadth escapes, and trials, Peter succeeded in obtaining his freedom.

Now he began to feel that he was really free, and the taste of liberty he found most sweet. He lay down in his hammock, and all night long dreamt of liberty and its attendant blessings, thanking God with a full heart for his happy deliverance. But he shall tell his happiness himself.

"When I look back, and think how I suffered by bein' beat, and banged, and whipt, and starved; and then my feelin's arter I got free, when I held up my head among men, and nobody pinted at me when I went by, and said, 'There goes this man's nigger, or that man's nigger;' why, I can't describe how I felt for two or three years, I was almost crazy with joy. What I got for work was my own, and if I had a dollar, I would slap my hand on my pocket and say, 'that's my own;' and if I hauled out my turnip, why it ticked for me and not for my master, and 'twas mine when it ticked. And I bought clothes, and good ones, and my own arms paid for 'em. In fact, I breathed, and thought, and acted, all different, and it was almost like what a person feels when he is changed from darkness into light. Besides, when gentlemen and ladies put a handle to my name, and called me Mr. Wheeler, why, for months, I felt odd enough; for you see, a slave han't got no name, only 'nig,' or 'cuss,' or 'shrunk,' or 'cuffee,' or 'darkey;" and then, besides, I was treated like a man; and if you show anybody any kindness, or attention, or good will, you improve their characters, for you make them respect you and themselves, and the whole human race a sight more than ever. Why, respect and kindness lifts up anybody, or thing, even the beast or dog, if you show 'em a kindness, they will never forget it, and they'll strut and show pride in treatin' on you well; and pity if man is of sich a natur' that he ain't as noble as that, then I give it up. Why, arter I come to myself, and I would git up and find all the family as pleasant as could be, and I would go out and look, and see the sun rise, and hear the bird's sing, and I felt so joyful that I fairly thought my heart would leap out of my body, and I would turn on my heel, and ask myself, 'is this Peter Wheeler or ain't it?' and if 'tis me, why, how changed I be! I felt as a body would after a long sickness, when they first got able to be out, and felt a light mornin' breeze comin' on 'em, and a fresh, cool kind of a feelin' comin' over 'em; and they would think they never see anything, or felt anything afore, for all seemed more brighter and more gloriouser than ever; and oh! it does seem to me that no Christian people in the world can help wantin' to see all free, for Christians love to see all God's crutters happy.

"I b'lieve that one of the wickedst and most awful things in creation, and the root, and bottom, and heart of all the evil, is prejudice agin colors! There is most, or quite as much of this at the North as there is at the South, for I can speak from experience. There is that disgrace upon us, that many people think it a disgrace to 'em to have us come into a room where they be, for fear they would be blacked, or disgraced by us poor off-scourin' of 'arth. But worse than this, this same disgrace is cast on our color in the sanctuary of the Living God. In enemost all the meetin'-houses, you see the 'nigger pew;' and when they come to administer the Lord's Supper, they send us off into some dark pew, in one corner by ourselves, as though they thought we would disgrace 'em, or black 'em, or somethin.' Why, 'twas only at the last Sacrament in our church, this took place. All communicants was axed to come and partake together, and I come down from the gallery, and as I come into the door, to go and set down among 'em, one of the elders stretched out his arm, with an air of disdain, and beckoned me away to a corner pew, where there was no soul within two or three pews on me, as though he had the power to save or cast off. Now think what a struggle I had, when I sot down, to git my mind into a proper state for the solemn business I was agoin' to do.

"We ain't suffered to attend any pleasant place, or enjoy the advantages of debating schools, or libraries, and societies, &c.; and all these things is jist what improves the whites so fast. And if we, by hook or by crook, git into any sich place, why some feller will step on our toes and give us a shove, and say, 'stand back, nig, you can see jist as well a little furder off.'

"Now all these things is what keeps us so much in the back ground; for, if we have a chance, we git up in the world as fast as anybody. For there is smart and respectable colored folks; and you sarch out their history, and you'll find they once had a good chance to git larnin', and they jumped arter it. I think one of the greatest things the abolition folks should be arter, is to help the free people of color to git up in the world, and grow respectable, and educated, and then we will prove false what our enemies say, 'that we are better off in chains than we be in freedom!' "

Still in the confidence of his employer, and a favorite with the crew, Peter prospered in the goodly ship. On the 22nd of October, 1806, they sailed for St. Bartholomew's, and none worked at the capstan, or danced among the spars with more alacrity than the liberated slave. Away they went on the waste of waters; the land grew blue and disappeared; and the sun set into a bed of gold, and the moon like a silver gem floated up from the silvery ocean. Night passed; and the morning star shot up red as quick coal, and the ship bounded over the waters like a bird, and all went happy "as a marriage bell." They hailed a French vessel and then sailed on. Then a storm broke forth, and the waves started up like huge wedges splitting the blue sky, while the wind rose higher and higher and stripped every sail to ribbons. Then the lightning struck the waves and hissed like red-hot iron, and the thunder followed crash on crash. All this time the crew laboured at the pumps, and Peter worked as hard as any, for he now felt life was worth saving. Then they passed the line, and Peter was called upon to pay his bottle or be tarred and feathered. Arrived at St. Bartholomew's, they sold cargo, and put off for Porto Rica. The climate was hot enough to scorch all the wool off a "nigger's" head, and the fever raged on shore. From Porto Rica, they sailed for New York. On this voyage, they saved a shipwrecked mariner, who was found floating on a buoy. He was brought on board and put to bed, and, says the captain, "we shall have a new sailor in a hurry." In twenty-one days they reached New York, and, as soon as the ship hauled up, Peter sprang ashore, and cried--"Here's a Free Nigger!"

Peter Wheeler, after passing through a variety of romantic life-scenes, died full of simple and earnest piety, an exemplification of what the slave is compelled to be in bondage, and what he is capable of becoming, when he has cast off his ignominious bonds.

CONCLUDING OBSERVATIONS.

THERE is not a single instance in the history of literature of a book having so wide a circulation, and creating so intense an enthusiasm, as "Uncle Tom's Cabin." The name has struck upon our ears, and the title met our eyes in every possible place. It has taken rank by the side of heavy literature on the shelves of weighty publishers. It has been placed side by side with serious works and flimsy novels. It has stood out in prominent relief among the cheap wares of the newsvenders. It has graced roadside and railway book-stalls. Whirled away in the fast train, the softly-cushioned first classes have turned its leaves with their kid-gloved fingers. Jogging along on the hard benches of government trains, less exquisite personages have left their thumb-prints upon its pages. In faraway country towns, where some local "Independent" brings the news of the week, and all else in the shape of literature seems torpid, it peeps at you through the dusty panes of the stationer who keeps the circulating library. Instead of saying, where Uncle Tom has penetrated, we ought to ask where it has not, and pause while echo answers, where. It has been not merely ubiquitous, but omnipresent. All sorts of people have read it. Gentlemen, who pore over the Edinburgh or the Quarterly; grave men of science, fit to write encyclopoedias; ladies who devour the productions of Colburn and Bentley; flippant idlers learned in play-bills, matter of fact folk who mainly confine themselves to the "Times." Hard-headed men of business have, for once in their lives, been betrayed into emotion; tender-hearted people have fairly moistened it with their tears, and boys and girls have loved Eva, and wondered what papa would do to them if they were like Topsy. No place has been too notorious, none too obscure, no mind too intellectual or rigid, none too simple, child-like, or ignorant. Like a pure bright sun ray it has gone forth to the world, adding to what light we already had, and calling up sympathizing thoughts for those immured in the darkness of slavery.

The thousands have stamped upon this book of Mrs. Stowe's the seal of something more fervent than mere approbation; but, amid the almost universal applause, a low growl of dissent has been here and there heard. A few reviewers have found specks in it, and magnified them. The craft of the critic is one which induces a mental habit of making mountains out of molehills. Mere criticism is too often allowed to degenerate into hypercriticism. It is hardly fair we should censure them, or expect that professional fault-finders should be all praise. If they once came to that pass. Othello's occupation would, indeed, be gone. To them no pen is inspired. By virtue of their craft, they are bound to let the world see that they are beyond the influence of the charmer, "charm he never so wisely;" and to make it apparent that, however much any one else may know about any particular subject, they, at least, are better informed. For these, and reasons like these, we are scarcely inclined to find fault with the dissecters of literature, because, amid the general acclamation, there has been a hoot as discordant as the cry of an owl among a full chorus of song birds, but we betake us to the task, in this our last gossip about Uncle Tom, of answering the gravest of their objections and charges.

It has been said by some gentlemen of a classical turn of mind, that Mrs. Stowe's book is faulty in its construction, and the tale is unartistic in its development. The minds to whom that will appear important, require the unities of the old Greek drama, strictly observed in a modern book bearing upon modern facts, and telling of a state of things without a parallel in the annals of civilization. Let us grant that Mrs. Stowe has disregarded the unities; that her construction is unartistic, and the development not according to the square and plumb-line of established fiction. What then? Does that detract from the merit of the work or impair its effect? If Euripides were to make his appearance to-morrow in company with Virgil, and declaim the most chaste and regular of their compositions in the most sonorous Greek, or manly Latin, or the most elegant translation, the effect would be as nothing to that of the poorest chapter of Uncle Tom, read out by a drawling schoolboy. Most authors have "a purpose" in writing, so has Mrs. Stowe; and she has taken the most effective means to secure its accomplishment. There is throughout the work true unity--the unity of aim and object. Other writers strive to make up a good story; to make time and fact keep pace with each other--to bring each character forward in due order--to put incident and action in their places dramatically speaking, to tie hard knots of suffering and despair and misery--then in due season to let in a little hope--then to get into smooth water, and wind up finally with testy fathers bothered scheming mothers thwarted, villains betrayed, misanthropes, cured, vice generally condemned, and virtue as generally rewarded--the single married, and the married happy. The formula for a good every-day novel, which critics would have pronounced artistic, would have been easily enough mastered by a woman of Mrs. Stowe's intellect, but such a production was not her object. She wanted to tell all the world of a monster evil, and tell it in language which all world listen to. If she had written for university men, she ought to have been severe and classical, for artists accurate, and finishedly elegant; but she was writing for the many, for perceptions of all grades, and intellects of all classes; for those who dote over the canvas of Landseer, and those who admire the genius of a strolling sign-painter; those who respect the unities of the strict drama, and the great number who cannot be moved by anything less powerful than melodrama; and, so that her book might be something more than a class-book, so that it might influence all, she secured effect, not by recourse to art, but by adherence to truth and nature; not by bursts of eloquence, but by the simple, homely, touching language of natural sympathy.

Others say, that Mrs. Stowe has indulged in exaggeration. To some extent possibly she has, but not in a greater degree than our best writers of fiction. She has as every one of deep feeling will, written up to a high standard existing in her own mind; but it would be as well to recollect what Bulwer says--that the ideal is as true as the real which it always underlies, and to which the real is always tending. Take any character in Uncle Tom, and compare it with Dickens' Tom Pinch, or Kate Nickleby, or Florence Dombey, or Thackeray's Amelia in Vanity Fair, and it will at once be seen that there is no more exaggeration in one than the other. But the truth is, that at the bottom of this charge, there is lurking a touch of that prejudice against color which is to be found even among Free Britons. Our writers have written of white people, sometimes beautiful beings, seldom or ever absolutely repulsive. Mrs. Stowe, while she has not violated this feeling so far as George and Eliza are concerned, has painted in the highest colors which can grace Christian heroism poor Uncle Tom "a nasty black nigger," and through the mist of their prejudices and instincts, some cannot recognize the possible truth of the picture. Of its probability we shall have something more to say afterwards.

Another count in the indictment runs, that Mrs. Stowe has painted all her whites devils, and all her blacks angels. Has she? This, if true, would be a grave impeachment of her impartiality, for even slavery cannot root out of the fair skinned masters all traces of the better part of humanity and no race, whether black or white, however purified by suffering, ever produced angels. But it is not true. We are utterly at a loss to conceive where the reviewer found the materials of his fiction. To prove what we say, let us take a picture or two from "Uncle Tom's Cabin." By the way, it would not be a bad suggestion for the Abolitionists to decorate their halls with pictures from Uncle Tom, which would adorn them as gracefully and as instructively as scenes from our own history can the hall in which our legislators assemble.

But to the question--are all the whites demons? Take the character of Mr. Shelby, Uncle Tom's first master. Allowing for the difference of circumstances, most of our readers may, among their own circle of acquaintance, find his parallel. A man certainly not bad, but rather negatively than positively good. He is what would be termed in any society in the world thoroughly respectable. Gentlemanly, courteous, educated, and sufficiently amiable to make the serfdom of his slaves endurable, and to cause them to love him. Born and educated in England, Mr. Shelby, from a mere sense of decency and right, would have been an Abolitionist; but, with one of those minds, over which custom is omnipotent, his lot cast in a Southern State, and where slavery was a familiar customary institution, he took it among the general run of things, and tolerated rather than supported it. He can scarcely repress his disgust and contempt for the slave-merchant, and is only led to deal with him by the danger of losing his position in society. He feels selling Uncle Tom as much as Uncle Tom himself feels being sold; and spite of the custom of the many swamping the feeling of the individual, can hardly bring himself to bear the parting, while the bargain for Eliza's child is forced on him against his will, and completed with shrinking repugnance. Can it be said that Mr. Shelby is an uncommon character, or that Mrs. Stowe has painted him with a cloven foot?

Take a glance at Mrs. Shelby. What of the devil is to be found in her portraiture? She is a woman, with a woman's sympathy, and an almost masculine intellect. No amount of use or familiarity can blind her to the wrong of slavery when it comes before her in its full force. The subtlest logic cannot blind her reason, nor the most specious appearance of piety impose on her morality. She meets argument, boldly faces expediency, and, with a woman's heart, goes to the right and wrong of the matter. She cannot think it is right that a kind master should be separated from an attached slave, but the instinct of her nature--the feelings of a mother--shrink, as from the direst wrong, at the thought of tearing a devoted mother from an affectionate child. Human nature is not yet so poor but that we can appreciate the excellence of Mrs. Shelby's character by the example of many such women at home, women who have been bred under more fortunate conditions, and who denounce slavery because it is wrong, without feeling its bad effects.

Look into the house of the Birds, as drawn by Mrs. Stowe, and see how little there is there to justify the accusation, that the whites are all described as bad. Mr. Bird is a striking example of a large class--men who are better than the doctrines they preach. He is a senator, and makes laws against fugitive slaves. With his brother legislators, he fortifies himself with speeches about abstract wisdom and practical expediency. The Union must be maintained, runaways must be hunted down and given up. He and his fellows find it easy to deal with the mass of suffering humanity not directly before their eyes; but, the business done, the mass resolves itself into the individuals, and the stern, cold, wisdom melts beneath the rays of sympathy like ice before a warm sun. One poor hunted fugitive appeals to the man, and upsets all the philosophy of the senator; and Mr. Bird turns away to wipe his eyes like an ordinary mortal. Like many others, he has the weakness to think himself firmer than he is, and to feel ashamed when he turns out better than he deemed himself to be. No doubt America has thousands of such sons. And little, insignificant, rosy Mrs. Bird, what a happy picture she is of the beings who make many a home happy. Not handsome, or even pretty, but lovely in the attractiveness of simple goodness. Not clever, nor learned, but acting on impulses more correct than mere intellectual conclusions can be. That meek woman, her whole strength in her absolute powerlessness, confronting the dictates of worldly wisdom and timid prudence, and beating them down with a touch of pure, homely, natural feeling, is enough to acquit a book of injustice to the race which owns her as a daughter. And what a commentary upon the hearts of good men, who make bad laws, is the description of Mr. Bird quitting his comfortable home for a toilsome night drive, so that the slave and her son may be placed in safety under, the care of Van Tromp.

Sturdy, gallant, chivalrous old Van Tromp! What will the reviewer, who would have us think Mrs. Stowe appreciates none but "niggers," say to him? The rough old man, who, without much knowledge, or refinement, or conventional delicacy, fished out of his rude, honest heart, the truth which lay there imbedded like a bright gem in a dark mine, that slavery is an accursed thing. That resolution once come to the strong, energetic, sincere man, not caring what his neighbors said or thought, made up his mind at once to wash his hands of it and, leading his slaves to freedom, retired to his log hut. What a graphic scene it is where Mr. Bird brings Eliza and her child to his door, and asks if, he is the man to protect a fugitive. We almost think we see the stalwart old man, stretching up his tall form in the low doorway, and answering as though he thought such a question ought not to be asked of him. The reader glows as the old Abolitionist says--"Here am I, six-foot-two, and here are my seven sons--each over six feet--and them as wants her will find us at home!" Peaceful as a man may be, he feels as though he would wish, if he were Van Tromp, that the slave-hunters would come and struggle for their prey; and, for once, the most intellectual sympathizes with force--mere physical force--, which seems to borrow a character of sacredness from the fact of its being enlisted upon the side of mercy and right. The character of Van Tromp is an eloquent truthful assertion of the inherent goodness which will spring up in the roughest natures, and amid the most unfavorable circumstances.

What shall we say of the Quakers--the quiet, peaceful men, ready to sacrifice themselves in the cause of justice--are they bad? Their characters are admirably drawn. They are the natural contrasts to the Van Tromps, but equally admirable. The old converted slaveholder, with "the ancient Adam" strong within him, and full of the instincts of force, recurs to open resistance naturally. The Quakers, with their passions subdued, and the consciousness of feebleness, seek safety in concealment and flight. Yet loving the right quite as much as more combative men, they are ready to brave persecution, and face danger to ensure its triumph. How our hearts open to the demure matron who tends the fugitives, and the pretty young wife who runs in with the warm socks for the slave child, and runs out to her own husband and baby. The back-woodsman who has married a Quakeress, and said to her in scriptural language--"Thy path shall be my path, and thy God my God," how deftly he is brought before us; his old habits peeping out of his prim garb, and his sharp eye gleaming from beneath the broad brim, from the moment he overhears the plans of the slavehunters, to the time when his two-handed nature rushing out, he pushes the foremost of the pursuers down the precipice.

What a graphic portraiture is St. Clair. How like many of those we meet with. A man of great capacity but of weak energy--one who might do great things if he could but rouse his soul from the physical torpor which hangs about it--a powerful thinking machine, without the strength to turn thoughts into facts--a human atom among the crowd who float down with the strong current which they have not the courage to breast. Like others of his class, he invests the familiar with the aspect of the inevitable, and submits to a necessity from which his heart recoils. Bred among slavery he tolerates rather than defends it, and endures it rather than tolerates it: but he loathes the attempt to reconcile it to right, to make it appear compatible with womanly tenderness, or to bestow upon it the sanction of that religion which makes tyranny a sin, and invites equally the bond and the free to share in its consolations. But though he suffers slavery; and takes his share in it, as a portion of the must be, he divests it of its terrors, and almost makes his slaves his masters.

One example more,--Miss Ophelia, the downright rigid, scrupulous, punctilious Yankee lady, as upright and unbending in mind as in body. The Christian upon principle, whose strong feelings lying deep under the surface, are not to be lightly touched nor quickly called into action. She is a fit descendant of those puritan mothers, who, flying with their husbands from religious persecution, preferred free consciences and the dangers of the savage and the wilderness, to a fettered faith gilded by the comforts of a more civilized home. She despises the system of slavery for its "shiftlessness," almost as much as she abhors it for its sinfulness, and scouts expediency when it runs counter to right. If St. Clair could have been imbued with her masculine spirit of stern determination, he would have been an agitator instead of a theorist, yet, however, she, a type of her race, shows her weak side in that loathing of the black skin, which would make English ladies, the denizens of a free country, the wives of free husbands, and the mothers of free children, shrink from the touch of a black.

We must have done with this class of examples, or, with the loquaciousness of a commentary, this gossip will run into a book as large as that which forms its subject. We cannot, however, help pointing to the angelic Eva, as a being almost too pure and bright to have lived, yet those who have read Dickens' pictures of Nelly and Paul Dombey, and perchance those too, who have watched the lives of children doomed to early decay, will acquit the portrait of exaggeration. We hope that enough has been said to show that Mrs. Stowe fully recognizes the fact, that warm hearts beat high below the palest skins.

It is true that some of the white men are pictured as fiends. The calculating slave-merchant Haley, who has his own notions of mercy, and practises it because it pays. Loker, the slave-hunter, who does the rough work, and Marks, his fellow, who backs force by fraud. Legree, the brutal planter, who buys slaves as the raw material to be used up in his cotton fields, and has made his fist as hard as iron, by knocking down "niggers." Granted that they could not well be made darker than they are, we ask, whether they appear worse than such a system as that of slavery is calculated to make men. A few high and pure natures may escape its contamination, and rise above its degradation, but in many minds the germs of kindness will be trodden down--in many breasts the springs of mercy will be dried up; it cannot be otherwise. Take any child, your own, reader, if you be a father, let him be a rosy-cheeked golden-haired boy, with eyes all love and merriment. Teach him to be cruel--not to delight in torment as a pastime, that is wantonness,--but to regard it with the deeper feeling that it is a serious lawful business. Think you that the result will be something assimilating to the angel or the monster? You cannot help knowing which--that the end must be evil--and if it be inevitable to the young soul running over with affection, what will happen to the ruined profligate, the impoverished debauchee, the men with lost characters, who take to slave-hunting as a business, for which, like that of the executioner, anybody is good enough. Such men must have the morality and the tenderness of humanity rooted up, before they could become what they are, and every day hardens their souls, as it did Legree's fist.

Unfortunately; however, we may leave the region of speculation for the world of facts, to show that Mrs. Stowe has not exaggerated the cruelties practiced upon slaves. The lives which this book contains, are authentic records, convincing us, beyond the possibility of doubt, that Mrs. Stowe has been more than impartial; merciful in her description of the horrors of bondage. Her vivid words have told us all the misery without charging all the crime. Over a multitude of sins she has thrown the mantle of charity.

We must examine the allegation that Mrs. Stowe takes. Uncle Tom with his endurance, patience, forgiveness, and heroism, as a type of the slave. The answer to it is, that the averment is untrue. Uncle Tom is an exceptional character. In the whole book there is not one which even approaches him. He is not a sample of what slaves are, or slavery would be an elevating institution, but an example of what the negro may approach to, when the best qualities of his nature are developed. Old Aunt Chloe--Uncle Tom's wife--is not resigned, but grumbles and curses her fate, and those who made it. Sam and Andy, who plague Haley, are specimens of that love of fun inherent in the black, and never to be suppressed, and of the lax morality which slavery is almost certain to induce. George, the mulatto, is not patient, but is patient to turn upon his pursuers with the fury of a tiger. Eliza is not submissive, when ruffians would tear asunder the dearest ties of blood and love. Dinah, St. Clair's cook, is a pattern of carelessness and willfulness. Topsy is the incarnation of heathenish mischief. The Creole servants are proud, lazy, and vain. The old black woman who serves the baker is a specimen of the deepest degradation to which wrong, vice, and gin, can lower humanity; and Legree's black slave-drivers are sneaking scoundrels, at once ferocious and cowardly. Mrs. Stowe, draws the blacks as they are, as slavery has made them, with one bright example to show what they were capable of becoming, but that course was prompted both by a regard for truth and by shrewd policy: for the worse the slaves are and the better they might be, the worse the condemnation against the system which forms them, and is answerable for what of evil exists under it.

The character of Uncle Tom himself, requires closer analysis. We do not know whether or not the portrait is professedly drawn from life, but it is so like what a

Christian ought to be, rather than what Christians are, that it may be taken for a possible rather than actual existence. If such a man as Uncle Tom ever did exist, we should be rather inclined to look for his advent among the degraded slaves than the happier free men. It is quite consistent to expect to find the greatest extremes in closest contact, and given an original nature capable of a near approach to goodness, once in a course of years, an Uncle Tom miglit be looked for among those whose daily life is suffering, and to whom endurance has become a habit of mind. It is there only that that passive humility and meek patience would spring up which could hardly take root in the mind of a free man smarting under a sense of injury.

We must remember too, that Mrs. Stowe expresses an opinion that the African race is peculiarly fitted to develop the affections and the softer feelings of our nature, and to exemplify Christianity in its most benignant aspect. In this opinion we concur. The blacks may have less intellect as a body, though the mixed race has produced men fitted to stand on the loftiest white platforms, but they are assuredly fuller of tenderness. If that were not so, they would have risen against their oppressors long before this. It would have been impossible to have kept any other race so long in such utter subjection, and to have perpetrated upon them so many atrocities without arousing the fiercest animosity. We cannot point to any group of men on the Continent of Europe, nay, nor in the East, nor at the Antipodes, who would have endured what the Africans have borne, without stretching forth the red Band, of vengeance. One of the pillars of negro slavery, is the mildness, gentleness, forbearance, and humor of the negro character, and in this sense Uncle Tom is a type of his brothers, who will not, except in isolated cases, take their liberty, or run or fight for it, but wait till it is given them, with Quaker-like patience, and more than Quaker-like resignation of endurance.

It may be startling, perhaps, to the Anglo-Saxon, or Celt, to be told that they are not fitted to become Christians in so high a sense of the word, as the black man whom they despise. Yet it is true. What are the highest attributes of Christianity, not the qualities which make men great, but those which make them good. Not the quick wit or the fertile invention--not the strong nerve or the ready hand--not prowess or physical courage, but charity, resignation, endurance, and faith. Can any white man point out any race which, through a long course of years, has evinced the possession of those latter qualities in so high a degree as the blacks.

It may be a fanciful theory, but one quite in keeping with the facts of the world, that each of the great races is peculiarly fitted to develop some special phase of our nature. We would example the race known as the Anglo-Saxon, as the industrial and practical; the Celtic as the ambitious, impulsive, and enthusiastic; the German as the abstract; the Sclavonic as the obedient, and the Orientals as the fatalistic. It may be that the Negro is characterised by sensibility, and that when industry, enthusiasm, obedience, and submission to destiny have failed, the great principle of love will work out the mission of Christianity.

On the whole, we should say, that Mrs. Stowe, where she has exaggerated, has but followed, and not exceeded the ordinary license of authors, and that altogether she has rather moderated than heightened the horrors of slavery. She is partial, it is true. How could she be otherwise than partial. She hates fervently what she denounces eloquently, but with a woman's delicacy, she shrinks from doing more than hinting at the worst feature of the horrid traffic in human life. . . . Female purity will not allow her to overstep one boundary behind which lies the darkest portion of the truth. We allude to the New Orleans market, to supply which, the most beautiful of the slave girls are bought, and sacrificed to purposes more easily imagined than described. Mrs. Stowe could not, partizan as she may be, venture on such a narrative. She would be more or less than woman, who could. It is difficult to touch pitch and not be defiled. She might look with a sad eye at the lace-rated back. She might view with bleeding heart the nearest relations torn from each other, but women sold to infamy was too demoralizing for pure woman's thoughts. Let any one notice how shudderingly any decent woman will recoil from our civilized open profligacy, as though from corruption, no matter how lightly and delicately it may be touched on, and then conceive how she would be repulsed from the idea of women not abandoning themselves to wrong, not led into evil, not betrayed to sin, but sold to pollution like sheep to the butcher. Sold, beyond help or hope from God or man, except through the dark avenue of death. Slavery has a blacker page than any Mrs. Stowe has painted.

Worse still. There are whispered hints which even we men cannot venture openly to translate to the world--scarcely to our own souls--rumours which sear the heart. The planters are notoriously profligate. Beside their own lawful children, infants of a darker hue run about. Often, indeed, in the majority of cases, the swart and the fair are brothers and sisters--the children of the same father. These Creole girls grow up in great beauty, not recognized by their white parent who may be as profligate as he will, but may not have natural affection for his offspring. Of their occasional fate it is impossible to speak out. Such deeds are perpetrated as we find among mythological legends, and glance at in the darkest family histories. Let any one remember the Cenci of Shelley, and our meaning will be plain. We fear these tales are too true, and if so, the system which so corrupts and demoralizes all that is good in the heart, and turns the well-spring of natural love into a putrid stagnant pool of lust, must be accursed beyond all the evils which have been permitted to exist upon earth.

Had Mrs. Stowe spoken more warmly than she has done, who could have blamed her? What being with a human heart and feeling, not blunted by familiarity with crime, could stand silently by, while sins against all laws, worth acknowledging, disgrace the earth and pollute the air. Diplomatists may blind themselves to right by their craft, and statesmen overlay their hearts with ambition, but right-minded men will say that before the enormity of the wrong all consideration of policy or expediency should vanish, that at the risk not only of dismembering the Union, but at any risk, the American people should vindicate their fame, and that, failing their doing so, the tribes of all the earth should rise to purge the world of what is repugnant to humanity. But, alas! the world is not yet a moral world. It has other laws than those of the New Testament--other codes than that of morality. Virtue is not yet enthroned. A mingled monster, compounded of men's interests, passions, and feelings, sways the sceptre. Of this Mrs. Stowe is as well aware as we are, and she evidently looks not to one influence but to many; not to religious truth alone, but to that in some, to right feeling aroused in others, to a sense of the shiftlessness and unprofitableness of slavery in another portion, and to the ears of its danger to rid us of its horrors. Added to this, there must be a means more or less safe of providing for the enfranchised black population, such as Liberia, for after they are set free, we must not expect the prejudices on the score of color, which prevail in the free as well as the slave States strongly enough to delay emancipation, to allow of the negros mingling in anything like equal terms with the whites. Mrs. Stowe has done her part toward the good work, and the true-hearted will pray that the spark she has kindled, may burst into a flame, which shall wither up the bonds of serfdom.

In conclusion we would say, let us be just to our American cousins. We are accustomed to glorify ourselves that we have abolished slavery. We must recollect, however, that the difference between our former position and that of America is very great. If we, instead of being called on to sacrifice twenty millions, had to set free some millions of slaves at our own hearths, to live among us--if instead of feeling slavery dimly in a distant colony, it had pressed upon us a familiar institution to which we were used, it is difficult to say, what we should have done. If we had proclaimed negro freedom then, we should have done something more difficult than England, great as she is, has ever had the courage to attempt, or the energy to accomplish.

APPENDIX.
REPORT OF THE SPEECH
OF
FREDERICK DOUGLASS,
THE AMERICAN SLAVE,
Delivered at a Public Meeting held at Finsbury Chapel, Moorfields, Joseph Sturge, Esq., in the chair.

F. DOUGLASS rose amid loud cheers, and said--I feel exceedingly glad of the opportunity now afforded me of presenting the claims of my brethren in bonds in the United States to so many in London, and from various parts of Britain, who have assembled here on the present occasion. I have nothing to commend me to your consideration in the way of learning, nothing in the way of education, to entitle me to your attention; and you are aware that slavery is a very bad school for rearing teachers of morality and religion. Twenty-one years of my life have been spent in slavery, personal slavery, surrounded by degrading influences such as can exist nowhere beyond the pale of slavery; and it will not be strange, if under such circumstances, I should betray in what I have to say to you a deficiency of that refinement which is seldom or never found, except among persons that have experienced superior advantages to those which I have enjoyed. (Hear, hear.). But I will take it for granted that you know something about the degrading influences of slavery, and that you will not expect great things from me this evening, but simply such facts as I may be able to advance immediately in connection with my own experience of slavery.

The subject of American slavery is beginning to attract the attention of philanthropists of all countries,--it is a matter to which philosophers, statesmen, and theologians, in all parts of the world, are turning their attention. It is a matter in which the people of this country especially, and of Scotland and Ireland, are taking the deepest interest,--it is a matter in which all persons, who speak the English language, must eventually become interested. It is no longer an unintelligible or obscure question, although there is much yet to be learned. In order to the proper understanding of the subject before us, allow me briefly to state the nature of the American Government, and the geographical location of slavery in the United States. There are at this time twenty-eight States, called the United States, each of which has a constitution of its own, under which constitution is convened, from year to year, what is called a local legislature--a legislature that has the power of making the local laws for that state. Each state is considered (within the limits of the constitution) sovereign in itself, but over all the states there is a general government, under a federal constitution, which constitutes these twenty-eight states, the United States. The general government in the Congress, under the constitution, has no right to interfere with the domestic arrangements of the individual states. The general government has the power of levying taxes, providing for the general welfare, regulating commerce, declaring war, and concluding peace. There are what are called free states and slave states; the latter are fifteen in number, the former thirteen. The free states are divided from the slave states by what is called Mason and Dixon's line, running east and west. All the states south of the line are slave states. Notwithstanding the general government has nothing to do with the domestic and the local civil institutions of the individual state, it becomes my duty to show that the general government does after all give support to the institution of slavery as it exists in the slave states. An attempt has been made in this country to establish the conviction that the free states of the Union have nothing whatever to do with the maintenance and perpetuity of slavery in the southern states, and many persons coming from the United States have represented themselves as coming from the free states, and have shirked all responsibility in regard to slavery on this ground. Now, I am here to maintain that slavery is not only a matter belonging to the states south of the line, but is an American institution--a United States institution--a system that derives its support as well from the non-slave-holding states, as they are called, as from the slave-holding states. The slave-holding states, to be sure, enjoy all the profits of slavery--the institution exists upon their soil; but if I were going to give the exact position of the northern and southern states it would be simply this--the slave states are the slave-holding states, while the non-slave states are the slavery-upholding states. The physical power necessary to keep the slaves in bondage lies north of the line. The southern states admit their inability to hold their slaves, except through protection afforded by the northern states. The constitution makes it the duty of the northern states to return the slave if he attempts to escape, to call out the army and navy to crush the slave into subjection, if he dare make an attempt to gain his freedom. The east and the west, the north and the south, the people of Massachusetts and the people of South Carolina have, through their representatives, each in their own official capacity, sworn before high Heaven, that the slave shall be a slave or die. So that while the free states of the American Union consent to what they call the compromise of the constitution of the United States, they are responsible for the existence of slavery in the southern states. (Loud cheers.) There are three millions of slaves, and I believe the largest estimate that has ever been made of the slave-holders does not exceed three hundred thousand. How do you suppose three hundred thousand men are capable of holding three millions of men in slavery? It cannot be. The slaves could by their own power crush their masters if they would, and take their freedom, or they could run away and defy their masters to bring them back. Why do they not do it? It is because the people of the United States are all pledged, bound by their oaths, bound by their citizenship in that country, to bring their whole physical power to bear against the slave if such an event should arise. (Cries of "Shame!") The slave has no hopes from the northern states, for they are in connexion with the slave states of America. Every defender of the American Union, of the compromise of the United States, no matter how much he may boast of his anti-slavery feeling, is, so far as his citizenship goes, a pledged enemy to the emancipation of the bondsman. I have thought it necessary to say thus much that you might see where slavery exists, and how it exists in the United States. The slave-holders admit that they are incapable of retaining their slaves. "Why," said one man, "we are surrounded by savages; if they could entertain the idea that immediate death would not be their portion, they would re-enact the St. Domingo tragedy." (Hear, hear.) The same gentleman goes on to advocate the existence of the slave-holding union between the states, and the utility of the union on the ground that, should it be dissolved, the slave would cross Mason and Dixon's line, and turn round and curse his master from the other side.

Now what is this system of slavery? This is the subject of my lecture this evening--what is the character of this institution? I am about to answer the inquiry, what is American slavery? I do this the more readily, since I have found persons in this country who have identified the term slavery with that which I think it is not, and in some instances, I have feared, in so doing have rather (unwittingly, I know) detracted much from the horror with which the term slavery is contemplated. It is common in this country to distinguish every bad thing by the name slavery. Intemperance is slavery (cheers); to be deprived of the right to vote is slavery, says one; to have to work hard is slavery, says another (laughter, and loud cheers); and I do not know but that if we should let them go on, they would say to eat when we are hungry, to walk when we desire to have exercise, or to minister to our necessities, or have necessities at all, is slavery. (Laughter.) I do not wish for a moment to detract from the horror with which the evil of intemperance is contemplated; not at all; nor do I wish to throw the slightest obstruction in the way of any political freedom that any class of persons in this country may desire to obtain. But I am here to say, that I think the term slavery is sometimes abused by identifying it with that which it is not. Slavery in the United States is the granting of that power by which one man exercises and enforces a right of property in the body and soul of another. The condition of a slave is simply that of the brute beast. He is a piece of property--a marketable commodity in the language of the law, to be bought or sold at the will and caprice of the master who claims him to be his property; he is spoken of, thought of, and treated as property. His own good, his conscience, his intellect, his affections, are all set aside by the master. The will and the wishes of the master are the law of the slave. He is as much a piece of property as a horse. If he is fed, he is fed because he is property. If he is clothed, it is with a view to the increase of his value as property. Whatever of comfort is necessary to him for his body or soul, that is inconsistent with his being property, is carefully wrested from him, not only by public opinion, but by the law of the country. He is carefully deprived of everything that tends in the slightest degree to detract from his value as property. He is deprived of education. God has given him an intellect--the slave-holder declares that it shall not be cultivated. If his moral perception leads him in a course contrary to his value as property, the slave-holder declares he shall not pursue it. The marriage institution cannot exist among slaves, and one sixth of the population of democratic America is denied its privileges by the law of the land. What is to be thought of a nation boasting of its liberty, boasting of its humanity, boasting of its Christianity, boasting of its love of justice and purity, and yet having within its own borders three millions of persons denied by law the right of marriage?--what must be the condition of that people? I need not lift up the veil by giving you any experience of my own. Every one that can put two ideas together, must see the most fearful results from such a state of things, as I have just mentioned. If any of these three millions find for themselves companions, and prove themselves honest, upright, virtuous persons to each other, yet in these cases--few as I am bound to confess they are--the virtuous live in constant apprehension of being torn asunder by the merciless men-stealers that claim them as their property. (Hear.) This is American slavery--no marriage--no education--the light of the Gospel shut out from the dark mind of the bondman--and he forbidden by law to learn to read. If a mother shall teach her children to read, the law in Louisiana proclaims that she may be hanged by the neck. (Sensation.) If the father attempt to give his son a knowledge of letters, he may be punished by the whip in one instance, and in another be killed, at the discretion of the court. Three millions of people shut out from the light of knowledge! It is easy for you to conceive the evil that must result from such a state of things. (Hear, hear.)

I now come to the physical evils of slavery. I do not wish to dwell at length upon these, but it seems right to speak of them, not so much to influence your minds on this question, as to let the slave-holders of America know that the curtain which conceals their crimes is being lifted abroad (loud cheers); that we are opening the dark cell, and leading the people into the dark recesses of what they are pleased to call their domestic institution. (Cheers.) We want them to know that a knowledge of their whippings, their scourgings, their brandings, their chainings, is not confined to their plantations, but that some negro of theirs has broken loose from his chains (loud applause)--has burst through the dark incrustation of slavery, and is now exposing their deeds of deep damnation to the gaze of the Christian people of England. (Immense cheers.)

The slave-holders resort to all kinds of cruelty. If I were disposed, I have matter enough to interest you on this question for five or six evenings, but I will not dwell at length upon these cruelties. Suffice it to say, that all the peculiar modes of torture that were resorted to in the West India Islands, are resorted to, I believe, even more frequently, in the United States of America. Starvation, the bloody whip, the chain, the gag, the thumb-screw, cat-hauling, the cat-o'-nine-tails, the dungeon, the blood-hound, are all in requisition to keep the slave in his condition as a slave in the United States. (Hear.) If any one has a doubt upon this point, I would ask him to read the chapter on slavery in Dickens' Notes on America. If any man has a doubt upon it, I have here the "testimony of a thousand witnesses," which I can give at any length, all going to prove the truth of my statement. The blood-hound is regularly trained in the United States, and advertisements are to be found in the southern papers of the Union, from persons advertising themselves as bloodhound trainers, and offering to hunt down slaves at fifteen dollars a-piece, recommending their hounds as the fleetest in the neighborhood, never known to fail. (Much sensation.) Advertisements are from time to time inserted, stating that slaves have escaped with iron collars, about their necks, with bands of iron about their feet, marked with the lash, branded with red hot irons, the initials of their master's name burned into their flesh; and the masters advertise the fact of their being thus branded with their own signature, thereby proving to the world, that however daring it may appear to non-slave-holders, such practices are not regarded discreditable or daring among the slave-holders themselves. Why, I believe if a man should brand his horse in this country,--burn the initials of his name into any of his cattle, and publish the ferocious deed here,--that the united execrations of Christians in Britian would descend upon him. (Cheers.) Yet, in the United States, human beings are thus branded. As Whittier says--

> "Our countrymen in chains,
> The whip on woman's shrinking flesh,
> Our soil yet reddening with the stains,
> Caught from her scourgings warm and fresh."

(Loud cheers.) The slave-dealer boldly publishes his infamous acts to the world. Of all things that have been said of slavery to which exception has been taken by slave-holders, this, the charge of cruelty, stands foremost, and yet there is no charge capable of clearer demonstration, than that of the most barbarous inhumanity on the part of the slave-holders towards their slaves. And all this is necessary--it is necessary to resort to these cruelties, in order to make the slave a slave, and to keep him a slave. Why, my experience all goes to prove the truth of what you will call a marvelous proposition, that the better you treat a slave, the more you destroy his value as a slave, and enhance the probability of his eluding the grasp of the slave-holder; the more kindly you treat him, the more wretched you make him, while you keep him in the condition of a slave. My experience, I say, confirms the truth of this proposition. When I was treated exceedingly ill, when my back was being scourged daily, when I was kept within an inch of my life, life was all I cared for. "Spare my life," was my continual prayer. When I was looking for the blow about to be inflicted upon my head, I was not thinking of my liberty; it was my life. But, as soon as the blow was not to be feared, then came the longing for liberty. (Cheers.) If a slave has a bad master, his ambition is to get a better; when he gets a better, he aspires to have the best; and when he gets the best, he aspires to be his own master. (Loud cheers.) But the slave must be brutalized to keep him as a slave. The slave-holder feels this necessity. I admit this necessity. If it be right to hold slaves at all, it is right to hold them in the only way in which they can be held; and this can be done only by shutting out the light of education from their minds and brutalizing their persons. The whip, the chain, the gag, the thumb-screw, the bloodhound, the stocks, and all the other bloody paraphernalia of the slave-system, are indispensably necessary to the relation of master and slave. (Cheers.) The slave must be subjected to these, or he ceases to be a slave. Let him know that the whip is burned, that the fetters have been turned to some useful and profitable employment, that the chain is no longer for his limbs, that the bloodhound is no longer to be put upon his track, that his master's authority over him is no longer to be enforced by taking his life, and immediately he walks out from the house of bondage and asserts his freedom as a man. (Loud cheers.) The slave-holder finds it necessary to have these implements to keep the slave in bondage; finds it necessary to be able to say,--"Unless you do so and so; unless you do as I bid you, I will take away your life!" (Hear, hear.) Some of the most awful scenes of cruelty are constantly taking place in the middle states of the Union. We have in those states what are called the slave-breeding states. Allow me to speak plainly. (Hear, hear.) Although it is harrowing to your feelings, it is necessary that the facts of the case should be stated. We have in the United States, slave-breeding states. The very state from which the Minister from our Court to yours comes is one of these states (cries of "Hear.")--Maryland, where men, women, and children are reared for the market just as horses, sheep, and swine are raised for the market. Slave-rearing is there looked upon as a legitimate trade, the law sanctions it, public opinion upholds it, the church does not condemn it. (Cries of "Shame!") It goes on in all its bloody horrors, sustained by the auctioneer's block. If you would see the cruelties of this system, hear the following narrative:--Not long since the following scene occurred.--A slave woman and a slave man had united themselves as man and wife in the absence of any law to protect them as man and wife. They had lived together by the permission, not by right, of their master, and they had reared a family. The master found it expedient, and for his interest to sell them. He did not ask them their wishes in regard to the matter at all; they were not consulted. The man and woman were brought to the auctioneer's block, under the sound of the hammer. The cry was raised, "Here goes; who bids cash?" Think of it, a man and wife to be sold. (Hear, hear.) The woman was placed on the auctioneer's block; her limbs, as is customary, were brutally exposed to the purchasers, who examined her with all the freedom with which they would examine a horse. There stood the husband powerless; no right to his wife; the master's right pre-eminent. She was sold. He was next brought to the auctioneer's block. His eyes followed his wife in the distance; and he looked beseechingly, imploringly to the man that had bought his wife, to buy him also. But he was at length bid off to another person. He was about to be separated from her he loved forever. No word of his, no work of his, could save him from this separation. He asked permission of his new master to go and take the hand of his wife at parting. It was denied him. In the agony of his soul he rushed from the man who had just bought him, that he might take a farewell of his wife; but his way was obstructed, he was struck over the head with a loaded whip, and was held for a moment; but his agony was too great. When he was let go, he fell a corpse at the feet of his master. (Much sensation.) His heart was broken. Such scenes are the every-day fruits of American slavery. Some two years since, the

Hon. Seth M. Yates, an anti-slavery gentleman of the State of New York, a representative in the Congress of the United States, told me he saw with his own eyes the following circumstance. In the national district of Columbia, over which the star-spangled emblem is constantly waving, where orators are ever holding forth on the subject of American liberty, American democracy, American republicanism, there are two slave prisons. When going across a bridge leading to one of these prisons, he saw a young woman run out, bare-footed and bare-headed, and with very little clothing on. She was running with all speed to the bridge he was approaching. His eye was fixed upon her, and he stopped to see what was the matter. He had not paused long before he saw three men run out after her. He now knew what the nature of the case was, a slave escaping from her chains, a young woman, a sister, escaping from the bondage in which she had been held. She made her way to the bridge, but had not reached it, ere from the Virginia side there came two slaveholders. As soon as they saw them, her pursuers called out, "Stop her." True to their Virginian instincts, they came to the rescue of their brother kidnappers--across the bridge. The poor girl now saw that there was no chance for her. It was a trying time. She knew if she went back, she must be a slave for ever, she must be dragged down to the scenes of pollution which the slaveholders continually provide for most of the poor, sinking, wretched young women, whom they call their property. She formed her resolution; and just as those who were about to take her, were going to put hands upon her, to drag her back, she leaped over the balustrades of the bridge, and down she went to rise no more. (Great sensation.) She chose death, rather than to go back into the hands of those Christian slaveholders from whom she had escaped. (Hear, hear.) Can it be possible that such things as these exist in the United States? Are not these the exceptions? Are any such scenes as this general? Are not such deeds condemned by the law and denounced by public opinion? (Cheers.) Let me read to you a few of the laws of the slaveholding states of America. I think no better exposure of slavery can be made than is made by the laws of the states in which slavery exists. I prefer reading the laws to making any statement in confirmation of what I have said myself; for the slaveholders cannot object to this testimony, since it is the calm, the cool, the deliberate enactment of their wisest heads, of their most clear-sighted, their own constituted representatives. (Hear, hear.) "If more than seven slaves together are found in any road without a white person, twenty lashes a piece; for visiting a plantation without a written pass, ten lashes: for letting loose a boat from where it is made fast, thirty-nine lashes for the first offence; and for the second, shall have cut off from his head one ear. For keeping or carrying a club, thirty-nine lashes. For having any article for sale, without a ticket from his master, ten lashes.

A Voice.--What is the name of the book?

Mr. Douglass.--I read from "American Slavery as it is: Testimony of a Thousand Witnesses." These are extracted from the Slave Laws. This publication has been before the public of the United States for the last seven years, and not a single fact or statement recorded therein has ever been called in question by a single slaveholder. (Loud cheers.) I read, therefore, with confidence. We have the testimony of the slaveholders themselves. "For travelling in any other than the most usual and accustomed road, when going alone to any place, forty lashes. For travelling in the night without a pass, forty lashes." I am afraid you do not understand the awful character of these lashes. You must bring it before your mind. A human being in a perfect state of nudity, tied hand and foot to a stake, and a strong man standing behind with a heavy whip, knotted at the end, each blow cutting into the flesh, and leaving the warm blood dripping to the feet (sensation); and for these trifles. "For being found in another person's negro-quarters, forty lashes; for hunting with dogs in the woods, thirty lashes; for being on horseback without the written permission of his master, twenty-five lashes; for riding or going abroad in the night, or riding horses in the day time without leave, a slave may be whipped, cropped, or branded in the check with the letter R, or otherwise punished, such punishment not extending to life, or so as to render him unfit for labor." The laws referred to may be found by consulting "Brevard's Digest"; "Haywood's Manual"; "Virginia Revised Code"; "Prince's Digest"; "Missouri Laws"; "Mississippi Revised Code"--

A Person in the Gallery.--Will you allow me to ask a question?

The Chairman.--I must beg that there may be no interruptions.

Mr. Douglass.--It is my custom to answer questions when they are put to me.

The Person in the Gallery.--What is the value of a good slave? (Hissing.)

Mr. Douglass.--Slaves vary in price in different parts of the United States. In the middle States, where they grow them for the market, they are much cheaper than in the far-south. The slave trader who purchases a slave in Maryland for seven hundred dollars, about one hundred and sixty pounds of your money, will sell him in Louisiana for one thousand dollars, or two hundred pounds. There is a great speculation in this matter, and here let me state, that when the price of cotton is high, so is that of the slave. I will give you an invariable rule by which to ascertain the price of human flesh in the United States. When cotton rises in the market in England, the price of human flesh rises in the United States. (Hear, hear.) How much responsibility attaches to you in the use of that commodity. (Loud cheers.) To return to my point. A man for going to visit his brethren, without the permission of his master, and in many instances he may not have that permission, his master from caprice or other reasons, may not be willing to allow it, may be caught on his way, dragged to a post, the branding iron heated, and the name of his master, or the letter

R, branded into his cheek or on his forehead. (Sensation.) They treat slaves thus on the principle that they must punish for light offences in order to prevent the commission of larger ones. I wish you to mark that in the single State of Virginia there are seventy-one crimes for which a colored-man may be executed; while there are only three of these crimes, which when committed by a white man will subject him to that punishment. (Hear, hear.) There are many of these crimes which if the white man did not commit, he would be regarded as a scoundrel and a coward. In South Maryland, there is a law to this effect:--that if a slave should strike his master, he may be hanged, his head severed from his body, his body quartered, and his head and quarters set up in the most prominent place in the neighborhood. (Sensation.) If a colored woman, in the defense of her own virtue--in defense of her own person-- should shield herself from the brutal attacks of her tyrannical master, or make the slightest resistance, she may be killed on the spot. (Loud cries of "Shame!") No law whatever will bring the guilty man to justice for the crime. But you will ask me, can these things be possible in a land professing Christianity? Yes, they are so; and this is not the worst. No, a darker feature is yet to be presented than the mere existence of these facts. I have to inform you that the religion of the Southern States, at this time, is the great supporter, the great sanctioner of the bloody atrocities to which I have referred. (Deep sensation.) While America is printing Tracts and Bibles; sending Missionaries abroad to convert the Heathen; expending her money in various ways for the promotion of the Gospel in foreign lands, the slave not only lies forgotten--uncared for, but is trampled underfoot by the very churches of the land. What have we in America? Why we have slavery made part of the religion of the land. Yes, the pulpit there stands up as the great defender of this cursed institution, as it is called. Ministers of religion come forward, and torture the hallowed pages of inspired wisdom to sanction the bloody deed. (Loud cries of "Shame!") They stand forth as the foremost, the strongest defenders of this "institution." As a proof of this, I need not do more than state the general fact, that slavery has existed, under the droppings of the sanctuary of the South, for the last two hundred years, and there has not been any war between the religion and slavery of the South. Whips, chains, gags, and thumb-screws have all lain under the droppings of the sanctuary, and instead of rusting from off the limbs of the bondman, those droppings have served to preserve them in all their strength. Instead of preaching the Gospel against this tyranny and rebuking the wrong, ministers of religion have sought, by all and every means, to throw in the background whatever in the Bible could be construed into opposition to slavery, and to bring forward that which they could torture into its support. (Cries of "Shame!") This I conceive to be the darkest feature of slavery, and the most difficult to attack, because it is identified with religion, and exposes those who denounce it to the charge of infidelity. Yes, those with whom I have been labouring, namely, the old organization Anti-Slavery Society of America, have been again and again stigmatized as infidels, and for what reason? Why, solely in consequence of the faithfulness of their attacks upon the slave-holding religion of the Southern States, and the northern religion that sympathizes with it. (Hear, hear.)

I have found it difficult to speak on this matter without persons coming forward and saying,

"Douglass, are you not afraid of injuring the cause of Christ? You do not desire to do so we know; but are you not undermining religion?" This has been said to me again and again, even since I came to this country, but I cannot be induced to leave off these exposures. (Loud cheers.) I love the religion of our blessed Saviour, I love that religion that comes from above, in the "wisdom of God, which is first pure, then peaceable, gentle, and easy to be entreated, full of mercy and good fruits, without partiality and without hypocrisy." I love that religion that sends its votaries to bind up the wounds of him that has fallen among thieves. I love that religion that makes it the duty of its disciples to visit the fatherless and widow in their affliction. I love that religion that is based upon the glorious principle, of love to God and love to man (cheers); which makes its followers do unto others as they themselves would be done by. If you demand liberty to yourself, it says, grant it to your neighbors. If you claim a right to think for yourselves, it says, allow your neighbors the some right. It is because I love this religion that I hate the slave-holding, woman-whipping, the mind-darkening, the soul-destroying religion that exists in the Southern States of America. (Immense cheering.) It is because I regard the one as good, and pure, and holy, that I cannot but regard the other as bad, corrupt, and wicked. Loving the one I must hate the other, holding to the one I must reject the other, and I, therefore, proclaim myself an infidel to the slave-holding religion of America. (Reiterated cheers.) Why, as I said in another place, to a smaller audience the other day, in answer to the question, "Mr. Douglass, are there not Methodist churches, Baptist churches, Congregational churches, Episcopal churches, Roman Catholic churches, Presbyterian churches in the United States, and in the Southern States of America, and do they not have revivals of religion, accessions to their ranks from day to day, and will you tell me that these men are not followers of the meek and lowly Savior?" Most unhesitatingly I do. Revivals in religion, and revivals in the slave-trade, go hand in hand together. (Cheers.) The church and the slave-prison stand next to each other; the groans and cries of the heart-broken slave often drowned in the pious devotions of his religious master. (Hear, hear.) The church-going bell and the auctioneer's bell chime in with each other; the pulpit and the auctioneer's block stand in the same neighborhood; while the blood-stained gold goes to support the pulpit, the pulpit covers the infernal business in the garb of Christianity. We have men sold to build churches, women sold to support missionaries, and babies sold to buy Bibles and communion-services for the churches. (Loud cheers.)

A Voice.--It is not true.

Mr. Douglass--Not true! Is it not? (Immense cheers.) Hear the following advertisement:--"Field Negros, by Thomas Gadsden." I read now from "The

American Churches, the Bulwarks of American Slavery;" by an American, or by J. G. Birney. This has been before the public in this country and the United States for the last six years; not a fact nor a statement in it has been called in question. (Cheers.) The following is taken from the "Charleston Courier" of Feb. 12, 1835:--"Field Negros, by Thomas Gadsden. On Tuesday, the 17th instant, will be sold, at the North of the Exchange, at 10 o'clock, a prime gang of ten negros, accustomed to the culture of cotton and provisions, belonging to the Independent Church, in Christchurch parish." (Loud cheers.) I could read other testimony on this point, but is it necessary? (Cries of "No," and "One more.") Is it required that one more be given? You shall have another. (Loud cheers.) A notice taken from a Savannah paper will show that slaves are often bequeathed to the missionary societies. "Bryan Superior Court. Between John J. Maxwell and others, executors of Ann Pray, complainants, and Mary Sleigh and others, devises and legatees under the will of Ann Pray, defendants, in equity. A bill having been filed for the distribution of the estate of the testatrix, Ann Pray, and it appearing that among other legacies in her will is the following:--viz., a legacy of one-fourth of certain negro slaves to the American Board of Commissioners for domestic (foreign it probably should have been) missions, for the purpose of sending the Gospel to the heathen, and particularly to the Indians of this continent; it is on motion of the solicitors of the complainants ordered, that all persons claiming the said legacy do appear and answer the bill of the complainants within four months from this day. And it is ordered, that this order be published in a public Gazette of the city of Savannah, and in one of the Gazettes of Philadelphia, once a month, for four months. Extract from the Minutes, December 2, 1832." (Cheers.) The bequest I am in duty bound to say, was not accepted by that board. (Cheers.) But let me tell you what would have been accepted by that board. Had those slaves been sold by Ann Pray, and the money bequeathed to that board, the price of their blood would have gone into the treasury, and they would have quoted Chalmers, Cunningham, and Candlish in support of the deed. (Cheers.) Not only are legacies left and slaves sold in this way to build churches, but the right is openly defended by the church. In 1836 the great Methodist Church in America, holding, through ministers, and elders, and members, in their own church 250,000 slaves, said in their general conference in Cincinnati that they had no right, no wish, no intention to interfere with the relation of master and slave as it existed in the slave states of the American Union. What was this but saying to the world, we have no right, no wish, no intention to release the bondman from his chains? The annual conference in the south took the broad round of the right of property in man, asserting it in a resolution, proclaiming it in an address, preaching it in thanksgiving sermons, putting it forth in 4th of July orations, and even quoting Scripture. I could tire your patience by reading, if it were required, extracts from documents, the genuineness of which has never been called in question, showing that the right is asserted by the slaveholder, to property in human beings. (Hear, hear.)

But I must hasten to another point--How are we to get rid of this system? This is the question which mostly concerns the people of this country. There are different ways by which you may operate against slavery. First let me state how it is upheld; it is upheld by public opinion. How is public opinion maintained? Mainly by the press and by the pulpit. How are we to get these committed on the side of freedom? How are we to change our pro-slavery pulpit into an anti-slavery one, our pro-slavery literature to anti-slavery literature, our pro-slavery press into an anti-slavery press? I can only point British abolitionists to the mode they adopted in their own country. Here, happily for you, the pulpit was already on your side to a considerable extent, at least the Dissenting pulpit. (Cheers.) The Wesleyans have retained a sufficiency of the spirit of their founder, John Wesley, to declare with him, that slavery is the sum of all villainies. (Cheers.) You had but to proclaim the sin of slavery in the people's cars, and they rallied around your standard on behalf of emancipation. Not so in our country. They have taken the strongest ground against us; but I am in duty bound to say that in the Northern States they are fast getting into your own way. I will, however, speak of this under another head. We have had the pulpit against us. I am not here to represent one class of abolitionists, particularly in the United States, but the cause of the slave, and the friends of the slave, at large. However, I am more interested in the religious aspect of this question than in its political aspect. There are two classes of abolitionists in the United States; one takes the ground that slavery is the creature of the law, that it must, therefore, be proceeded against as such; and they have formed themselves into what is called, "The liberty party." There is another class--that with which I am particularly associated, and they take the ground that our energies should be devoted to the purifying of the moral sentiment of the country, by directing its energies to the purification of the church, and the exclusion of slaveholders from communion with it. (Loud cheers.) We have proceeded at once to expose the inconsistency of retaining men-stealers as members of the Church of Christ. Our attention was more particularly turned to this, by this able collection of facts by J. G. Birney, who was in this country about six years since. He brought together a number of facts, showing that the American churches were the bulwarks of American slavery. Finding this to be the case, we brought the denunciations of the inspired volume to bear against slave-holding and slaveholders; for after all, it is with the slaveholder that we have to do, and not with the system. It is easy to denounce the system; many of the slave-holders will hold up their hands to denounce the system; the Free Church of Scotland will denounce the system, but the brand of infamy is to be fixed upon the brow of the slaveholder. (Cheers.) Here alone we can successfully meet and overthrow this system of iniquity. The abolitionists have been labouring for the last fifteen years, in season and out of season, in the midst of obloquy and reproach, in the midst of mobs and various kinds of opposition, to establish the conviction that slave-holding is a sin, and that the slaveholder is a sinner, and ought to be treated as such. (Loud cheers.) Thanks to heaven, we have succeeded to a considerable extent in establishing this conviction in the minds of the people in the North, and to some extent in the South. Our efforts have been devoted to bringing the denunciations of religion against it. In this way we have succeeded in expelling pro-slavery, and putting in their stead, anti-slavery publications. Half-a-dozen faithful abolitionists in the North were found sufficient to purify a church. Never was the truth of that saying in the Scriptures more beautifully illustrated, that "one should chase a thousand, and two put ten thousand to flight," than in the history of this movement as regards members of the church. Five or six members would band together and say to the minister, "We want you to remember the poor slave in your prayers. We hear you thank God that you live in a land of civil and religious liberty, and yet you make no reference to the three millions who are denied the privilege of learning the name of the God that made them. We ask you to pray for the slave." He would say, "No; I cannot pray for the slave, I should give offence to that rich member of my church who contributes largely to my salary. I may drive him from the church, and may be the means of destroying his soul. (Laughter.) Is it not better that I should preach such doctrines as would retain him in the church, and thereby, by enunciating great principles, be the means eventually--mark, eventually--of bringing him to a sense of his duty in this matter? I cannot mention the slave." But the brethren insisted upon it, growing more and more firm. In the prayer-meeting they would pray for the slave. (Cheers.) In the conference meeting they would exhort for the slave; they would tell of his woes, and beg their brethren to unite with them; the consequence would be, that in a short time they must be put out of the church, or they must leave the church. Often they would say to the minister, "Unless you remember the bondman we cannot support you; we must leave our pews vacant." One vacant pew is all-powerful in asserting a great and glorious principle, when it is vacant in consequence of adherence to it. A few vacant seats would soon make the minister see that something must be done for the slave, and he would commit himself by opening his mouth in prayer. To be sure this is not the highest motive by which he could be influenced; but this was one of the motives, and I think a legitimate one, by which the friends might operate on the man. For, after all, bread and butter has a great influence on the subject. (Laughter and cheers.) I am convinced, however, that a great number of northern pulpits, came up to this glorious work from higher motives than self-interest; and I believe their hearts were always on the side of the slave, and their only fear was, they could not live, and preach the Gospel. They thought it was necessary for them to live. George Bradburn, an individual whom some of you may remember was present at the World's Convention in 1840, said, he was once met by a minister, who said to him, "Brother Bradburn, I think you abolitionists are too severe upon us poor ministers; we have to take a great deal; you do not seem to remember it is necessary we should live." Said George Bradburn, in his peculiar way, "I do not admit any such necessity. (Laughter.) I hold that it is not necessary for any man to live unless he can live honestly." (Cheers.) Our proceedings with the church have had the effect of dissolving several very important connections with the slave states. Previously to this movement the slave-holding minister could come to the North and preach in our pulpits; the northern minister could go to the South and preach in their pulpits; the slave-holding minister of a church could come and join a northern church; and the northern church minister could go and join the southern church. All were woven and interwoven, linked and interlinked together; they had a common cause to maintain. Now we have succeeded in making it unpopular and discreditable to hold Christian fellowship with slaveholders. (Cheers.) The great Methodist General Conference in 1844, came to the decision that it was at least not expedient, or rather it was inexpedient, for a bishop to hold slaves. This was a great step. (Hear, hear.) I must dwell upon this, not, however, to reflect on our Methodist brethren, but as an illustration of the state of morals in the church. A slave-holding bishop, Bishop Andrews, of South Carolina, married a slave-holding wife, and became the possessor of fifteen slaves. At this time, the Methodist church in the North were of opinion that bishops should not hold slaves. They remonstrated with the Conference to induce Bishop Andrews to emancipate his slaves. The Conference did it in this way if they did it at all. A resolution was brought in, when the bishop was present, to the following effect:-- "Whereas Bishop Andrews has connected himself with slavery, and has thereby injured his itinerancy as a bishop,"--it was not, "Whereas Bishop Andrews has connected himself with slavery, and has thereby become guilty, or has done a great wrong;"--but "has thereby injured his itinerancy as a bishop; we therefore resolve that Bishop Andrews be, and he hereby is,"--what?--"requested to suspend his labors as bishop till he can get rid of"--what?--slavery?--"his impediment." (Laughter.) This was the name given to slavery. One might have inferred from the preamble that it was to get rid of his wife. (Laughter and loud cheers.) How long did it take to pass that resolution? They remained in New York discussing this question three weeks. They had fasting and prayers; they had various kinds of meeting. Part of the slave-holding ministers remonstrated against the resolution, as an insult to the slave-holding members of the Conference. The resolution, however, was passed, although it was partly recalled by subsequent action on the part of the General Conference. Such was the determination of the slave-holding members of that Conference to adhere to the institution of slavery, that they at once moved for a dissolution of fellowship with the northern anti-slavery members of that Conference. It was not the northern members that came out from the slave-holding members, but the slave-holding members that came out from the northern members. (Hear, hear.) I am glad the secession took place; it was our efforts in the North that made it necessary. "Coming events cast their shadows before them." They saw that the spirit that was manifested in 1844, that the holding of slaves was injurious to the itinerancy of the bishop, would in 1848, in all probability, go so far as to say that it was not only injurious to his itinerancy, but at variance with the law of God, and they have now seceded. It was to get rid of the anti-slavery men, but they took the wrong course to preserve their institution. What we want is to get the slaveholders pent up by themselves; too little distinction has been drawn between the slaveholder and the anti-slavery man, between the pure and the base. We want to get slave-holding politics, slave-holding civility, slave-holding religion, slave-holding ministers, slave-holding bishops, slave-holding church members, slave-holding churches, and slave-holding everything, in a position where the eyes of the world can look at them, without looking through any other things. (Cheers.) This we are doing. The Baptists have dissolved their connections. The Free-will Baptists have long done so. The Covenanters have always been separated. The Society of Friends, many years ago, set an example to the world of excluding slaveholders. (Loud cheers.) We have succeeded in creating a warm and determined religious feeling against slavery. Even political abolitionists are opposed to slavery on religious ground; although I feel that they have not been so active on religious grounds as they ought to have been, yet I would not say that they have been without religious influence in bringing forward this question. Although they could not do so in their party, they have done so as individuals. Gerrit Smith has taken a leading part. William Goodell is calling for separation from slaveholders; and a great mass of the abolitionists of New York are taking ground against the union with slaveholders in a religious form. We have succeeded in divorcing slaveholders from the church to a considerable extent. I fear that I am proceeding at too great a length. (Cries of "No, no." I therefore come back hastily to what I wish you to do.

A Voice.--Who is your legal owner?

Mr. Douglass.--I ran away from Thomas Auld, of St. Michael's, Talbot county, Maryland, who was my legal owner. Since I came to this country, I have, as our president has said, published a narrative of my experience, and I kindly sent a copy to my master. (Laughter, and cheers.) He has become so offended with me, that he says he will not own me any longer, and, in his boundless generosity, he has transferred his legal right in my body and soul to his brother, Hugh Auld (laughter), who now lives in Baltimore, and who declares that he will have me if ever I set my foot on American soil. (Hear, hear.)

I may be asked, why I am so anxious to bring this subject before the British public--why I do not confine my efforts to the United States? My answer is, first, that slavery is the common enemy of mankind, and all mankind should be made acquainted with its abominable character. (Cheers.) My next answer is, that the slave is a man, and, as such, is entitled to your sympathy as a brother. (Hear, hear.) All the feelings, all the susceptibilities, all the capacities, which you have, he has. He is a part of the human family. He has been the prey--the common prey--of Christendom for the last three hundred years, and it is but right, it is but just, it is but proper, that his wrongs should be known throughout the world. (Cheers.) I have another reason for bringing this matter before the British public, and it is this, slavery is a system of wrong, so blinding to all around, so hardening to the heart, so corrupting to the morals, so deleterious to religion, so sapping to all the principles of justice in its immediate vicinity, that the community surrounding it lack the moral stamina necessary to its removal. It is a system of such gigantic evil, so strong, so overwhelming in its power, that no one nation is equal to its removal. It requires the humanity of Christendom, the morality of the world, to remove it. (Cheers.) Hence I call upon the people of Britain to look at this matter, and to exert the influence I am about to show they possess, for the removal of slavery from America. I can appeal to them, as strongly by their regard for the slaveholder as for the slave, to labor in this cause. (Hear, hear.) I am here because you have an influence on America that no other nation can have. You have been drawn together by the power of steam to a marvelous extent; the distance between London and Boston is now reduced to twelve or fourteen days, so that the denunciations against slavery uttered in London this week, may be heard in a fortnight in the streets of Boston, and reverberating amidst the hills of Massachusetts. There is nothing said here against slavery, that will not be recorded in the United States. (Hear, hear.) I am here also, because the slaveholders do not want me to be here; they would rather that I was not here. (Cheers.) I have adopted a maxim laid down by Napoleon, never to occupy ground which the enemy would like me to occupy. The slaveholders would much rather have me, if I will denounce slavery, denounce it in the Northern States, where their friends and supporters are, who will stand by and mob me for denouncing it. (Cheers.) They feel something like the man felt, when he uttered his prayer, in which he made out a most horrible case for himself, and one of his neighbors touched him and said, "My friend, I had always the opinion of you that you have now expressed for yourself--that you are a very great sinner." Coming from himself it was all very well, but coming from a stranger it was rather cutting. (Cheers.) The slaveholders felt that when slavery was denounced among themselves, it was not so bad, but let one of the slaves get loose, let him summon the people of Britain, and make known to them the conduct of the slaveholders towards their slaves, and it cuts them to the quick, and produces a sensation such as would be produced by nothing else. (Cheers.) The power I exert now is something like the power that is exerted by the man at the end of the lever; my influence now is just in proportion to the distance that I am from the United States. My exposure of slavery abroad will tell more upon the hearts and consciences of slaveholders, than if I was attacking them in America, for almost every paper that I now receive from the United States comes teeming with statements about this fugitive negro, calling him a "glib-tongued scoundrel" (laughter), and saying that he is running out against the institutions and people of America. I deny the charge, that I am saying a word against the institutions of America or the people as such. What I have to say is against slavery and slaveholders. I feel at liberty to speak on this subject. I have on my back the marks of the lash; I have four sisters and one brother now under the galling chain. I feel it my duty to cry aloud and spare not. (Loud cheers.) I am not averse to having the good opinion of my fellow-creatures. I am not averse to being kindly regarded by all men, but I am bound, even at the hazard of making a large class of religionists in this country hate me, oppose me, and malign me as they have done--I am bound by the prayers and tears and entreaties of three millions of kneeling bondmen, to have no compromise with men who are in any shape or form connected with the slaveholders of America. (Reiterated cheers.) I expose slavery in this country, because to expose it is to kill it. Slavery is one of those monsters of darkness to whom the light of truth is death. Expose slavery, and it dies. Light is to slavery what the heat of the sun is to the root of a tree, it must die under it. All the slaveholder asks of me, is silence. He does not ask me to go abroad and preach in favor of slavery; he does not ask anyone to do that. He would not say that slavery is a good thing, but the best under the circumstances. The slaveholders want total darkness on the subject. They want the hatchway shut down, that the monster may crawl in his den of darkness, crushing human hopes and happiness, destroying the bondman at his will, and having no one to reprove or rebuke him. Slavery shrinks from the light, it hateth the light, neither cometh to the light, lest its deeds should be reproved. (Cheers.) To tear off the mask from this abominable system, to expose it to the light of heaven, aye, to the heat of the sun, that it may burn and wither it out of existence, is my object in coming to this country. (Cheers.) But I am here because certain individuals have seen fit to come to this land, to misrepresent the character of the abolitionists, misrepresent the character of the slaves, misrepresent the character of the colored-people, and have sought to turn off attention from the slave system of America. I am here to revive this attention, and to fix it on the slaveholders. What would I have you then to do? I would have the church, in the first place--Methodist, Baptist, Congregationalist, all persuasions--to declare, in their Conventions, Associations, Synods, Conferences, or whatever be their ecclesiastical meetings, "no Christian fellowship with slaveholders." (Loud cheers.) I want the slaveholder surrounded, as by a wall of anti-slavery fire, so that he may see the condemnation of himself and his system glaring down in letters of light. I want him to feel that he has no sympathy in England, Scotland, or Ireland; that he has none in Canada, none in Mexico, none among the poor wild Indians; that the voice of the civilized, aye, and savage world, is against him. I would have condemnation blaze down upon him in every, direction, till stunned and overwhelmed with shame and confusion, he is compelled to let go the grasp he holds upon the persons of his victims, and restore them to their long-lost rights. (Loud cheers.) Here, then, is work for us all to do. Let me say to the churches that have spoken on the subject, I thank you with my whole heart. I thank the Evangelical Alliance, though I would rather they had taken stronger ground, and not only have said, "Slaveholders shall not be invited," but "Slaveholders shall not be admitted."*

 * *Alas, the Evangelical Alliance has since done worse.*

(Loud cheers.) I am a great lover of music, but I never heard any music half so sweet to my ears, as the voice of our president last night at another meeting--the Temperance meeting at Exeter Hall--where a motion was made to the following effect:--"That this meeting learns with pleasure the determination of the National Temperance Society to hold a world's convention in August next." On that resolution, our worthy president said that the fifty pounds he was to give to that society would be withheld if they admitted slaveholders to that convention. (Loud cheers.) The fact is out: it has gone careering across the Atlantic, and it will fall amidst slaveholders like a bomb-shell. I have to say to those who have spoken on the subject, that they have not only my gratitude, but the gratitude of the millions ready to perish. But I have to say to you further, although you have done much, there is much more to be done. If you have whispered truth, whisper no longer: speak as the tempest does--stronger and stronger. Let your voices be heard through the press, through the pulpit, in all directions. Let the atmosphere of Britain be such that the slaveholder may not be able to breathe it. Let him feel his lungs oppressed the moment he steps on British soil. (Loud cheers.) Why should the slaveholder breathe British atmosphere when it is such as it is? (Hear, hear.) I had heard of Britain long before I got out of slavery. I had not heard of it in the eloquent strains and language of Curran; but I had heard of the great truth embodied in that eloquent sentence which proclaims that the moment a slave sets his foot on British soil his body swells beyond the measure of his chains--they burst from around him, and he stands redeemed, regenerated, disenthralled, by the irresistible genius of universal emancipation. (Loud cheers.)

One word about the Free Church of Scotland. (Cheers.) The facts ought to be stated. The Free Church of Scotland--do you know what Church that is? I have been talking to a people who do not need any explanation on the subject; for I have been in Scotland recently. About two years ago the Free Church of Scotland sent a deputation to the United States, composed of the Rev. Dr. Cunningham, Mr. Chalmers, of this city, Mr. Lewis of Dundee, Mr. Fergusson, and Dr. Burns, for the purpose of explaining the disruption that occurred in Scotland to the people of America, and of soliciting pecuniary aid to enable the Free Church to build churches and to pay their ministers. On reaching the United States, the deputation were very early addressed by the committee of the American and Foreign Anti-Slavery Society, beseeching them, in the most Christian and powerful manner, not to go into the slave states and solicit aid from slaveholders, not to take the price of blood to build free churches and pay free church ministers in Scotland. (Hear, hear.) The deputation did not heed this advice; they went at the invitation of a slaveholder, Dr. Smyth, into the slave states. They were admitted into the pulpits of slaveholders; they were welcomed to the houses of slaveholders; they enjoyed all the hospitalities and attentions that the slaveholders were capable of showering upon them; and they took the slaveholders money, or rather the money of which the slaveholders had robbed the slaves. (Hear, hear.) They have returned to Scotland, and have deliberately attempted, and persevered in their attempt, to show that slavery in itself is not inconsistent with Christian fellowship. (Cries of "Shame!" and hisses.) I hear a hiss. ("Not at you.") I am used to being hissed in Scotland on this subject (laughter), for they do not like me to state the thing in my own language. They have undertaken to show, that neither Christ nor his Apostles, had any objection to slaveholders being admitted to church fellowship. They have undertaken to show, that the Apostle Paul, in sending Onesimus back to Philemon, sanctioned the relation of master and slave. (Hear, hear.) Their arguments on this question are vain, being quoted in the United States by the slaveholding, pro-slavery papers against the abolitionists, and against those who are separating from the slaveholder. (Hear.) Now I have to bring certain charges against that deputation. I charge them, in the first place, with having struck hands in Christian fellowship with men-stealers. (Cheers.) I charge them, in the next place, with having taken the produce of human blood to build free churches, and to pay free church ministers in Scotland. I charge them with having done this knowingly (Cheers), they having been met by a remonstrance against such conduct by the executive committee of the American and Foreign Anti-Slavery Society. I have to charge them with going among men-stealers, with a perfect knowledge that they were such. (Cheers.) I have to charge them with taking money that not only was stolen, but which they knew to be stolen. I have to charge them, moreover, with going into a country where they saw three millions of people deprived of every right, stripped of every privilege, driven like brutes from time into eternity in the dark, robbed of all that makes life dear, the marriage institution destroyed, men herded together like beasts, deprived of the privilege of learning to read the name of the God who made them; and yet that deputation did not utter a word of denunciation against the man-stealer, or a word of sympathy for these poor, outraged, long-neglected people. (Loud cries of "Shame!") What I want the brethren of England to do is this; to tell the Free Church of Scotland, the words you have just heard--"Send back the money." (Cheers.) They can never remonstrate against the slaveholder while they hold on to the money; therefore they should send it back. I want you to aid my friend, my eloquent friend, the slaves' friend, Mr. George Thompson. (Loud cheers.) My friend Mr. Thompson and myself expect to leave early to-morrow for Scotland; we are going there with few of the wealthy, few of the influential, to second our efforts. We believe that it is the duty of the Free Church of Scotland to send back the money. I believe it is in our power, under God, to induce a state of feeling in Scotland which will demand the sending back of that money. We now want your aid; we want you to raise your voices and your sympathies. Let us have your sympathy. Write, "Send back the money." Speak, "Send back the money," Preachs, "Send back the money." (Immense cheering.) I believe that the sending back of that money to the United States, will do more to unrivet the fetters, to break the chains of the bondman, and to hasten the day of emancipation, than years of lecturing by the most eloquent abolitionists. It would produce such an effect, that it would send slavery staggering to its grave, as if struck by the voice of Heaven. The truth is, the slaveholders have scarcely anywhere to lean. They leaned against the northern states--the abolitionists have removed their prop. They used to lean a good deal on their religious fellowship in England. It was once said to a person, "You come from Maryland: are you a slaveholder?" "Yes." "Then you cannot come in." (Cheers.) The Christian people of England are beginning to see the inconsistency of holding fellowship with these men, and are breaking loose from them. The United

Secession Synod has declared, unanimously, that it will no longer strike hands in Christian fellowship with the men-stealers in America. (Cheers.) The Relief Synod, whose meeting is now in session in Edinburgh, has come to the same unanimous conclusion. (Cheers.) The Evangelical Alliance has said, through Dr. Candlish, one of the Free Church leaders, that the slaveholders ought not to be invited. I tell you slavery cannot live with all these stabs. "Send back the money--send back the money." (Loud cheers.) If it is not inconsistent with this meeting, allow me to do what I have done in Scotland. I want to have all the children writing about the streets "Send back the money." I want to have all the people saying "Send back the money;" and in order to rivet these words in the minds of the audience, I propose that they give three cheers, not hurrahs, but say "Send back the money." (The vast assembly spontaneously complied with Mr. Douglass' request. The effect produced was indescribable. Mr. Douglass then sat down amid reiterated rounds of applause.)

Uncle Tom's Companions

Uncle Tom's Companions

EMANCIPATION OF THE SLAVES.
Proclaimed on the 22d September 1862, by ABRAHAM LINCOLN, President of the United States of North America.

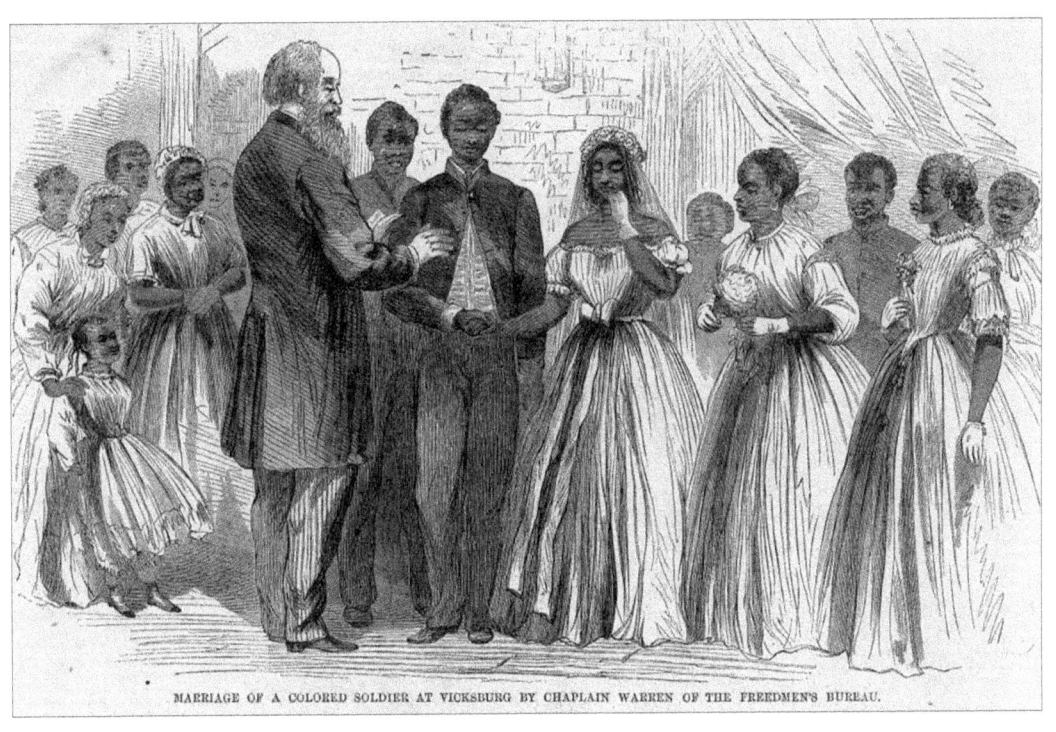

MARRIAGE OF A COLORED SOLDIER AT VICKSBURG BY CHAPLAIN WARREN OF THE FREEDMEN'S BUREAU.

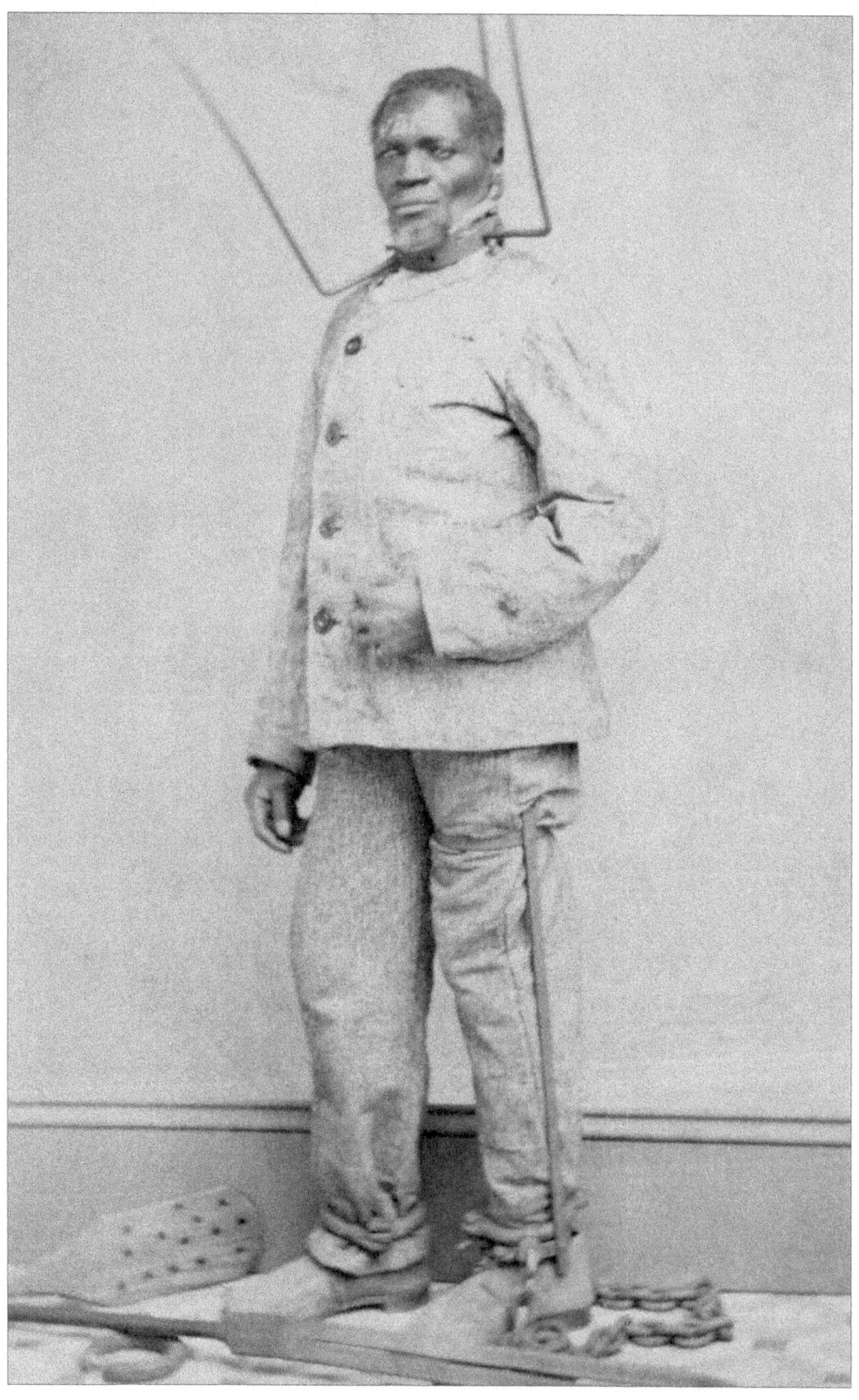

CELEBRATION OF THE ABOLITION OF SLAVERY IN THE DISTRICT OF COLUMBIA BY THE COLORED PEOPLE, IN WASHINGTON, April 19, 1866.—[Sketched by F. Dielman.]

SLAVES FOR SALE: A SCENE IN NEW ORLEANS

HISTORIC PUBLISHING
©2017

www.ingramcontent.com/pod-product-compliance
Lightning Source LLC
Chambersburg PA
CBHW080638170426
43200CB00015B/2881